PARAESTHETICS
FOUCAULT • LYOTARD • DERRIDA

PARAESTHETICS
FOUCAULT · LYOTARD · DERRIDA

DAVID CARROLL

ROUTLEDGE: NEW YORK & LONDON

First Published in 1987 by Methuen, Inc.
Reprinted in 1989 by
Routledge, an imprint of
Routledge, Chapman and Hall, Inc.
29 West 35th Street, New York, N.Y. 10001

Published in Great Britain by
Routledge
11 New Fetter Lane, London EC4P 4EE

© 1987 Methuen, Inc.

Printed in the United States of America

Library of Congress Cataloging in Publication Data

Carroll, David, 1944–
    Paraesthetics: Foucault, Lyotard, Derrida.

    Bibliography: p.
    Includes index.
    1. Foucault, Michel.   2. Lyotard, Jean Francois.
3. Derrida, Jacques.   4. Aesthetics, Modern—20th
century.   I. Title.
B2430.F724C37   1987   111'.85'0922   87-11296
ISBN 0-416-01721-5
ISBN 0-415-90291-6 (pbk.)

British Library Cataloguing in Publication Data

Carroll, David, 1944–
    Paraesthetics: Foucault, Lyotard, Derrida.
    1 . Aesthetics
    I. Title
    700'.1   N65

    ISBN 0-416-01721-5
    ISBN 0-415-90291-6 (pbk.)

FOR THOMAS AND HIS MOTHER

C O N T E N T S

ix
ACKNOWLEDGMENTS

xi
PREFACE
Paraesthetics: The Displacement of Theory and the Question of Art

1
CHAPTER ONE
Beyond Theorisms and Aestheticisms / *Nietzsche*
1. The Critical Force of Art and Literature   1
2. The Contamination of Philosophy   7
3. Literature as Rhetoric   11
4. Rethinking the Literary   17

23
CHAPTER TWO
Aesthetic Antagonisms / *Lyotard*
1. Art as Critique   23
2. The Disruption of the Theoretical   30
3. Desire and the Figural   37
4. Libidinal Politics   43

53
CHAPTER THREE
Self-Reflexivity and Critical Theory / *Foucault*
1. The *Mise en abyme* of Historical Representation   53
2. A Poetics of Absence   67
3. Thinking the Outside   77

81
CHAPTER FOUR
Deconstruction and the Question of Literature / *Derrida*
1. Writing and the Priority of Literature   81
2. The Trials of Philosophy   89
3. The Crisis of Literature and the Displacement of Theory   95

107
CHAPTER FIVE
Disruptive Discourse and Critical Power / *Foucault*
1. Madness and Literature 107
2. The Theaters of Power 118

131
CHAPTER SIX
Borderline Aesthetics / *Derrida*
1. Working the Frame 131
2. Framing the Work 144

155
CHAPTER SEVEN
The Aesthetic and the Political / *Lyotard*
1. The Rules of the Game 155
2. Phrasing the Political 164
3. Auschwitz and the "Signs of History" 169
4. A Critique of Political Judgment 173

185
CHAPTER EIGHT
The Undetermined Ends of Theory and Art

189
NOTES

215
INDEX

ACKNOWLEDGMENTS

I want to thank the "first readers" (and first critics) of this book, Suzanne Gearhart and Richard Regosin, for their insightful critiques and numerous suggestions for improvement. I know that I could not have written the book without them.

I have also profited from discussions through the years with Jacques Derrida and Jean-François Lyotard, not only on problems treated in the chapters devoted to their work but also on a wide range of topics. They of course are not responsible for the interpretations I give their work.

I also want to acknowledge that I have benefited in the last four years from discussions and debates with my colleagues at Irvine in the Focused Research Program in Contemporary Critical Theory. I want to single out especially Mark Poster and Murray Krieger, who from very different critical perspectives have, through their questions and interventions, often forced me to rethink my own position on various problems.

In 1985, I received an Irvine Faculty Research Fellowship, which allowed me during one quarter to devote my full attention to research on this book at a crucial moment of its development.

Parts of this book have previously appeared in print: Chapter 5 appeared in a slightly different form in *Humanities in Society*, v. 5, nos. 3–4 (Summer–Fall 1982), and a part of the second half of Chapter 6 appeared as a section of an essay on Derrida whose title was "Institutional Authority vs. Critical Power, or the Uneasy Relations of Psychoanalysis and Literature," in *Taking chances: Derrida, Psychoanalysis, and Literature*, Joseph H. Smith and William Kerrigan, eds. (Baltimore: Johns Hopkins University Press, 1984).

P R E F A C E
PARAESTHETICS:
The Displacement of Theory and the Question of Art

This book is about theory and its limitations. It is not, however, an anti-theoretical book, a book "against theory," as seems to be the rage today. On the contrary, I have chosen to focus on Michel Foucault, Jean-François Lyotard, and Jacques Derrida because they are all critical philosophers whose awareness of the limitations of theory has led them not to reject theory but rather to work at and on the borders of theory in order to stretch, bend, or exceed its limitations. An effect of such "critical work"—and without this *work* claims that are made about the transgression, excess, openness, or even deconstruction of theory are no more than slogans—is that theory is continually displaced and in this way revitalized, that is, given a different form and critical function. It seems to me extremely important at the present juncture, when the theoretical advances of the last two decades are more and more often distorted, blindly attacked, or simply dismissed, that such *work* be better understood. The principal argument of this book is that this cannot be done if one ignores the crucial role given to the questions of art and literature in the critical strategies of Foucault, Lyotard, and Derrida.

There have been a number of signs in recent years that we are perhaps approaching the end of what has been labeled (erroneously, I would say) the "poststructuralist" phase of theory and criticism. The gradual demise (or dispersion) of the so-called "Yale School of Criticism" and its notion of "deconstruction as literary criticism" undoubtedly constitutes the most obvious of these signs. It could be argued that the demise of any important school and the orthodoxy inevitably associated with it often brings about a general reevaluation of critical positions, more diversified debates, and increased experimentation with alternative critical strategies. If this general process of reevaluation and experimentation could in some sense be said to be underway at the present time, we are also, however, witnessing at the same time a definite hardening of positions on all sides of the theoretical spectrum. A battle is now raging on many fronts to impose or reimpose forms of previously challenged orthodoxies in order to cut short debate and experimentation and reestablish what is sometimes claimed to be more solid foundations for humanistic inquiry: namely, history, the real, man, subjectivity, etc. This increase in what I would call theoretical "reactivity" is much more disturbing than the short reign of a formalist, poststructuralist, or deconstructive school of criticism, which in fact had the merit of challenging and undermining the grounds for many of the positions now reemerging with vengeance to fill in the space left vacant by its demise.

By using a term such as reactivity, I am not referring to so-called political reactionaries alone, for reactivity is as much a phenomenon of the "left" and even the liberal "center" as the "right." It consists in the rejection of particular types of theoretical questions as illegitimate in themselves, the condemnation of certain strategies of interpretation for being morally or politically suspect, and in general in the imposition of a way of reading (most often a way of *not* reading), a way of approaching problems, to the exclusion or devaluation of all others. In short, all reactivity perpetuates theoretical dogmatism.

I argue in the chapters that follow that one of the ways in which the work of Foucault, Lyotard, and Derrida can be considered critical is precisely in its search for alternatives to theoretical orthodoxies and dogmatisms. This does not mean that in the hands of some, their work itself could not be the basis for a new orthodoxy: at least in the case of Foucault and Derrida, it seems quite evident that their "orthodoxization" has already taken place. But this should surprise no one, for no critical position can ever claim to be completely immune to this possibility. The best that critical thought can do is provide weapons for undoing orthodoxy, even one that might eventually be created in its own name. I shall insist especially on those elements of the work of Foucault and Derrida that do not fit nicely within the orthodoxies formed in their name—not in order to free them from all responsibility for the "schools" formed around them but rather to show that something is at stake in their work of even more critical import than their most vocal followers, as well as their most ferocious opponents, have allowed.

A few years ago, I gave a graduate seminar on the critical role of a certain notion of art and literature in the work of Jacques Derrida. After the first class, in which I attempted to describe what I felt was the complexity of the questions of "the aesthetic" and "the literary" in his work, as well as what their radical theoretical implications might be, a first-year student approached me with a discouraged look on his face. He felt very uneasy listening to me, he said, because what I seemed to be saying went against everything he believed and everything he had been taught to believe in his undergraduate classes on literature and theory. He could not conceive of the possibility that any approach to "aesthetics" could, even under the best of conditions, have *critical* rather than idealist or aestheticist effects. Because he claimed he had always been taught to be "suspicious" of all forms of aesthetics, the choice of how to deal with art and literature was for him stark and uncompromising: either one treated art and literature from an historical-political perspective or one approached it with formalist-aesthetic categories. In the first case, one was a critical thinker; in the second, an idealist or an aestheticist. It was as simple as that.

Even though few would express their distrust of aesthetics and of approaches concerned with issues such as the specificity, or better, the singularity of art and literature in as straightforward terms as this student, the distrust he expressed is quite widespread, and not just among first-year graduate students. And as I think I answered him at the time, it is probably not in itself a bad thing, at least as long as it doesn't result in the dismissal of the question of the aesthetic as a valid and important critical question. There may be many good reasons to be suspicious of aesthetics and of what many do with and to art and literature; the elevated place it often holds in theories whose chief purpose is to negate or trivialize historical-political questions invites suspicion and criticism. Aestheticism is certainly a risk whenever a theory deals with the questions of art and literature, and it is important to analyze the specific effects of aestheticist tendencies in the theories in which they occur.

Thus, as I had to admit to my despairing student, I too have always been suspicious of aesthetics and of theories that postulate art and literature as ends in themselves. I would even say, in fact, that I could never have imagined myself writing a book such as the one that follows in which the problem of the aesthetic was the central focus—that is, I couldn't imagine writing such a book until there no longer seemed any way to avoid confronting the issue head-on, given its importance in the work of three French philosophers generally considered to be at the forefront of contemporary critical thought. For it became more and more clear to me as I worked on Foucault, Lyotard, and Derrida that there was no way to separate the questions of art and literature from the most important philosophical, historical, and political issues raise by their work. But I would not be exaggerating at all to say that the project for this book was born more in distrust than in any certainty or confidence in either the inherent critical or transcendent powers of art or literature.

I have attempted as much as possible to remain suspicious of the "critical powers" of the aesthetic throughout the book, while at the same time, continually confronting the assumptions underlying not only my student's dismissal of aesthetics but also those supporting the perhaps more sophisticated but yet just as reductive positions of certain important "historically"- or "politically"-oriented theorists. This book constitutes neither a defense nor an indictment of aesthetics as such but rather a critical evaluation of the place of the question of art and literature in the work of three important critical philosophers. It is an attempt to understand why "art" (in its general sense as art and literature) is not for them "a thing of the past," as Hegel proclaimed in order to subsume it under philosophy and theology, but why it is rather a "thing of the future" and continues to be a difficult but pressing question for critical thought.

I have chosen to follow the question of the aesthetic in its various formulations in the work of all three philosophers. My justification for following this path rather than some other is that in the work of each, art and literature hold a pivotal, strategic place; for each, larger theoretical, political, historical issues are approached and reformulated in terms of critical openings or a critical distance provided by art and/or literature. The question I treat in their work is not aesthetics per se, for aesthetics implies the establishment of a theory of art and literature or the application of a general theory to the area of art. I am interested rather in the critical possibilities of art and literature and the particular problems the aesthetic raises for theory. At stake are precisely the boundaries separating and linking art, literature, and theory, and the relations that exist within and across these boundaries.

This book is not focused on aesthetics, but rather on what I call *paraesthetics*. I use this term to indicate that I am here approaching art in terms of its relations with the *extra*-aesthetic in general. I am, for example, interested in the philosophical, historical, and political issues raised by the question of form or the problem of beauty rather than in form and beauty as narrow aestheticist questions. The OED gives the following definition of "para," which indicates various disruptive effects of this prefix that are crucial to my use of the term paraesthetics:

> As a preposition, Gr. παρά had the sense "by the side of, beside," whence "alongside of, by, past, beyond," etc. In composition it had the same senses, with such cognate adverbial ones as "to one side, aside, amiss, faulty, irregular, disordered, improper, wrong": also expressing subsidiary relation, alteration, perversion, simulation, etc.

Paraesthetics indicates something like an aesthetics turned against itself or pushed beyond or beside itself, a faulty, irregular, disordered, improper aesthetics—one not content to remain within the area defined by the aesthetic. Paraesthetics describes a critical approach to aesthetics for which art is a question not a given, an aesthetics in which art does not have a determined place or a fixed definition.

This term seemed to me more appropriate than any other to situate the question of the aesthetic in the work of Foucault, Lyotard, and Derrida, for the multiple and even contradictory senses of *para* suggest the complexity of the problem of art and literature in their work. Certainly none of them attempts to construct a "new" aesthetics or provide an alternate theory of art. They are all concerned, however, with how art resists (even its own) theorization, and for this reason they attempt through various strategies to push the question of art beyond itself and its theoretical representation. Paraesthetics indicates, then, more of a bastard, parasitical, transgressive, critical aesthetics than a "true" aesthetics. Neither aestheticist nor anti-aesthetic in its approach to art, it considers the links with the "outside," with what is not aesthetic, to be fundamental to the aesthetic and vice-versa. Paraesthetics has to do with the often contradictory, disordered forms the question of art and literature takes after the "end of art" has been proclaimed by philosophy or history, with how art and literature live on after their philosophical-historical death(s).

The critical force of the questions of art and literature in the work of Foucault, Lyotard, and Derrida has to do with the fact that these terms are called

CHAPTER ONE
BEYOND THEORISMS AND AESTHETICISMS

N I E T Z S C H E

Our religion, morality, and philosophy are decadence forms of man. The *countermovement: art.*

L'art pour l'art: . . . The virtuoso croaking of shivering frogs, despairing in their swamp.
——Friedrich Nietzsche, *The Will to Power*

1. The Critical Force of Art and Literature

At a time when one hears more and more often from representatives of the most diverse positions that we must limit or even leave behind theoretical concerns and get back to practical analysis again—whether it be in the form of reading literary texts, interpreting historical facts, or formulating "no-non-sense" philosophical arguments—it seems to me urgent to look at what is at stake in such demands. There is, of course, the standard argument "against theory" that is always being made, an argument that sees the extended questioning of fundamental premises of critical methodology, the systematic analysis of the implications of strategies of interpretation, and the critique of established logic (as well as the alternative critical methodologies, strategies, and "(para)logics" resulting from such critiques), to constitute, at best, detours from the real task at hand—practical analysis—and, at worst, threats to the pristine purity of criticism, history, or philosophy. From this perspective, theory is something to be tolerated only if it remains marginal and subservient, to be referred to and used only in those instances when it confirms the critical principles already held and refuted, or more likely, ignored in all other instances. Such anti-theoretical dogmatism has often been chal-

1

lenged, and there is no reason to rehearse its shortcomings once again. Suffice it to say that what is most evident and problematical in this stance against theory in general is its failure, or even explicit refusal, to question its own, supposedly "atheoretical" position and its (usually) loud and polemical dismissal of all those who challenge its position.

But more important than the anti-theoretical argument, a complaint against theory is beginning to be heard from sectors not previously opposed to theory but now fatigued by having had to deal—for what obviously seems to some as an intolerably long time—with theoretical problems that do not appear any closer to being resolved now than they were when the current (that is, structuralist-poststructuralist) phase of theoretical emphasis began about twenty years ago. If anything, the theoretical problems have multiplied and become more diverse and difficult to resolve since the importation of the "structuralist controversy" to the United States—(where, incidently, it has had a much longer life than in the exporting country, France). Whatever the reason for this complaint, many scholars today seem to think theory has worn out its welcome—assuming that it was ever really welcome in the first place— and that it would be "healthier" for the various disciplines of the humanities to return to more empirical, practical investigations and spend less time debating abstract theoretical issues. The renewed interest in pragmatism, sociology, and performance theory may very well all be signs of theoretical weariness and of a desire to "get back to basics" or, at least, to a somewhat more solid ground that can support a more practical form of theorization and criticism, signs of a longing to deal with problems that have definite solutions and with questions that have specific answers to them.

There may indeed be good reasons to be weary of theory, or at least weary of forms of theorizing that tend toward abstraction, universalization, idealism. A weariness of this type could lead to increased critical vigilance and sophistication, and thus produce a more active, energetic form of critical theory. And yet the danger is now, as it has always been, that weariness with theory will lead to another type of reaction, to the reinstitution of naïve, unscrutinized theoretical concepts as alternatives to theory. One can already see the reemergence of such concepts as the subject, man, history, the social context, morality, the poetic object, literary tradition, rhetoric, dialogue, consensus, etc., in a naïve, *pre*-theoretical form—as if they had never been challenged at all. For the most part, these concepts are being championed, in order to combat theory in general and to make reading, analysis, interpretation, and communication in their direct, uncomplicated forms possible once again. But attractive as such a return to "simplicity" might seem at times, we must always ask ourselves what price we pay for simplification and what ends are being served when "common sense," logic, historical certainty, dialogue, and consensus are the ends of (that is, put an end to) theoretical questioning. What

2

values are being defended and perpetuated in such a return to simplicity or "normalcy?"[1]

There are obviously better, more effective ways of dealing with the limitations of theory than to reject theory outright; and the three critical philosophers who are the principal focus of the present work, Foucault, Lyotard, and Derrida, all use as important components of their theoretical projects the questioning of theory and the undermining of its limitations. To question theory has not, for them, meant to reject or ignore theory, but rather to undo the closures constituted by theory *from within* and to develop critical strategies that are capable of pointing to, or linking up with, what is "beyond theory." For each of them, a certain "art" or "literature" (the quotation marks indicate that the meaning of these terms is to be determined), a certain radical notion of "aesthetics" or "poetics," has an important role to play in the struggle of critical theory to move beyond the limitations of theory. For each, a critical approach to art and literature—what I call "paraesthetics"—has made it possible to begin to develop, if not *a* "critical theory," then at least alternative critical strategies that confront and attempt to undermine and move beyond the closure of theory in its systematic, philosophical form.

Foucault, Lyotard, and Derrida have many important predecessors in this critical project (Blanchot, Merleau-Ponty, Adorno, Benjamin, Heidegger, the German Romantics, and Kant, to name only these), but of all their predecessors, Nietzsche is undoubtedly the one who most explicitly laid the groundwork for something like a critical or a para- aesthetics in the sense this term will be given in the course of the book. For it is in terms of Nietzsche that I can best highlight both the possibilities and the risks of a critical strategy that assumes, in some sense, the perspective of "art" to counter the limitations of theory.[2] For Nietzsche, "art" (a category including literature: the poetic, the tragic, the fictive) is *the* "countermovement" to religion, morality, and philosophy, and, as such, has a privileged affirmative and disruptive force. But the danger of privileging any term (and this is especially true of art), is that it will begin to take on the very characteristics it is supposed to counter. The use of art "against" theory (philosophy and religion in Nietzsche's case) can very easily end up being a mystification of art. Although Nietzsche constantly evokes art as a means to combat the truth, that same art, when posited as "sovereign and universal," will become yet another version of the truth. If placed above "the struggle between power-complexes," art becomes a repressive force preventing or resolving all struggle, rather than being "a means in the struggle" of forces that Nietzsche considers to be essential to "life."[3]

The problem can be formulated in reference to Nietzsche in the following way: can the aesthetic be used to point to the limitations of the theoretical, the speculative, the moral-religious, without becoming a replacement for them and a transcendent order in itself? Can the aestheticist temptation, to which literary theorists frequently (and philosophers and historians occa-

3

sionally) give in, be avoided without at the same time canceling the critical, disruptive powers the aesthetic is called upon to provide in the work of a philosopher such as Nietzsche? The question is not one of an alternative system or method, or even of a better theoretical model, but rather of developing critical strategies to be used within a field of conflicting forces where no one force has absolute priority over the others and where the temptation to grant a term transcendent status must continually be resisted. If "art" is to function critically and indicate a movement "beyond theory," it must also move "beyond art" and function outside of all forms of aestheticism.

There would seem to be little disagreement that within the history of philosophy Nietzsche could be considered "the most literary of philosophers." Not only do art and literary-rhetorical questions have a central place in his work, but the form of his writing and his use of rhetorical techniques and discursive strategies (more associated with literature than with traditional philosophical argumentation) make his work as much literary as philosophical—assuming for a moment that we know what each of these terms means and what differentiates them. But even if his work has been dismissed by certain schools of philosophy for not being sufficiently "philosophical" (that is, analytical) others, more sympathetic to his overall critical project and perhaps less willing to accept any rigid definition of philosophical specificity, consider the literary characteristics of his work not to be an abuse of philosophy, but, rather, to have a legitimate philosophical function. Certainly at least since Heidegger, a reading of Nietzsche that places the question of the aesthetic at the center of his philosophical project and judges it to be a legitimate means of raising fundamental philosophical questions cannot be considered unphilosophical, except by the most dogmatic of philosophers.

From this perspective, it is tempting to generalize the description that Eugen Fink gives of *The Birth of Tragedy* and apply it to Nietzsche's entire work:

> The aesthetic theme acquires for him the status of a fundamental ontological principle. Art, the tragic poem, becomes for him the key that will open up the essence [*Wesen*] of the world. Art is raised into an organ of philosophy and taken as the most serious, authentic entryway for the most original comprehension [*als das ursprünglichste Verstehen*], the concept at the very best coming after. . . . Nietzsche uses aesthetic categories to formulate his fundamental vision of being. The phenomenon of art is placed at the center: in it and from it the world can be deciphered. (*Nietzsches Philosophie* [Stuttgart: Verlag, 1960], 16–17)[4]

One way to save Nietzsche for philosophy, to keep him from becoming "too aesthetic or literary," is to consider art or literature in his work as the means

4

of successfully and "originally" entering into true philosophical thought and formulating the most fundamental of philosophical visions, that of being. Art, though privileged—it can even at times be considered more originally philosophical than philosophy itself—remains a tool or organ of philosophy and its concept of being. To put it another way, the ends of art in Fink's reading of *The Birth of Tragedy* are postulated as being philosophical, and the purpose of art is thus to come to its end in philosophy. But conceived in such terms, one would have to say that Nietzsche, that ferocious opponent of dialectical thinking, had not really left Hegel very far behind at all (as Nietzsche himself admitted, at least as concerns *The Birth of Tragedy*) and deserves to be considered a (in Heidegger's analysis, the last) metaphysician, one who comes to being through art.

Certainly no serious discussion of the role of art in Nietzsche can ignore Heidegger's meticulous reading, which emphasizes the central role given to art in Nietzsche's concept of will to power and argues that this is Nietzsche's fundamental response to the "question of being": *"An interpretation of the nucleus of will to power must begin precisely here, with art,"* for "art is not merely one configuration of will to power among others but the *supreme* configuration."[5] For Heidegger, art is at the nucleus of the central question of Nietzsche's philosophy as the figure of all figures of will to power, which necessitates that in reading Nietzsche it is necessary to *begin with* the question of art: "The innermost essence of Being is will to power. In the being of the artist we encounter the most perspicuous and most familiar mode of will to power. Since it is a matter of illuminating the Being of beings, meditation on art has in this regard decisive priority" (*Nietzsche*, I, 70). But even if we agree with Heidegger on the priority of the question of art in Nietzsche and on the necessity of beginning with art in reading *The Will to Power*, the problem remains as to whether art is really a question that can be contained within metaphysics, whether art in Nietzsche has only metaphysical ends, as Heidegger claims.

Heidegger may argue that Nietzsche's treatment of art is the "reversal of Platonism" (*Nietzsche*, v. I, 162), but his own reading also demonstrates that there is more at stake here than a simple reversal.[6] Heidegger shows how Nietzsche's positing of the question of art at the center of his interrogation of being leads not to harmony between truth and art, or the dominance of one over the other, but to a "raging discordance that arouses dread" (142—"The Raging Discordance between Truth and Art" is also Heidegger's title for the entire section 19 of his *Nietzsche*).[7] This in itself, however, is not enough to ensure that art will not constitute such a reversal—for no matter how much discordance might rage, a resolution for it, or at least a context in which to contain it, does seem to be readily available for Nietzsche in art. Art not only counters philosophy and its truth but also seems to rise above the discordance its relation to the truth provokes. "Art is *worth more* than truth," says Nietzsche, because art is "the only superior counterforce to all will to denial of life, as that which is anti-Christian, anti-Buddhist, antinihilist *par excellence*." It is "the *redemption of the man of knowledge . . . the man of action . . . the sufferer*" (*The Will to Power*, 453, 452—Kaufmann argues that this section, a fragment of a draft for a preface for a new edition of *The Birth of Tragedy*, probably dates from the fall of 1886 [451]).[8] If art redeems in this way, it puts an end to discordance and the dread provoked by it. As Heidegger argues, the choice of art over truth in Nietzsche's work constitutes a "reversal of metaphysics," signifying that art's worth is to provide a better, non-nihilistic form of truth than the truth of philosophy or religion.

For Heidegger, the problem with such a resolution of discordance in the form of a reversal is that the choice is a bit too easy. The reversal of Platonism and Christianity ultimately obscures "the essence of the truth," because the path to the essence by way of art moves away from the essence rather than toward it:

> According to what we have shown, we must first ask upon which route of meaning the word "truth" moves for Nietzsche in the context of his discussion of the relation between art and truth. The answer is that it moves along the route which deviates from the essential route. This means that in the fundamental question which arouses dread Nietzsche nevertheless does not arrive at the proper question of truth, in the sense of a discussion of the essence of the true. The essence is presupposed as evident. . . . It is of decisive importance to know that Nietzsche does not pose the question of truth proper. (*Nietzsche*, v. I, 148)

In Heidegger's reading, Nietzsche takes his place within the long history of metaphysics; for him, Nietzsche assumes rather than questions the essence of truth, and, in so doing, continues to obscure it: "That the question of the essence of truth is missing in Nietzsche's thought is an oversight unlike any other; it cannot be blamed on him alone, on him first of all—if it can be blamed on anyone. The 'oversight' pervades the entire history of occidental philosophy since Plato and Aristotle" (149). For Heidegger, Nietzsche's privileging of art does not arrive at its destination in the truth and thus obscures this essential question.

But if, for Heidegger, Nietzsche is guilty of such an "oversight" and "deviates from the essential route," what interests me is how Heidegger's insistence that art be evaluated principally in terms of the essence of the truth might itself be considered a serious and deeply-rooted oversight, a way of deflecting or (in Philippe Lacoue-Labarthe's terms) "obliterating" the critical potential of the question of art—a question that may have less to do with "the essential" than with the questioning of and movement away from or beyond the essen-

6

tial. It is not perhaps as a reversal of the truth, but as a deviation or "detour" that, in all instances, does not return to the truth, that art raises its most disruptive, discordant questions with regard to truth.[9] This is probably what philosophy from the very beginning has most dreaded in its relations with art: not that the discordances would be resolved in art (as a superior or more original form of philosophy) but that they would remain unresolved to undermine the integrity of both philosophy and art, of philosophy as art or art as philosophy.

The problem that Nietzsche's work raises and that Heidegger's reading both leads to and obliterates is whether it is possible to "live with" the raging discordance without dread, whether it is possible to keep this discordance unresolved and use it as part of an affirmative critical strategy. The two epigraphs from *The Will to Power* used to inaugurate this chapter address this very problem: whether it is possible to exploit the critical force of art (and literature) as a countermovement to philosophy without, through a process of reversal, elevating art to a transcendent status above the fray. For to elevate art is to mystify its powers and reduce it to the "virtuoso croaking," not only "of shivering frogs despairing in their swamps," but of all other forms of aestheticism, wherever they may breed.

2. The Contamination of Philosophy

One of the moments in Nietzsche's work which most forcefully dramatizes the discordant, antagonistic relations of art and truth (here in the form of the relations of literature and philosophy), is in *The Birth of Tragedy*, an "early work," which is, at least in terms of this problem, as complicated as any of Nietzsche's texts. It is the well-known moment when Euripides brings Socrates onto the theatrical stage, with what Nietzsche considers to be disastrous results for tragedy per se, a moment that determines the whole history of the relations of philosophy and literature in terms of the dominance of philosophy. With what Nietzsche calls "aesthetic Socratism, whose supreme law reads roughly as follows, 'To be beautiful everything must be intelligible,'"[10] the Dionysian/Apollonian opposition of forces basic to authentic tragedy is replaced by another: a Dionysian/Socratic (or as Paul de Man argues), a Dionysian/Apollonian/Socratic opposition[11] that brings about the wreck of Greek tragedy. The historical schema delineated here seems, on the surface, simple enough: the alien (to art and tragedy) force of philosophy, a force rooted in essential truth, enters on stage and transforms or corrupts the originally tragic dimensions of the stage and the actors by giving meaning to them, by relating them to the truth. For Nietzsche, this is an indication of the repressive power of nihilism (philosophy) to infer the "essential perversity and reprehensibility of what exists," and thus to take on itself the "duty to correct existence" (*The Birth of Tragedy*, 87). With Socrates, true tragedy is

7

thus destroyed, and its Dionysian/Apollonian forces tamed; philosophical tragedy takes its place so that philosophy will thereafter dominate the stage.

On closer scrutiny, however, the story of the fall or "tragic suicide" of tragedy (76) is not as simple as the above schema would imply. First of all, the "original" Dionysian/Apollonian form of tragedy was never itself pure, for an "anti-Dionysian tendency was operating even prior to Socrates" (92). In the very play and opposition of forces basic to tragedy, in the very necessity for tragedy to produce figures and forms, to partake of the realm of appearances (however artistic, dream-like, narcotic, or unreal this realm is), the philosophical questions of intelligibility and truth are not completely absent, even if not dominant. In Nietzsche's schema, they become dominant with the entry of Socrates, even though they never succeed in canceling out the more disruptive Dionysian forces. Secondly, and perhaps more importantly, Socrates (philosophy) does not conquer without giving up something: as philosophy transforms tragedy, it is transformed, made more "aesthetic" in turn. Socrates may "wreck" tragedy by upsetting the delicate balance of forces, but he also "wrecks" philosophy at its origin by having it brought on a stage that is not its own and that it does not completely control. In their "pure" forms both tragedy and philosophy are lost; they survive, in their contaminated forms, to tell their stories over and over again. The struggle between them continues, although the form of this struggle and the place and power of the combatant forces constantly changes.

The fiction or drama of the "tragic suicide" or murder of tragedy in *The Birth of Tragedy* is well-known but in this context worth looking at again.[12] Nietzsche begins the drama off-stage, with Plato burning his poems in order to become a disciple of Socrates. This double act of rejecting poetry and accepting philosophy as his unique master transforms the relation of the forces associated with poetry and redirects rather than eliminates them: "The youthful tragic poet Plato first burned his poems that he might become a student of Socrates. But where unconquerable propensities struggled against the Socratic maxims, their power together with the impact of his tremendous character, was still great enough to force poetry itself into new and hitherto unknown channels" (90). For Nietzsche, Plato will turn out to be not the first "*artist*-philosopher"—which in *The Will to Power* is associated with a "higher concept of art" (Section 795, [1885–1886], 419)—but the first *philosopher*-artist, a figure who in strict philosophical terms is a lower form of the philosopher and in artistic terms is a compromised form of the artist. But is there really an essential difference between the artist-philosopher and the philosopher-artist? Is it not a question of degree rather than nature, and who or what is to decide which figure is the lower or the higher? Once philosophy and art are contaminated by each other—that is, from the very beginning—can either be assumed to be able to provide a reliable perspective from which to determine such a hierarchy?

In following his master, Socrates, and condemning tragedy as a deviation from the truth, Plato ends up creating a new form of art (and philosophy):

> An instance of this is Plato who in condemning tragedy and art in general certainly did not lag behind the naïve cynicism of his master; he was constrained by sheer artistic necessity to create an art form that was related to those forms of art which he repudiated. . . . Thus Plato, the thinker, arrived by a detour where he had always been at home as a poet. . . . If tragedy had absorbed into itself all the earlier types of art, the same might also be said in an eccentric sense of the Platonic dialogue which, a mixture of all extant styles and forms, hovers midway between narrative, lyric, and drama, between prose and poetry, and so has also broken the strict old law of the unity of linguistic form. (90)

For Nietzsche, the Platonic dialogue is a hybrid form that attempts to combat art on its own terms and, that in doing so, blurs those very boundaries between art and philosophy that it is hoping to defend. The "victory" of philosophy over art is achieved only at the expense of the unity and purity of philosophy; art may pay a terrible price because of philosophy's desire to master it, but so does philosophy.

The price paid by art, according to Nietzsche, is that its scope is greatly reduced:

> The Platonic dialogue was, as it were, the barge on which the ship-wrecked ancient poetry saved herself with all her children: crowded into a narrow space and timidly submitting to the single pilot, Socrates, they now sailed into a new world, which never tired of looking at the fantastic spectacle of this procession. Indeed Plato has given to all posterity the model of a new art form, the model of the *novel*—which may be described as an infinitely enhanced Aesopian fable, in which poetry holds the same rank in relation to dialectical philosophy as this same philosophy held for many centuries in relation to theology: namely, the rank of *ancilla*. This was the new position into which Plato, under the pressure of the demonic Socrates, forced poetry. (90–91)[13]

Within the dialogue, art becomes the servant of philosophy and is forced to accept the course determined by its pilot, Socrates; yet, at the same time, the dialogue is itself a new art form that is "fictive" ("an infinitely enhanced Aesopian fable") rather than philosophical. Art is now compelled by philosophy to "cling to the trunk of dialectic" (91), but this trunk has become less solid, less firmly rooted in the ground than it was before philosophy was

9

contaminated by the fictive or poetic, before philosophy turned into the same sort of bastard mixture of forms as the tragic art it was attempting to pilot. In the dialogue, philosophy cannot pilot and control art as easily as it would like; the philosophical barge is drifting off its intended course from the very beginning of its voyage.

Nietzsche is forced to admit that there are definite "aesthetic" benefits from the mutual transformation of tragedy and philosophy. After insisting on the tragic loss imposed upon tragedy when music (the "essence" of tragedy) is driven off by "Socratic optimism," he reveals that Socrates cannot be seen as a totally negative force, and that the opposition between the philosophical and the poetic cannot be taken as hard and fast.

> For in view of the Platonic dialogues we are certainly not entitled to regard [a phenomenon such as Socrates] as a merely disintegrating, negative force. And though there can be no doubt that the most immediate effect of the Socratic impulse tended to the dissolution of Dionysian tragedy, yet a profound experience in Socrates' own life impels us to ask whether there is *necessarily* only an antipodal relation between Socratism and art, and whether the birth of an "artistic Socrates" is altogether a contradiction in terms. (92)

This Nietzschean narrative (novel) of the birth of tragedy is also, then, the narrative of the birth of the novel, which comes about with the disintegration, murder, or suicide of what, at times, seems to be a pure poetic force—tragedy before Socrates—but which is really already a contamination of forms and a conflict of forces. The Nietzschean narrative reveals that the momentary dominance of one set of forces or forms is never accomplished without affecting the dominating as well as the dominated forces, and that no one force ever emerges totally victorious from the conflict, no single reversal can ever be taken as conclusive.

In his narrative, Nietzsche gives us one more look at Socrates, and this version of Socrates is further proof that philosophy has not emerged totally victorious; the battle that began with him is still being fought by Nietzsche. The last Socrates we see in *The Birth of Tragedy* is a "Nietzschean" Socrates who in prison is told in a dream to practice music, and who, thus, is led to recognize, in spite of himself, the force of art and the limits of philosophy:

> The voice of the Socratic dream vision is the only sign of any misgivings about the limits of logic: Perhaps—thus he must have asked himself—what is not intelligible to me is not necessarily unintelligent? Perhaps there is a realm of wisdom from which the logician is exiled? Perhaps art is even a necessary correlative of, and supplement for science? (93)

10

The words Nietzsche attributes hypothetically to Socrates—the fiction he creates as to what Socrates must have asked himself—admit that logic (science, philosophy) is not universal. The limits of the intelligible are thus indicated to him by the necessity of art—or at least by the demand for art, a demand that the dream apparition repeatedly makes: "Socrates, practice music." Nietzsche has Socrates die for the truth, all the while doubting whether truth is enough.

In the realm of dreams, apparitions, and fictions, art is considered a necessary supplement for science; it indicates a realm "beyond" the intelligible and the theoretical. If this "beyond" is also a "realm of wisdom," it is nevertheless radically different in form and logic from the wisdom of philosophy. In the story of the birth and death of tragedy narrated by Nietzsche, it is the contamination of these two realms that produces the most powerful weapons against both the dogmatic philosopher and the aestheticist, the dreams (fictions) of the philosopher and the "wisdom" of the dreamer being the weapons Nietzsche constantly uses against each. "We have *art* lest we *perish of the truth*," says Nietzsche in *The Will to Power* (Section 822 [1888], 435, translation slightly modified). But the way "we have art"—if it is not to lead to raising art above the fray, if it is not to make of art a transcendent term, the reversal of philosophical truth—must continually confront art with the philosophical tradition to which it is inextricably bound and whose traces and forms it carries within it. Today, it seems to me just as urgent to say, and in a way that is anything but anti-Nietzschean, that there is just as great a danger of our perishing of art as of the truth, and that it is this double danger that confronts critical theory and art after Nietzsche.

3. Literature as Rhetoric

Of all the recent work done on Nietzsche, essays by Paul de Man and Philippe Lacoue-Labarthe focus most directly and persistently on the question of art (explicitly as literature or fiction) and its relation to philosophy. Their approaches to Nietzsche are similar in many ways, for both follow and, at the same time, complicate and even challenge the Heideggerean reading of Nietzsche. They both also emphasize the fundamental role played by rhetoric in Nietzsche's attack on philosophy, as well as his strategic use of literature or fiction as the principal means of undermining the truth. And yet in spite of these similarities, there is a seemingly minor, but, I would argue, crucial difference between their interpretative strategies: in particular, a difference in the way each deals with the question of rhetoric each finds central to Nietzsche's work, and the way each determines the function of art and literature both in Nietzsche's overall strategy and in their own. Both may be convinced that rhetoric is crucial to our "survival," an important critical weapon that helps keep us from "perishing of the truth," but they differ over how the question of rhetoric is to be treated as well as over the specific relation it has to the question of literature.

In the three chapters devoted to Nietzsche in *Allegories of Reading*, Paul de Man, like Heidegger, puts the question of the relationship of "art" and philosophy at the center of his reading. For de Man, "art" is not art in general but quite specifically literature: "For Nietzsche is obviously one of those figures like Plato, Augustine, Montaigne, or Rousseau whose work straddles the two activities of the human intellect that are both the closest and the most impenetrable to each other—literature and philosophy" (103). For de Man, the question of literature in Nietzsche's work cannot be confined (as it is for the most part by Heidegger) to one of content or theme; it is also, or even primarily, one of form: "the complex question of his reflection on literature and on the specifically literary aspects of his own philosophical discourse" (103). If, as Heidegger claims, art is the entry Nietzsche uses to raise the most fundamental philosophical questions, rhetoric is the entry de Man uses to raise fundamental questions concerning both literature and philosophy and their coimplication in Nietzsche.

Strangely enough, de Man announces that it might seem "far-fetched" to concentrate on what seems to be an "eccentric and minor part of Nietzsche's enterprise," especially when "an abundance of other, less oblique approaches to the question may appear preferable" (103). For anyone who knows de Man's work at all, this must be taken as a rhetorical ploy; but it is still important to notice that he characterizes a rhetorical approach as far-fetched, eccentric, minor, and oblique. This characterization serves de Man as a definition (of sorts) of literature itself: literature is opposed to the reasonableness, essentiality, and directness of philosophy. Because of the heritage of structuralism and its emphasis on rhetoric and form (as well as the importance of de Man's own work in this area), it probably seems far-fetched to very few literary critics (perhaps de Man was addressing only philosophers?) that de Man chose in this instance to concentrate on the problem of rhetoric in Nietzsche. For de Man, and the many critics influenced by his work, this is an absolutely essential way to proceed—not only as it concerns Nietzsche, the most literary of philosophers, but also as it concerns even the most philosophical of philosophers.

If few today would deny that philosophical discourse is first and foremost *discourse*, a form of writing that necessarily uses rhetorical strategies and tropes like any other form, there is, however, still much controversy concerning the implications to be derived from the rhetorical nature of philosophy and the place of Nietzsche in determining these implications.[14] The question that de Man forces us to ask is what is accomplished when the problem of the relation between philosophy and literature is recast in terms of the oblique but more fundamental problem of rhetoric—especially if rhetoric is seen as "grounding," in a very particular way, both philosophy and literature and thus playing a determining role in the very formation of that relation?

Before the effects of this recasting of philosophy and literature can be understood, we first need to have a sense of what rhetoric is and how it works. If rhetoric is such a fundamental question, it is important to know who or what determines what rhetoric is in the first place, as well as how we are to have access to this determination. De Man's reading emphasizes how Nietzsche radicalizes the classical concept of rhetoric by deriving literature and philosophy (aesthetics and meaning) from tropes or figures, rather than the reverse. If de Man rejects Heidegger's characterization of Nietzsche's work as the reversal of Platonism (*Allegories*, 109), he seems in turn to be treating it as the reversal of classical rhetoric (of Aristotelianism?): "Tropes are not understood aesthetically, as ornament, nor are they understood semantically as a figurative meaning that derives from literal, proper denomination. Rather the reverse is the case. The trope is not a derived, marginal, or aberrant form of language but *the linguistic paradigm par excellence*. The figurative structure is not one linguistic mode among others but *characterizes language as such*" (105, my emphasis). The seemingly eccentric, far-fetched, marginal or aberrant forms of language have here become the essential characteristics of language.

There remains, however, the problem of how de Man, once philosophy and classical rhetoric have been shown to be faulty in their definitions of rhetoric, can speak with such certainty, how he can be sure that he has seized the essence of "language as such" and chosen the true and unique "linguistic paradigm par excellence." Has not Nietzsche (and de Man, himself, after him) undercut the very grounds on which to make such assertions about tropes and figurative structures? If this is so, on what basis can one continue to assert such things? If we cannot know the essence of truth, if "metaphysics, morality, religion, science . . . merit consideration only as various forms of lies" (*The Will to Power*, Section 853 [1886?], 451), how can we *know* that a particular linguistic paradigm is *the* linguistic paradigm or what characterizes language as such?

Nietzsche gives the task of "solving" problems such as these to the "liar" or the "artist" that "man must be" (451); de Man looks to literature to provide "answers" to all such questions. Rejecting literature as the mere reversal of metaphysics, there nevertheless slips into de Man's reading from the beginning, if not an equation between literature and "true" rhetoric or "authentic" language use, then at least an assertion—and it must remain only an assertion for it cannot be proved, because to prove it would be to make rhetoric, language, and literature all organs of philosophy and its logic—of the proximity of literature to rhetoric (language as such) that ultimately functions as a kind of equation: "We can legitimately assert therefore," says de Man, "that the key to Nietzsche's critique of metaphysics . . . lies in the rhetorical model

13

of the trope or, if one prefers to call it that way, in literature as the language most explicitly grounded in rhetoric" (109). Literature as the language most explicitly grounded in the ground of literature and philosophy, that is, most explicitly grounded in the ground of all grounds, comes in to assure us or at least to allow us legitimately to assert that all language works the way it asserts (and shows) that its own language works, or, better yet, that it itself works as language. Literature is the key to the relationship between philosophy and literature because it is explicitly grounded in language, *the ultimate ground.*

De Man indicates that he himself does not want to glorify literature by such assertions and that Nietzsche certainly didn't want to either: "A text like *On Truth and Lie,* although it presents itself legitimately as a demystification of literary rhetoric, remains entirely literary, rhetorical, and deceptive itself. Does this mean that it will end up in a glorification of literature over science or, as is sometimes claimed of Nietzsche, in a purely literary conception of philosophy?" (113). Even though de Man obviously intends such questions to be answered more in the negative than in the positive, he does not himself answer them directly. They are for him rhetorical questions, and this means that they have no simple answer, that they cannot be answered unambiguously either affirmatively or negatively. In this case, the glorification of literature and a purely literary conception of philosophy are both to be avoided insomuch as they imply an original separation between philosophy and literature and thus a traditional definition of literature as the other of philosophy. At the same time, it would be extremely difficult to argue that de Man's approach to philosophy is in no way dependent on a "literary" conception of philosophy and literature—as long as we come to an agreement as to what he means by literature, which is not an easy task at all. The task of deciding how to answer is here difficult, if not impossible.[15]

What is certain is that in de Man's interpretation of Nietzsche, philosophy can no longer be taken for the dominant term in its relationship with literature, and if this results in literature being privileged, de Man does not want this privilege to be the result of a simple, unambiguous reversal. In other words, the insight offered by a literature that admits its own deceitful, that is, rhetorical, tropological character, cannot be presented as a simple (ie. philosophical) insight without immediately being lost as an insight:

> The critical deconstruction that leads to the discoveries of the literary, rhetorical nature of the philosophical claim to truth is genuine enough and cannot be refuted: literature turns out to be the main topic of philosophy and the model for the kind of truth to which it aspires. But when literature seduces us with the freedom of its figural combinations . . . it is not the less deceitful because it asserts its own deceitful properties. (115)

14

There is no escape from untruth or deceit, even, or, especially in literature; even by admitting or asserting explicitly that it is deceitful, literature can do no more than remain deceitful—it certainly cannot claim to attain the truth, even the truth of deceit.

Thus neither a philosophy that denies its own deceitful status, nor a literature or philosophy-as-literature that acknowledges it, succeeds in mastering or escaping from the disruptive rhetorical forces of untruth. And yet the desire to escape and master deceit seems to be, for de Man, one of the principal dynamic elements of the relationship between philosophy and literature. For if "philosophy turns out to be an endless reflection on its own destruction at the hands of literature [deceit]," this is the ultimate proof of the legitimacy of de Man's assertions: "the endless reflection is itself a rhetorical mode, since it is unable even to escape from the rhetorical deceit it denounces" (115). Deceit leads to more deceit, rhetoric leads to more rhetoric; the inescapable ground continues to assert itself as the ground—no matter how unstable it might be—and the end of both philosophy and literature, of philosophy as literature.

There would seem to be no room left for wisdom in such a configuration; yet de Man does claim that Nietzsche's text possesses a certain form of wisdom: the wisdom of all texts as such (that is, all texts that he would call literary), a wisdom of self-destruction, repetition, and reversal. "The wisdom of the text is self-destructive (art is true but truth kills itself), but this self-destruction is infinitely displaced in a series of successive rhetorical reversals which, by the endless repetition of the same figure, keep it suspended between truth and the death of this truth" (115). The complex play and conflict of forces of life and death, truth and deceit, that de Man is attempting to describe here, cannot, I would claim, in any way be considered a form of quietism or acquiescence, as some have argued. The repetition of the same figure may result in its suspension "between truth and the death of this truth," but this suspension is active, even productive, precisely because it is infinite. If this "allegory of errors is the very model of philosophical rigor" (118), as de Man claims at the end of the essay, it is because such a structure of repetition or infinite reversal constitutes a critical process that takes no form of truth and no form of deceit (the death of truth) as its truth. It may continually make affirmations about truth and deceit and their relations, but its affirmations are themselves susceptible to reversal. Philosophical rigor is here a synonym for non-closure and the perpetual rearrangement of forces.

There remains the problem of rhetoric and literature. De Man avoids almost all the traps into which readers of Nietzsche have traditionally fallen, and he does this by refusing to give in to the temptation to take literature literally (that is, to take it as the mere reversal of truth), or to posit literary-rhetorical strategies and figures as alternatives to philosophical logic or argumentation. In de Man's reading of Nietzsche, truth's positing and undoing function si-

15

multaneously, in a conflictual process of reversal within the dynamics of any text—in both literature and philosophy. On this level of his analysis literature has no privilege.

And yet on another level literature is privileged. In not questioning sufficiently the concept of rhetoric (a concept he manipulates with great skill) and by accepting the trope as given (as linguistic paradigm par excellence, given each time by and through literature, or, at least, through the underlying "literary" grounds of philosophy), de Man delimits the play and conflict of textual forces in terms of a particular notion of language—a notion that literature practices (performs) more explicitly than does philosophy or any other form or genre of discourse. In its proximity to rhetoric, being at heart nothing but rhetoric, literature is there to give us access to the sense, form, and function of language. Rhetoric is the only given that is not given by anything but itself, that gives itself as given, because what gives it, literature, is nothing but rhetoric. We always come back to rhetoric (and literature) because there is no escape from it (them), and we can be sure we have come back to it (them) in the right way if we follow the way literature leads us back to them, that is, back to itself. A limitation is thus imposed on a process that is supposed to be without limitations.[16]

At the end of de Man's third and final chapter on Nietzsche in *Allegories of Reading*, "Rhetoric of Persuasion," the consequences of his concept of rhetoric and his rhetorical strategy in presenting and performing this concept are especially evident:

> And since, if one wants to conserve the term "literature," one should not hesitate to assimilate it with rhetoric, then it would follow that the deconstruction of metaphysics, or "philosophy," is an impossibility to the precise extent that it is "literary." This by no means resolves the problem of the relationship between literature and philosophy in Nietzsche, but it at least establishes a somewhat more reliable point of "reference" from which to ask the question. (131)

Again, de Man's argument is incredibly dense, as much in a state of active suspension and reversal as the text it is commenting on. But what grounds its instability and makes sense out of, or gives form to, its own reversibility is, not surprisingly, literature. To the extent that "philosophy" is "literary," it has no need of being, and de Man asserts, cannot be deconstructed. It cannot be deconstructed (from without, by the reader) because it has always-already deconstructed itself, for such is the nature of rhetoric for de Man. Rhetoric (and the literature de Man assimilates it to) becomes "a somewhat more reliable point of 'reference' from which to ask the question" of the relationship between literature and philosophy—at the very least, somewhat (and much rests on how much weight is to be given to this word) more reliable than philosophy,[17] because literature-as-rhetoric is both the unstable ground of the relationship and the repeated undoing of any particular form of the relationship; it is the infinite repetition of the construction, reversal, and deconstruction of the truth. Literature wins out in the struggle of forces by refusing to allow there to be a winner.

No matter how complicated, nuanced, and ironic de Man's argument is, it is precisely the "somewhat more reliable" position literature occupies that is the problem. This position limits and controls the interplay between philosophy and literature, and accounts for and finally resolves in each instance the conflict and discordance inherent in the relationship. But it cannot be stressed enough that it resolves them only after it has followed them at great length, after it has let them disrupt and undermine the obvious and immediate resolutions that might be imposed on them. De Man's assimilation of literature with rhetoric (a certain concept of rhetoric) is certainly no simple glorification of literature, as some have claimed: it is probably the most powerful, subtle, nuanced, and complicated "glorification" of recent years. The contradictory complexity de Man attributes to literature-as-rhetoric constitutes the critical, disruptive force of his position. The "reliability" of literature, no matter how relative or ironic this reliability is, as well as the equation of "the rhetorical potentiality of language with literature itself" (10), constitute its ultimate limitations.

4. Rethinking the Literary

Is there a way to push the question of the relationship between philosophy and literature beyond the limitations that an equation of rhetoric with literature imposes upon it? To be sure, it is already an important critical step to undermine the hierarchy that has allowed philosophical-theoretical language and categories (such as truth, referent, context, and even form) to determine literature; the limitations imposed by a strategy such as de Man's are undoubtedly less restrictive than those most often passively accepted and applied to, or actively imposed on, both philosophy and literature. This is especially true, I should add, of the approaches of most of those critics and theorists who have reacted with great vehemence against de Man's work (in most cases against the caricature of his work that they themselves have created) in the name of either traditional humanistic thought, authentic literary history, or socio-political concerns. In analyzing the differences between Lacoue-Labarthe's essays on Nietzsche in *Le Sujet de la philosophie* and de Man's from *Allegories of Reading* (two sets of essays, I have indicated, which focus on the problem of rhetoric in Nietzsche), my purpose is to give a sense of how these limitations might begin to be confronted—which does not necessarily mean that they will ever go away or be definitively transgressed.

Lacoue-Labarthe's central concern in *Le Sujet de la philosophie* is to specify

17

the limits of philosophical discourse, to analyze the source, form, and limitations of the critical power of philosophy by studying its relationship to that against which, "under the name of poetry, fiction or literature," it has always "attempted to delimit itself" (6). It is not surprising, that the central figure studied in this collection is Nietzsche and that his chief interlocutor is Heidegger. At first, Lacoue-Labarthe's project seems identical to de Man's, and the various references in *Allegories of Reading* to one of these essays, "Le Détour," indicate the affinity de Man has with such a critical project. But it is precisely because these two approaches to Nietzsche share so much in common that the differences between them are so revealing.[18]

In "La Fable," the first essay in *Le Sujet de la philosophie*, Lacoue-Labarthe argues that the ultimate problem raised by Nietzsche's attack on philosophical truth is not what it does to philosophy but what it does to fiction. Is it really possible, he asks, to conceive of fiction as the opposite of truth, as being located totally outside the oppositions determined by philosophy, the very field that fiction is being used to attack? Or, as he puts it: "To think fiction outside of philosophy is not to oppose appearance to reality because appearance is nothing other than the product of reality. It is precisely to think without recourse to this opposition, *outside* this opposition: to think the world as fable. Is it possible?" (16). Like de Man's "rhetorical question," this one cannot be answered simply with a yes or a no: therefore, the project of moving in the direction of an affirmative answer must always be aware that it might be doing nothing more than reinstituting the very oppositional logic of philosophy it is attempting to move beyond. In other words, fiction is as risky a "ground" to stand on as philosophy, because it may in fact be another form of the same ground.

Like de Man, Lacoue-Labarthe sees that the dangers of a "mere reversal" of the traditional hierarchy determining the relations between philosophy and literature and resulting in the simple "glorification" of literature are constant for any critical strategy using literature as a weapon "against" the limitations of philosophy. In almost all cases positing or affirming an alternative to philosophy turns out to be more within philosophy than outside it.[19] But what is also revealed here is Lacoue-Labarthe's uneasiness with the term fiction (or literature, or poetry, or art in general), one which is greater than de Man's; thus, the kinds of limits that de Man ultimately places around his critical investigation are themselves one of the objects of Lacoue-Labarthe's critique. In other words, Lacoue-Labarthe is unwilling to accept literature as the ground or ultimate destination of his critique, or even as a somewhat more reliable point of view for his investigation, because literature, even when it is allowed to speak for itself in its "own words" and on its "own terms," does not for him offer an alternative to philosophy: "Literature cannot speak of itself except in borrowing more or less shamefully the language of philosophy"[20]

18

Because the question here is of literature when it *speaks* of itself, of the language of literature, it is quite certain that de Man would not have been opposed to Lacoue-Labarthe's formulation. For speaking as such, even literature speaking of itself and being conscious of itself, was not the essential characteristic of literary discourse for de Man—at least it no longer was in his later work. From the perspective of de Man's later position, a response such as the following could be made to Lacoue-Labarthe's statement: granted that literature, when it speaks of itself, speaks in the language of, that is, as philosophy. Is there not something more basic in literature (and in philosophy) than speaking per se, something that makes speaking possible but that cannot be equated with it? In its proximity to, and even assimilation with, rhetoric (the defining characteristic of language), cannot literature be argued to figure or trope itself "unphilosophically?" The issue, therefore, is where Lacoue-Labarthe's uneasiness concerning fiction and any other proclaimed "outside" of philosophy leaves the question of rhetoric.

In "Le Détour," Lacoue-Labarthe begins his investigation of the question of rhetoric in Nietzsche with the caveat that Nietzsche's critical project and strategy should not be thought of as originating with him. The strategy of using the figurative forces of fiction (myth, poetry, rhetoric, literature) against philosophy and determining all language as "originally figurative," a determination that means that no language can free itself from its tropic status except by "forgetting, mistaking or dissimulating its own origin" (33–34), may be, Lacoue-Labarthe claims, as old as philosophy itself. In any case, he argues, it is most definitely "linked to a certain *epoch* of modern philosophy and the science of language it commands. And in its principle, regardless of the brutality or subtlety of its strategic intentions, it is abslutely subjected to a whole conceptual apparatus that is metaphysical from start to finish" (34). Perhaps even more important than his recognition that rhetorical strategies have an important role in the history of philosophy is Lacoue-Labarthe's admission that an emphasis on rhetoric is very likely one of the distinguishing characteristics of the "modern epoch" and thus an unthought condition of Nietzsche's and our own way of conceiving the problem in the first place. Rhetoric may be as much the modern epoch's way of avoiding critical thought as a critical weapon to be used against tradition.

For these reasons, Lacoue-Labarthe distrusts rhetoric as much as he does philosophy. Rhetoric is itself philosophical, dependent on a philosophical conceptualization of language, and in no way can it be thought to be simply given as a neutral ground for language or as giving itself by itself. Following Derrida,[21] Lacoue-Labarthe argues that a strategy that assumes, either in the first or last instance, the simple exteriority of metaphor or troping to philosophy will never succeed in resisting very effectively, or escaping from, the power of philosophy to incorporate into itself what *it* constitutes as its other. Such a strategy—even if it might initially be capable of disturbing philosophy's internal security—will ultimately reinforce the power of philosophy and reveal that rhetoric and a concept of literature based on the primacy of figurative language are ultimately philosophical concepts through and through. The question remains, therefore, whether it is possible to use rhetoric in some other fashion, fully aware that one is using a tool that has been given by the very tradition one is attempting to use it against.

Lacoue-Labarthe proceeds to show that Nietzsche's inability to construct an "innocent" concept of rhetoric (and it is not just his inability but that of any philosopher, writer or critic), is a limitation in his critical strategy against which he constantly struggles; and that this struggle is one of the most forceful aspects of his work. The problem is that there cannot be "a concept of rhetoric as such. An innocent concept. . . . If Nietzsche persists in constructing one, it is immediately displaced, effaced, dragged outside itself. The reason for this is actually quite simple: rhetoric is considered only for what it reveals of the essence of language itself. Or, if you prefer, there cannot be a very stable concept of rhetoric when rhetoric is at bottom the essence of what in principle it is only a certain use" (42). Rhetoric is not a concept, but a process or use of language perpetually in search of its concept whose definition or realization must be infinitely postponed—precisely because the rhetorical realization of the concept would at the same time displace it, derealize it. The lack of innocence of all concepts of rhetoric affects the concept of language (whose essence they might be assumed to constitute) and, certainly, any discursive form (literature, for example) that might be claimed to be associated with it.

Not only is philosophy undermined and transformed, Lacoue-Labarthe claims, when its relationship to literature (or to itself) is questioned in terms of rhetoric, but art and literature are also undermined and transformed in the same process of questioning: "The introduction of rhetoric finally touches less the theory of language than it subverts the conception of *art* itself. More precisely, the introduction of rhetoric, because it pushes the question of language to the forefront, demands that one think art in terms of language and not the reverse—and in this movement art and language are transformed together, neither remains what is was" (61). It is not, then, the equation of literature with rhetoric that provides a critical perspective from which to undo the limitations of philosophy; it is rather the mutual transformation of art by language and language by art that subverts philosophy, language, and art. In this process of mutual transformation and subversion, there is really no reliable perspective on the question of the relationship of the various elements. No perspective or positioning can be considered to be more than strategic, a part of the conflict of forces and shifting boundaries between entities with no one perspective or position dominating the field.

If displacement, excessiveness, instability are the characteristics of rhetoric, then one cannot fall back on rhetoric or on a notion of literature revealing itself to be fundamentally or explicitly rhetorical without immediately being drawn into the non- or para-rhetorical, the non- or para-literary. "Rhetoric," Lacoue-Labarthe concludes from all this, "is a monstrosity" (63). The radical place it holds in Nietzsche's work undermines boundaries and makes it impossible to locate definitively any pure exteriority: "The boundary that separates philosophy from its *other* then begins to be blurred. The emphasis on rhetoric leads to a point where it is no longer possible to turn against philosophy, as if from its pure 'outside' (that is, dialectically speaking, from its purest intimacy), any musical, mythical, etc. originality. Rhetoric contaminates an entire system of belief" (65–66). Rhetoric problematizes an entire system of belief in mythical or musical purity, in origins of all sorts, even or especially a belief in any form of "original language." In the same way, it has "contaminated" the belief in literature as originally exterior to philosophy, as well as the belief in a form of rhetoric which would also remain exterior to philosophy—because it could provide *the linguistic paradigm*, the origin and truth of language itself. For Lacoue-Labarthe, the "lesson of Nietzsche" is that it is precisely the "unreliability" or "monstrous" character of rhetoric that makes it an important critical tool, a means (and not the only one) of questioning the integrity not only of philosophy but also of literature. Rhetoric is no more characteristic of literature than of philosophy, no more exterior to one than to the other.

It could be argued that de Man's reading of Nietzsche also leads us to the point where philosophy and literature contaminate each other, where the distinctions between the two are not fixed by either but continually put into question. This is undeniably so, but the differences of emphasis and strategy of Lacoue-Labarthe's readings of Nietzsche point more explicitly than de Man's readings to the risks in the strategy of relying on literature as a means of undermining philosophy (theory in general). It is taken almost as a truism today that philosophy (theory) does not have, and should not be given, the upper hand in its relationship with literature. But it is equally important, I would insist, to understand why literatuure or fiction or art cannot, in turn, be attributed a position of dominance "above the fray"—and this is what important elements of "our age" most resist. This resistance, which takes the form of privileging the literary or the aesthetic as the opposite of the theoretical, is just as restrictive and dogmatic in its effect on literature and theory as is the reduction of the aesthetic to "outside" (philosophical, social, historical or political) determination.

In the following chapters, I shall analyze the critical strategies of three of the most important contemporary thinkers, all of whom rely in one way or another on the critical powers of art and literature to combat the restrictions of philosophy, political theory, history, and even aesthetics and literary criticism. In this way, they are indebted to Nietzsche and explicitly involved in the questions I have raised in this introductory chapter through an analysis of aspects of Nietzsche's critical and combative use of "art" and that of two of his most powerful contemporary interlocutors. My goal is to understand how each of the critical philosophers I shall treat deals with the questions of art and literature and is led not to construct an aesthetics but to develop what I call "paraesthetic" strategies. For each of them, I shall be arguing, "paraesthetic" strategies function as a nondogmatic way of developing and situating their own critical positions. What follows is an attempt to understand how Foucault, Lyotard, and Derrida all use art and literature as critical weapons "against" theoretical dogmatism and, at the same time, resist, undermine, and move beyond the aestheticist limitations that aesthetic and literary-poetic strategies inevitably carry along with them.

C H A P T E R　T W O
A E S T H E T I C　A N T A G O N I S M S

L　Y　O　T　A　R　D

What I am interested in, even if this isn't the way one is supposed to approach such things, is the fact that, politically, we have no theory, although important segments of theory could take their inspiration from what is being produced in what is commonly called the "arts."
　　　　—Jean-François Lyotard, "On Theory: An Interview"

Art is the social antithesis of society.
　　　　—Theodor Adorno, *Aesthetic Theory*

1. Art as Critique

Few would deny that art has "a certain" exteriority and autonomy in relation to philosophy, history, and the socio-political sphere, that everything in art cannot be accounted for, or, is not determined, in all its aspects by these other fields. And yet the extent and importance of this exteriority or autonomy is much debated: some would want to diminish it as much as possible in order to derive the essence of art from these other fields, while others would insist that the superiority, universality, transcendency, or simply critical force of art rests on it being *other*, and that this alterity should be respected and protected at all costs.

These debates are as old as philosophy itself, but they took on a new importance with Kant, when the specificity of aesthetic judgment became a central issue for philosophy. In spite of Hegel's attempt to rectify what he considered to be Kant's subjectivist approach to art and his desire to make art a mere stage on the way to absolute knowledge, an incomplete form of

23

philosophy, the problem of the relative exteriority of art to philosophy, history, politics, etc. continues to be the subject of much controversy in contemporary critical theory. The interest in such debates over the status of art is that they very rarely remain narrowly focused on art alone—for the place given to art and the way the question of the aesthetic in general is approached affect not only theories of art (aesthetics in the narrow sense), but also the theories of all the fields art relates to, even if at a distance.

Probably no critical philosopher in recent times has made more radical and sweeping claims in the name of the exteriority of art—not just to theory but to discourse in general (at least to discourse as it is defined by philosophy and linguistics)—than Jean-François Lyotard. From *Discours, figure* (Paris: Klincksieck, 1971) through at least *Economie libidinale* (Paris: Minuit, 1974), the aesthetic could be considered to constitute for Lyotard both the privileged space of all critical activity and the model for all unrestricted affirmation and radical socio-political transformation. The first work consists of a series of essays on art, linguistics, philosophy, and psychoanalysis; it lays the groundwork for a radical critical aesthetics by using art to reveal the limitations of theory. It treats the figural as a disruptive element that is, at the same time, within and outside discourse in general. The second work proposes a libidinal politics modeled after an energetics derived, in great part, from a radical notion of the aesthetic as the realm where libidinal drives remain uncathected and desire unfulfilled and disruptive. The aesthetic is treated as a space relatively untouched, or, at the very least, not determined by what Lyotard would argue are the restrictions of meaning and form governing discourse in general. Even more, Lyotard argues that when these restrictions are imposed on art, it resists and overcomes them and continues to function critically and/or affirmatively.

Juxtaposed out of context, many of Lyotard's claims for art appear to constitute an acritical and exaggerated attempt to compensate for the failures and inadequacies of the theoretical and historical-political realms. In the name of the radical exteriority of art, he legitimizes his own critical strategy and presents it as a radical alternative to what he argues are the fruitless attempts to criticize and radically transform philosophy and political theory and practice from within. At times, it even seems that Lyotard takes a bit too literally Nietzsche's claim that art is the "countermovement" to the "decadence forms of humanity" called religion and morality—and, we should add in Lyotard's case, politics—and that to an even greater extent than Nietzsche, he treats art as the reversal of philosophy-metaphysics. As was the case with Nietzsche, however, I would argue that more is at stake here than a simple reversal.

Lyotard characterizes his first major work, *Discours, figure*, as a "detour leading to the practical critique of ideology" (19). Why such a detour is necessary in the first place, and, why, for Lyotard, to be critically effective it must pass through the aesthetic field are two of the principal questions I find necessary to ask of this book. In the history of theory, there is certainly no shortage of attempts to link aesthetics with politics, art with society, literature with history. When carried through with subtlety and a concern for the relative specificity of the two realms, historical or sociological approaches to art and literature can raise fundamental questions about the nature of art, as well as the foundations of history and society. Too often, however, art and literature are reduced to mere reflections of their socio-historical context and judged according to criteria established for the presentation and evaluation of historical "facts"; they are placed in socio-historical totalities having no specifically aesthetic dimension. This is especially a problem when it comes to forms of art and literature that could be considered "experimental," for experimental art is not easily classified in terms of socio-historical totalities except as their negation; for most historians or sociologists, the "negation of history" is the greatest threat to history, the sign that one is attempting to flee or do away with history.[1]

Sociologists of literature, for instance, have traditionally shown little patience when dealing with movements or theories that could be classified under the rubrics "art for art's sake" and "experimental or avant-garde art"—perhaps because these movements seem to play with and even reject the most fundamental premises underlying the entire historical or sociological project: that there is *one* social or historical reality which all discourse and art represent either negatively or positively. To choose an obvious example, Jean-Paul Sartre—whose work constitutes an historical-political defense of a non-experimental, communicational notion of literature—condemned what he called "aesthetic purism" as a retreat from political responsibility: "We know very well that pure art and empty art are the same thing and that aesthetic purism was only a brilliant defensive maneuver of certain bourgeois of the last century who prefered to see themselves denounced as philistines rather than as exploiters" (*What is Literature?*, translated by Bernard Frechtman [New York: Washington Square Press, 1966], 17, translation modified). The alternative offered by Sartre is a simple one: either one is with or against history, for or against exploitation, and the sign of which side one is on is the kind of literature one writes, the form of art one paints,—and, following from this, the kind of criticism or theory one does. Even today, when the precise Sartrean notion of *engagement* is no longer in fashion, a too explicit or extended experimentation with form or a too developed questioning of the nature of the aesthetic or the literary as such can still be considered, at best, a "defensive maneuver" and, at worst, a sign of a conservative or even reactionary political ideology.

In *Discours, figure* and *Dérive à partir de Marx et Freud* (Paris: U.G.E., 1973)—parts of which have been translated as *Driftworks*[2]—Lyotard explicitly confronts this devaluation of the aesthetic in political and social theory,

25

what he calls the Marxist-French contempt for art, even if it is really much more than just French or Marxist. He sees this contempt as a definite sign of conservatism and dogmatism, of an unwillingness to question seriously the premises governing the construction of the socio-political field:

> The word aesthetic in Marxist-French is practically an insult, which reveals the connections of this language with that of the bourgeoisie: a contempt for art by treating it as a frivolous pastime, by considering the artist as a buffoon and aesthetic problems as false problems screening real ones—all formal concerns being considered as superstructural irrealities. And feeding this contempt is an active repression of affective intensities on the pretext that Rothko's painting, Cage's music, Baruchello's films serve no purpose, that they are not in any way effective, that they are elitist and do nothing but maintain the cultural domination of the bourgeoisie. (*Driftworks*, 15, t.m.)

Lyotard attacks this contempt for art with as much vehemence and frustration as Sartre attacked aesthetic purism—because just as much is at stake for him in the questions raised by art, by even or especially forms of "art for art's sake" or "aesthetic purism" as was at stake for Sartre in his notion of "littérature engagée." At stake is not only art but also questions of the social and the political: the possibility of critical thought itself. If Sartre saw aesthetic purism as a defensive maneuver, Lyotard sees what could be called "political purism" as an even more serious defensive maneuver, one that prohibits the questions raised by art from being treated seriously, not only in the aesthetic but in the theoretical-political realm as well.

In fact, Lyotard goes so far as to claim that a certain form of art, because it is not formed in terms of established social organizations or forms, practices an effective, that is to say, critical politics that no form of political activity in and of itself has succeeded in practicing:

> I believe it is absolutely obvious today, and it has been for quite some time, that, for one thing, the reconstitution of traditional political organizations is bound to fail, for this kind of reconstitution settles precisely into the order of the social surface where its organizations are "appropriated." They perpetuate the type of activity the system has instituted as political; they are necessarily alienated, ineffective. The other thing is that all deconstruction[3], which might appear as an aesthetic formalism, "avant-garde" research, etc., actually constitutes the only type of activity that is effective, and this is because it is functionally—the word is very bad; it would be better to say straight out ontologically—located outside the system, and by defi-

26

nition its function is to deconstruct everything that presents itself as an order, to show that all "order" conceals something else, something that is repressed in this order. (*Driftworks*, 29, t.m.)

The claim that art is ontologically outside the social-political universe grants it an enormous privilege and seems, at first glance, to be loaded with the most traditional kinds of idealist, aestheticist implications. It will, of course, all depend on what Lyotard means by "ontologically outside" and how well he keeps the radical distance between the aesthetic and the political—one he wants to maintain at all costs—from becoming the simple negation or repression of the political in the name of a higher ideal, art.

If Lyotard grants art the privilege of being ontologically outside, he also, at the same time, warns against attempts to institute art (or anything else) as an ideal or pseudo-religion. For him, "what art does—what it ought to do—is always to unmask all attempts to reconstitute a pseudo-religion" (72). The privilege of being "outside" is not given to all art but just to those forms of art that do what art "ought to do," and when art does what it ought to do, it undoes ontology, religion, and even itself. Aesthetic ideals, then, are not meant to replace political ideals, but a certain form of art is evoked as a way of undoing all ideals and all ends imposed on the critical process.

In order to accomplish this task, art, in Lyotard's sense, always has a double and contradictory status. First of all, it has a transcendent function that allows it to be situated outside the political and all other orders and, thus, be able to intervene effectively in these orders to expose what is repressed in them for order to be imposed. Secondly, art has a critical and self-critical function; it unmasks all attempts to raise any force or entity above the conflict of forces and orders to the level of a transcendent ideal or absolute. In a contradictory fashion, Lyotard thus demands that art be simultaneously transcendent and critical, constructive and deconstructive, apolitical and radically and profoundly political: to put it another way, he demands that all art, to fulfill its critical function as art, be art and anti-art at the same time.[4]

The ontological alterity of art, what Lyotard claims are its critical and even revolutionary characteristics, is rooted in its form, or rather, in a certain *work* of form. In "Désirévolution," (an essay from *Dérive* not translated in *Driftworks*), Lyotard claims that "form alone can express the movement of revolution *form is revolution*" ([Dérive, 31). And in "On Theory," he elaborates on this assertion: "And I would be tempted to say, even given how much of a political activist I am, that the best, the most radical critical activity bears on the formal, the most overtly plastic aspect of painting, photography or cinema, and not so much on the *signified*, be it social or anything else, of the objects with which it is concerned" (*Driftworks*, 28, t.m.). Formal experimentation and critical activity are thus intimately linked in Lyotard's work, but only insomuch as each is a radical undoing of established orders and forms, a relentless search for, and eventual release of, forces and forms hidden or repressed through the imposition of order or meaning.

The experimentation with form at the expense of the signified—at least at the expense of a certain level of the signified predetermined by the social, historical or political realms—amounts not to a rejection of the signified but to the search for alternative possibilities buried beneath it. Lyotard puts it this way: "Something is always happening in the arts . . . that incandesces the embers glowing in the depths of society" (*Driftworks*, 15, t.m.). What glows in the depths of society is not some ideal of society or essence of the social but the possibility of critical alternatives to the concept and practices of the existing social order. What has not yet happened in society and may in fact never occur as such "happens" in the arts:

> "Aesthetics" has been for the political activist I was (and still am?), not an alibi, a comfortable retreat, but the fault and fracture giving access to the underground of the political scene, the great vault of a cave in which the undersides of this scene could be seen being overturned or reversed, a pathway allowing me to skirt or divert the political scene itself. . . . Hence the equation: aesthetics = the workshop for the forging of the most discriminating critical concepts. (*Driftworks*, 16, t.m.)

For Lyotard, critical discourse is thus in some sense a derivative of art: to be effective it must follow in art's wake, attempt to penetrate the fissures created by art, and in this way be equal to the task of developing the tools and concepts forged in the workshop art constitutes. The aesthetic precedes the critical and sets very high, "the most discriminating," standards for it.

Lyotard is not always consistent, however, in his equation of art with the critical, for his position on art does change, even in the course of this one work. In *Discours, figure* and *Economie libidinale*, as well as the two collections of essays written at the same period, *Dérive à partir de Marx et Freud* and *Des dispositifs pulsionnels* (Paris: Bourgois, 1980—originally published in 1973), he confronts his reader with two very different, even opposed sets of statements concerning the equation of the aesthetic with the critical, as well as with differing evaluations of the strengths and weaknesses of these various works themselves. One of the problems with reading these works in conjunction with each other is to decide how much weight to give each of these sets of statements and how to decide among the different privileges each work gives to art. In the various positions taken on the relation between art and critical theory and practice, what at first glance seems like an idealization of art turns out to be, on closer scrutiny, something very different.

For example, by the time the essays of *Dérive* were published and Lyotard had written his preface to the collection, entitled "Dérives" (1972), he had already shifted perspectives and begun to see these essays and *Discours, figure* as being *too critical* and not affirmative, that is, in his new vocabulary, not libidinal enough: "The affirmative idea of a [libidinal] apparatus is, I repeat, what is missing from almost all these essays. The category of the figure remains thus emprisoned in the network of a negative, nihilistic way of thinking" (*Dérive*, 18). This critique of his prior work also challenges critical discourse in general; it challenges it to do more than forge and apply critical concepts and move beyond the category of negation. Here, too, the way is shown by art.

Certain forms of art, Lyotard now claims, have moved beyond the critical phase of art, and demand more of critical discourse than even "the most discriminating critical concepts":

> The most modern trends [in art] . . . place critical thought and negative dialectics before a considerable challenge: the works they produce are affirmative, not critical. . . . The philosopher and political activist you are about to read would have been satisfied, after Adorno, with using the arts as formal matrices of reversal; . . . the new position . . . is the end of all critique. (*Driftworks*, 16–17)

As Hegel announced the "end of art," Lyotard in much the same way announces "the end of all critique." If philosophy, for Hegel, incorporates art into itself and thus moves beyond it to a higher level, art, for Lyotard, moves beyond critical discourse and thus a certain stage of itself in a different way: not by incorporating the critical into itself but by jumping outside it and leaving it totally behind. The postcritical condition announced here by Lyotard could even be taken to signal the end of all aesthetics, for a radical energetics, a libidinal economy, not only moves art beyond all critique but also beyond what has traditionally been considered as art.

These comments on libidinal affirmations and the end of critical thought must be compared, however, with those found in the preface to the second edition of *Des dispositifs pulsionnels*, written in 1979. Here the libidinal position is itself challenged for being naïvely affirmative and not critical or self-critical enough, for being another form of metaphysics: "As for the metaphysics of desire or of drives that gushes forth here, let it at least be taken for what it was: a *coup* [a blow, a thrust, a move]" (*Dispositifs*, III). The only defense of his affirmative, libidinal position that Lyotard seems willing to make in this preface is that it shakes things up; its "metaphysical" underpinnings, he admits, are indefensible. In other words, the ontological outside in this case has become too ontologically determined.

Rather than consider these radical changes in Lyotard's position to be simply different stages in a sequential process of critical development, I feel that they are signs of the contradictory status of the aesthetic in his work in general. Taken together as conflicting positions on how to characterize the distance established by the aesthetic, they indicate that, for Lyotard, the problem with the aesthetic is that it is at the same time too negative or critical (a negative dialectics of reversal) and too assertive and acritical (metaphysical). Paradoxically, these are also its advantages.

In order to understand the critical force of art in his work, I would argue that it is important not to resolve these contradictions too quickly, not to decide which aspect of art wins out over the others, which preface or text has the final word as concerns the political effects of art. Depending on how it is approached, art has very different critical effects in his various works, which makes it possible to argue that the so-called ontological exteriority of art does not determine a space in which the essence of art can be located, but, rather, posits a distance in which critical alternatives—not just to the historical-political order, but also to the aesthetic realm itself—can be formulated. The ambivalence in Lyotard's use of the aesthetic is thus intimately related to the exorbitant privilege he grants it. Were he to decide definitively what art is and how it functions, his privileging of art would be as dogmatic as the political dogmatisms it is meant to undermine, and the ontological exteriority of art would, in that case, determine just another form of ontology.

2. The Disruption of the Theoretical

Probably no philosopher since Maurice Merleau-Ponty has been as concerned with the problem of the relation and/or non-relation of painting and critical discourse as has Lyotard, with the way art offers critical perspectives on discourse in general. *Discours, figure*, for example, begins by postulating two radically different realms: the realm of language, communication, discourse, on the one hand, and that of form, color, visual figures and designs (that is, of art in the sense of painting), on the other. Lyotard considers the first to be old, used-up, determined by a long historical-philosophical tradition and limited to what can be *read*, identified, and given meaning within a closed linguistic system. What can and will be said has, in some sense, already been anticipated or programmed by the system itself, which negates and appropriates into itself all oppositions, all breaks, all alterity of any kind. Within discourse, at least when it is taken in its restrained, linguistic-philosophical sense, nothing new or different really *happens*. Linguistic-philosophical closure thus promotes the repetition of identity at the expense of any opening toward irreducible difference or alterity.

Lyotard posits the figural, on the other hand, as not being determined by any philosophical tradition or linguistic system and as relatively free of the demands of meaning. The figural is disruptive of discursive systems and destructive of signification in general, a radical exteriority to discourse, what discourse is unable to *say*. In the figural realm, things *happen* that have never

30

happened before and whose occurrence could not have been anticipated. Here meaning is not produced and communicated, but intensities are felt. The figural continually displaces the viewer and leaves him without a fixed identity rather than situating him in the position of addressee. It is the realm of movement, difference, reversal, transgression, and affirmation, that is to say, it is everything the discursive is not.

The initial opposition between discourse and figure seems, at first glance, to make discourse in all its forms a reduced, inferior mode of expression when compared to painting; it seems to imply that the critical philosopher should risk giving up the security of knowledge and the satisfaction of appropriation for the intensity of being moved (in both senses of the word) and the insecurity of disruption and transgression.[5] And yet the entire work does everything it can to undo and complicate the opposition it initially postulates. For if Lyotard privileges the figural in order to open up the closure imposed on the discursive, he does not seek to encourage all critical philosophers or theorists to give up their theoretical projects—and even the use of language itself—and become painters or amateurs of art. He hopes, rather, to demonstrate how the critical force of the figural is at work as much within as outside discourse: "Only from within discourse can one move to and into the figure. . . . One can move into the figure without leaving language because the figure is lodged there. . . . The figure is both outside and inside" (*Discours, figure,* 13). The figural is not confined to painting or the visual arts per se, for it is also a particular function within language, an alterity within the discursive itself.

Much of the first part of *Discours, figure* consists of a series of very specific critiques of various linguistic and philosophical restraints imposed on discourse to keep it from opening up to this alterity, this figurality it carries within itself: "an exteriority that it cannot interiorize through the process of signification" (13). The principal enemy of the figural, and of art in general, is theoretical discourse, because it restrains, if not represses, alterity by incorporating into its system what is fundamentally nonsystematic. The task of the critical philosopher is not to become an artist, however, but to indicate in some way the exteriority that discourse carries within itself but cannot signify: "What is wanted is to have words *say* the preeminence of the figure, to *signify* the other of signification" (18).

The uneasy situation of the philosopher is that when he successfully completes his task he is at the same time unsuccessful. For if the other of signification is signified, it is no longer the other—unless, of course, a form of signification is found that maintains alterity while signifying it. This seemingly impossible pursuit for what could be called an open, transgressive form of discourse is not, however, the romantic, nostalgic pursuit of the ineffable, of what is before or outside language and what language vainly attempts to capture. It is much closer to what Lyotard will later call the *différend,* a

31

situation where what cannot be said (phrased) must be said, where critical discourse has, as its task, to find idioms for *différends* not permitted to be phrased according to the linguistic, philosophical, and political rules governing discourse (see Chapter 7). The figural is first and foremost the opening "within" language that makes the transgression of signification and critical alternatives to discourse possible.

It would be very difficult to define in a few sentences or paragraphs what Lyotard means by the figural, for Lyotard does everything he can to keep the term as elusive as possible and even drastically changes the terms used to characterize it in the course of the work. The early chapters characterize the figural in predominantly visual terms and privilege perception over language in a similar fashion to the later work of Merleau-Ponty. Lyotard even goes so far as to claim that "this book is a defense of the eye" (11). In the later chapters, Lyotard analyzes and figures the figural more in terms of libidinal drives, and the references to Husserl and Merleau-Ponty are replaced by analyses of Freud. Since the figural, whatever its particular characteristics, is predominantly a space of displacement for Lyotard, he tries to keep it from becoming too determined, too easy to locate, so that the possibility of a critical practice more radical than the critical discourse that calls for it will be kept open. The figural must continue to resist and be somewhat other than what it is signified to be, and this resistance and exteriority is what critical discourse has as its goal to signify, or perhaps more accurately, to figure as being beyond signification.

In the first part of *Discours, figure*, the Hegelian dialectic seems to be the principal obstacle to heterogeneity and alterity, and Lyotard's disputes with Hegel are largely over Hegel's way of "saying" the unsayable, that is, Hegel's attempt to "place it within a semantic field that links it to universality. But he does not succeed in incorporating showing, manifestation itself" (41). Hegel cannot incorporate the act of showing itself because he cannot overcome the difference between the two senses of sense, or using Hegelian terminology, cannot make form (the sensible) into category (the meaningful): "The negativity that inscribes its distance between eye and object is that of form, not of category. The sensible is insuppressably separated from the meaningful" (41). I would argue that this irreducible separation between the sensible and the discursive constitutes the fundamental principle of the first part of *Discours, figure*; against the entire Hegelian dialectic—whose purpose is in fact to overcome such separation and difference—Lyotard repeatedly insists that the separation or difference cannot be negated and overcome. Only by first transforming the sensible and making it discursive can the dialectic succeed, but in doing so it also fails because it has not accounted for the sensible as such.

Lyotard feels that the task of critical philosophy is, on the contrary, to develop strategies to keep discourse open to the uncertainties and complications of sensible experience:

> So long as the philosopher does not make himself equally into a painter, he must remain in the orbit of language, of the structural unconscious. But speech is still capable of the effort of inflicting on its very language the transgression of spacings, the mobility, the profondity that characterizes the referential aspect of discourse and that structuralism omits. This is not to draw or to paint as such; it is to draw and paint with and in words. Merleau-Ponty called this surreflexion.[6] (53)

"To paint with words" is to refuse to respect the intervals determined by the language system that serve as the foundation for meaning. To paint with words is to make metaphor or figure the primary critical characteristic of language. Indirection, ambiguity, suggestiveness, uncertainty are all demanded of critical discourse here, for what matters more than the "manifest meaning of each word and of each image" are the "lateral relations, the kinships that are implicated in their transfers [*virements*] and their exchanges" (*The Visible and the Invisible*, translated by Alphonso Lingis [Evanston: Northwestern University Press, 1968], 125). As long as critical discourse disrupts the established system of meaning and keeps open the possibility of unforeseen relations and connections, it is fulfilling its function of linking up with, without negating, the sensible. In this sense, the function of critical discourse is to be more than discursive.

Lyotard emphasizes how closely connected to a certain notion of poetry or dreams Merleau-Ponty's idea of surreflexion is, for "the one like the other, of course, supposes language, but disordered language; each, of course, supposes the invariable intervals of the linguistic table, but these intervals worked on and forced to undergo distortion, 'vibrating up to the point of disjunction.' To undo the code without, however, destroying the message but on the contrary delivering meaning, that is, lateral semantic reserves, is to accomplish a set of operations Freud named the dream-work" (*Discours, figura*, 55). Critical discourse as surreflexion has, as one of its tasks, to work on, bend, and distort the linguistic-philosophical code. By means of this work on the code, it seeks to make possible meanings that cannot be produced or presented directly or immediately within the linguistic code: meanings that are not extra-linguistic in nature, but not entirely linguistic or discursive in nature either. In the first part of this work, the transgression of the code is the key concept for Lyotard; as critical discourse approaches dreams and poetry, it is considered to be more effective as transgression. Lateral meanings are, potentially, more critically effective because they exceed all codes and systems and thus open up the possibility of the inscription of an alterity that is extra-discursive. In this context, transgression and excess are openings onto otherness, and poetry and dreams serve as models for how discourse can be transgressed.[7]

There can be no method or rules for transgression, for were there rules, transgression would simply be an alternate code or system. And yet there are models for critical philosophy—alternately called by Lyotard deconstruction or surreflexion—models not to follow slavishly and apply to other cases, but whose existence testifies to the fact that an alternative, figural function is fundamental to discourse as well as art. The models are provided by artists, and, in this particular context poets, because the problem confronted by the critical philosopher is how to exceed language while using language. "Surreflexion is interested in how the two forms of negation intersect, how the negation of showing can enter into that of telling, how the text can become figure; this is what can guide it. It will surprise no one that here too philosophy arrives too late and has everything to learn from poets" (60).

But what exactly can be *learned* from poets, from a Mallarmé, for instance—the poet Lyotard chooses here to illustrate the priority of the poet over the philosopher? Lyotard claims that what he calls Mallarmé's "radical poetry" penetrates the various levels of language and in the process undoes the various hierarchies and distinctions fixed within the historical heritage of language. For Lyotard, Mallarmé's poetics constitute a process of agitation and insurrection that has ramifications just as much outside as within poetry:

> It descends way down into the lowest echalons of the hierarchy of linguistic unities and brings with it agitation and insurrection, not only into traditional prosody . . . but into the fundamental rules of communicative discourse itself. With *Un coup de dés jamais n'abolira le hasard*, Mallarmé radically strips articulated language of its prosaic function of communication; he reveals in it a power that exceeds it, the power to be "seen" and not merely read or understood, the power to figure and not merely signify. (62)

The "power of language to figure" is rooted in its spatial nature—not in the arrangement of space as linguistics determines it, but in the fundamental spacing before arrangement of any sort. This extradiscursive power of discourse is what is highlighted in the figure,—the figure defined first as the visual shape of the poem, the way it delineates itself in space, and, as we shall see, the figure defined also as the figurative or metaphoric function of language in general.

As in perhaps all radical poetics or aesthetics, there is in Mallarmé a movement away from "the world,"—from history, society, and even from the subject and its sensations—which pushes to an extreme the distance from the world established by all language through both its signifying and referential functions: not only the regulated distances between terms within the code, but also the distance between language and the objects it designates outside itself. For Lyotard, radical poetry has nothing to do with the originality of a pure poetic voice or the inviolability of the poetic object. Rather, it has to do with pushing to an extreme a fundamental attribute of all language: "It is a radicalization of the spacing of reference defined as an irreducible distance that separates word and thing and guarantees to the first its measure of ideality" (63). The "measure of ideality" of the word is, then, not "the simple abolition of reference," were it possible to conceive of such a thing, but a radical form of the distancing *of reference*. One definition of aestheticism might be that this distancing is taken as an end in itself, through processes that are claimed to eliminate all designation or reference. "Radical poetry" and critical discourse have, on the contrary, the project of radicalizing the distancing of reference and recasting designation rather than eliminating it.

It is not a question, then, of choosing between critical, self-reflexive language and reference, poetry and the world—as some would have it—but rather of making language and its other communicate:

> What the *Coup de dés* says is that language does not abolish its other, that the work itself participates in the sensible, that the choice is not between choosing the written or renouncing it. . . . That language and its other are inseparable is the lesson of the *Coup de dés* and *Igitur* of Mallarmé. We will see why it is that Mallarmé feels that one acknowledges and submits oneself to this indissociability not by *signifying* it with a tip of the hat politely given at the heart of language but by making it be *seen*. (64)

For Lyotard, Mallarmé's poems undo the closed and hierarchized space of language to reveal the distance of language (and to an even more radical degree, the poem) from the world, making this distance be seen; in this way, they constitute a possible source of relations with the world different from those already determined either by language itself or by the world as it is defined by philosophy, history, sociology, or any other determined and/or determining discourse.

If Lyotard finds in Mallarmé's poetry a form of discourse that participates fully in the visible, a discourse that is to be seen as much as read or heard, he also discovers a visibility that speaks as much as it stands forth to be seen, for Mallarmé's is a text that

> makes the sensible enter into it; it no longer speaks only through its signification but expresses through its blanks, its body, the folds of its pages. . . . In this way, radical poetry demonstrates that there is the potentiality of the sensible in the meaningful, . . . not in the 'mat-

ter' of words . . . but in their arrangement. . . . Poetic dispersion on
a page is a disarrangement of the arrangement that produces signification; it disrupts communication. . . . The other of discourse
takes form in it. (68–9)

With the example of Mallarmé, the opposition between figure and discourse
is broken down—for his poetry is simultaneously discourse *and* figure, the
sensible taking shape out of the meaningful, and by doing so, greatly extending
its possibilities. Moving in the opposite direction from the Hegelian dialectic,
the sensible here negates and assumes the discursive into itself, and if it does
not raise it to a higher level, it does push it into a different realm. This "anti-"
or even "negative dialectic," a dialectic working against itself in a paradoxical fashion, does not have as its end the overcoming of difference and
the establishment of identity, but rather the overcoming of identity and the
"figuring" of otherness.

Mallarmé's radical poetry, what he himself called "critical poetry," is for
Lyotard a strange object, a *discourse-figure*[8] which does not transcend the
differences between the two realms but instead inhabits these differences,
exhibits them, radicalizes them. Discourse drifting into figure and "designation immigrating into signification" produce a crisis in discourse, one
which Lyotard intends to make as difficult as possible to resolve. This is not
only the "crisis of verse" proclaimed by Mallarmé but also a profound "crisis
of knowledge" (70),[9] because the discursive foundation for knowledge has
been undermined by this slippage. The critical poem is, thus, that form of
discourse that Hegel could not conceptualize, a non- or para-dialectical linkage of language and experience, meaning and form, discourse and figure.

For Lyotard, Mallarmé allows us to put Hegel behind us once and for all,
and, in doing so, perpetuate and extend the crisis that critical poetry provokes
in the discursive. The first part of *Discours, figure* could rightfully be considered a "critical aesthetics," that is, an aesthetics or poetics of crisis, a
disarrangement, disruption or "deconstruction" of the discursive through the
intervention of the figural. For, Lyotard would argue, only out of the crisis
provoked by the undoing of the arranged, the continuous or the constructed
can alterity be figured. The figural, as both a radical exteriority and an opening
within the discursive, points to what discourse as such cannot contain within
itself. Critical aesthetics or poetics opens the way for a form of critical discourse that is certainly not identical to poetry, but that "has learned" something about the figural from poetry. If nothing else, it has learned that the
closure of the discursive universe can never be accepted as determining, that
the discursive is not self-contained or self-sufficient. In a certain sense, even
though his notion of the figural and his approach to the aesthetic in general
will change, I would argue that Lyotard's entire critical project is rooted in
this "poetic" or "aesthetic" opening at the very (non)foundation of discourse.

36

In his terms, critical alternatives are always possible because the discursive cannot in fact eliminate, that is "theorize," the figural alterity disrupting it from within.

3. Desire and the Figural

As mentioned earlier, *Discours, figure* shifts abruptly when Lyotard begins to conceive of the notion of the figural in libidnal (Freudian) rather than visual, phenomenological terms. This shift occurs not long after his discussion of Mallarmé, which I would consider the culmination of the entire first part of the book. There is, in fact, a kind of dialectic at work in this first part, a dialectic that is Hegelian in its general form but anti-Hegelian in its content: its chief moments are the chapters devoted to Hegel, Saussure, Merleau-Ponty, and finally Mallarmé. If Hegel represents for Lyotard the dialectical-metaphysical moment of totalization, a synthesis of all philosophy from Plato on, structuralism (Saussure) and critical phenomenology (Merleau-Ponty) are treated as different forms of fragmentation of this process of totalization and then played off against each other to reveal the limitations of each form of fragmentation and undialectizable negation. The role of Mallarmé's critical poetics is to embody the point of extreme limit of both forms of negation. Lyotard thus presents Mallarmé as the triumph of poetics over dialectics insomuch as his poetry exceeds the limitations of dialectics and the theoretical in general more than either critical alternative coming after him is able to. *Enfin Mallarmé vint.*

With the triumph of the poetic, however, an impasse of sorts is reached in *Discours, figure.* For when the alternative between the discursive and the figural—defined in predominately visual terms—is overcome in Mallarmé's poetry, not only the alternative, but the notion of art supporting such a definition of the figure, can now be seen as deficient. It is as if the figural had become too stable, too visible, too easily located in a particular poetic practice—no matter how radical it is claimed to be—to continue to serve a critical function. In other words, I am arguing that certain aspects of Lyotard's use of Mallarmé's critical poetics represent, in this work, a reversal of the hierarchy of discourse over figure and a synthesis of the critical elements of each: a solution to, or resolution of, the antagonisms of discourse and figure, theory and art. In his desire to oppose and exceed all theoretical-discursive limitations, Lyotard might even be accused of assigning a determined end to the critical process in one particular form of poetry; this poetic reversal of discourse ends up, in its own way, limiting critical possibilities and alternatives. Poetic closure and theoretical-philosophical closure are, in fact, two sides of the same coin. The interpenetration of discourse and figure that this work as a whole seeks to produce, however, implies that no form of theory or art can resolve the conflicts of discourse and figure.

37

Lyotard never confronts this problem directly in these terms, but in turning now to Freud, he complicates his position on art and poetry. He moves away from a critical aesthetics, one which champions the visual, sensible nature of a certain discourse-practice, to a notion of the figural that sees art and poetry as the not strictly visible work of desire:

> We can't remain in the alternative of these two spaces, the space of the system and that of the subject, between which discourse slides. There is another space, a figural space. It must be supposed as buried; it gives itself neither to be seen nor to be thought. It is indicated in a lateral or fugitive fashion at the heart of discourse and perception as that which troubles them. It is the proper space of desire, the stakes of the struggle that painters and poets have never ceased waging against the return of the Ego and the return of the text. (135)

In the sections of *Discours, figure* dealing with Freud, the figural is no longer the irruption of the visible in the discursive, but, rather, what disturbs both. The visibility of the figure itself is now seen as a limitation (of sorts) of the figural, and not its defining characteristic. The crisis of verse and of knowledge is equally a crisis of visible form. It affects not just the order of discourse but the order of art as well. The irreducible distancing of perception has become the even more radically irreducible distancing of desire; if the object of perception is never attained as such but only approximated, the object of desire is in an even stronger sense unattainable.

The ultimate force of disruption and disarrangement for Lyotard is now desire, a self-presupposing principle that depends on nothing but itself for its existence, and, because it is unbounded, that manifests itself everywhere. Desire is even transgressive of the figure itself, thus making possible another notion of the figural, one even more destructive of established orders and forms than the predominately visual notion. This means that for Lyotard, aesthetics must now become an energetics if it is to measure up to desire, to the force and not the form of the figure:

> Every figure is linguistically charged, that is to say, it constitutes a linguistic event because it is a *discharge* effect coming from another order. . . . The figure presents itself as an incoherent *trace* that defies reading, that is not a letter, and that can only be understood in energetic terms. The figure is supported by displacements, condensations, and deformations. This means that *before* its incorporation into the order of language (for example, as a rhetorical form), the figure is the mark on the unities and rules of language of a force that treats these unities and rules as things. It is the trace of work (*travail*) and

not of knowledge achieved through signification. Through this work, what is realized is desire. (146)

From assertions such as these, it could be deduced that Lyotard feels that no type of formalism or aesthetics in the traditional sense could account for the force of desire and the disruption to form it produces. The energetics proposed here by Lyotard is thus an anti-formalism, or even an anti-aesthetics. It is concerned more with how in art and poetry the unities and rules of language and form are played with and misapplied than with how they are applied, more with how unfinished, unformed, even "bad" forms are produced than how completed, "good" forms are.

Lyotard's reading of Freud focuses on remarks Freud makes at the end of the chapter in *The Interpretation of Dreams* entitled "The Dream-Work." Freud formulates what Lyotard considers to be a radical distinction between *Traumarbeit* and *Traumgedanke* when he says that the dream-work is "qualitatively completely different from [waking thought]."[10] The difference between work and thought here is, in fact, similar to the difference between the sensible and the conceptual in Hegel—one which, as we have seen, Lyotard argued the Hegelian dialectic strives to negate and overcome. With the Freudian notion of the unconscious, this distinction is transposed onto another level; the sensible (and with it the aesthetic) are freed from the limitations of consciousness. Energetics could thus be considered an aesthetics of what is not strictly visible, an aesthetics where the work on form, the deformation of form, is more fundamental than the formation of form (which remains too closely linked to consciousness and thought to constitute the essence of the dream or to be considered libidinal).

For Lyotard, the key phrase from Freud (a part of which he uses as the title of one of his chapters), is the following: "The dream-work does not think, calculate or judge in any way at all; it restricts itself to giving things a new form [transforming things]" (*S.E.*, v. V, 507). And in a footnote added in 1909, Freud adds: "It is the *dream-work* which creates that form, and it alone is the essence of dreaming—the explanation of its particular nature" (506–7). Freud here links the notion of work to that of form and form to a process of transformation, a process that has other origins and ends than those of thought. Form is conceived in terms of a dynamics of change, dispersion, and displacement, rather than of stasis, completion, unity, or integrity.

Lyotard distinguishes three levels of the figure—the image-figure, the form-figure, and the matrix-figure—each of which is a complication of the visible nature of the figure.[11] Only the matrix-figure is invisible, or, rather, on the "other side" of visibility and art itself, if art is considered primarily to be form:

Not only is it not seen, but it is no more visible than readable. It does not belong to plastic space, nor to textual space either; it is difference

39

itself, and as such, it doesn't at all tolerate being put in the form of an *opposition*, which is what its spoken expression would demand, or in the form of an image or form, which its plastic expression would suppose. Discourse, image, and form all miss it equally because it resides in all three spaces together. The works of any individual are never more than the offshoots of this matrix. (278–79).

The matrix can be deduced, but never seen; as such, it is a kind of original phantasy, an object of an original repression (271).[12] It is a space of pure difference where "the confusion of spaces reigns 'at the origin,'" a space that is a transgression of the notion of space and of the very "place where the matrix is located" (279). The matrix, buried beneath the other two levels, supports the entire system of categories, but it supports it with a kind of nonsupport, an absence of any specific origin: "The phantasmatic matrix, far from being an origin, attests to the opposite, that our origin is an absence of origin and that everything presenting itself as the object of an original discourse is an hallucinatory *image-figure* placed precisely in this initial non-space" (271).

The matrix underlies the other categories of figures as a radical alterity of which they are the visible transformations, out of which they in some sense emerge and to which they *indirectly* refer. But when the matrix itself is made visible or intelligible, what is lost is its link to the unconscious: "In substituting an intelligible schema for it, its immersion in the unconscious is made unintelligible. This attests, however, to the fact that what is at stake is definitely the other of discourse and intelligibility" (271). No figure or form is equivalent to the matrix, but, at the same time, no indication of the matrix is possible outside of the approximations and distortions offered by figures and forms. The alterity of the matrix is never contained *in* either figure or form but lies as a potentiality *beyond* them.

The matrix never appears in itself because it is never itself; it appears only in its disappearance, as lost, repressed, already other. It participates in what cannot be communicated: "It is of all the orders of the figure, the furthest removed from communicability, the most isolated: it harbors within it the uncommunicable. It does engender forms and images, and it is only *of* these forms and images, which are its products, that discourse eventually begins to speak" (327). By definition, any discourse, no matter how critical, remains at a distance from the matrix, from the unrepresentable "origin" of image and figure, of representation itself. The alternative Lyotard now places critical discourse before is the following: either admit its own irrelevancy or else attempt in some way to deal with this distance, approach it without reducing it, situate itself in terms of it. Discourse can, in any case, never hope to contain or master it, and to claim that it has done so would be for Lyotard a sign that it has confused either image or form with matrix, the conscious with the unconscious, the discursive with the libidinal.

Lyotard gives two examples from Freud of the spatial and temporal complexity—the irrepresentable characteristics—of the matrix. The first, from *Civilization and its Discontents*, is Freud's reference to the coexistence of three different historical periods in modern Rome—ancient, Christian, and modern—to illustrate the intemporality of the unconscious. None of the stages totally effaces the stage or stages that come before it, and each is obliged to occupy the same site as the stages coming both before and after it. There is, strictly speaking, no present in which any of the stages is present in and as itself. Rome is "unpresentable" as such because no simultaneity of space and no evolution in time is adequate to the task of presenting this mixture of times and spaces. As Lyotard argues, this is an example of the space/time of desire:

> The space where the formations of desire reside is not merely a space of a topological type; what makes any representation of it impossible is that it is the corollary in visible space of the *atemporality* or *omnitemporality* of the primary process, which does not admit negation. Each drive-formation is always conserved, for an unconscious cathexis is never abandoned, . . . one never returns to the blank page. Nothing is effaced, but localizations are added one on top of the other. (337)

The radically heterogeneous coexistence of various times at one moment of time, of various spaces in one space, of multiple cathexes with countercathexes, of constructions with deconstructions, formations with deformations, makes such a site the unrepresentable site of "difference itself." Beyond discourse, there is image; beyond image, form; beyond form, matrix or difference itself. In other words, beyond critical discourse, there is art, and beyond art, the differential play of forces that art in some sense both manifests and represses in its formation and deformation of form.

The second and more developed example Lyotard gives is Freud's analysis of the phantasy, "A Child is being Beaten." Lyotard is especially interested in the way Freud shows how its "apparent coherence in psychic life contains within it a multiplicity of incomposable 'phrases'" (338).[13] In the "same" phantasy, Freud discovers a number of conflicting phantasies; in the "same" impulse, various and contradictory impulses; in the "same" desire, many opposed desires; in the "same" phase of development, a number of different phases experienced; in the "same" figure, different figures projected and identified with; in the "same" sex, another sex. In other words, the matrix works to "block together what is not composable" (339), and this blocking together retains the extreme heterogeneity of the primary process itself. In the second

41

part of *Discours, figure*, Lyotard's project is to focus on those instances when Freud refuses to reduce through interpretation the instability and heterogeneity of the primary process, those moments when his own critical discourse points to but does not attempt to master the disruptive effects of desire.

According to Lyotard, the mistake of all psychoanalytical approaches to art and literature—and this includes Freud's own applications of psychoanalysis to art and literature—is to treat the work as a symptom, to treat literature, for example, as "an exteriorization in words of a profound phantasmatics" (355). To do this is to imply that desire is fulfilled in the work, that there takes place in art and literature a "reconciliation between primary and secondary processes, between the ego and the id" (356). Such a reconciliation would make possible a psychoanalysis of art or even a psychoanalytical aesthetics, one in which desire was representable in the forms it produced. Lyotard insists that Freud's most important contributions in this area are not contained in his analyses of specific art works, but, rather, in the way his theory at its most radical moments indicates that the work "does not fulfill desire but unfulfills it" (385). Lyotard goes even further and claims that it is the role of all art worthy of its name, and thus of critical discourse that takes seriously the problems raised by art, to confront and perhaps even exacerbate this unfulfillment. Unfulfillment is the sign that neither discourse nor art is the end of the process of disruption and transformation.

This affirmation of the lack of finality of art, and, in art, of the disruptive-productive effects of desire brings *Discours, figure* to a fairly abrupt end. Lyotard's Freudian energetics raise serious questions concerning the limitations of both conceptual thinking and figurative expression, of both discourse and figure—for the disordered clash of libidinal forces breaks with and excedes all discursive and pictorial formations and can be indicated only in the breaks and disruptions inflicted on them. Insomuch as a certain art indicates indirectly what in art is "beyond art," what in form is unformed or deformed, it can be said to open the way for a critical approach to art, perhaps even for a libidinal paraesthetics that refuses to accept any of the theoretical or formal limitations that have traditionally been imposed on art.

In the disruptive effects or traces of libidinal energy found in a certain form of art, the heterogeneity basic to the aesthetic reaches a kind of absolute limit—for the unformed characteristics of the libidinal also indicate the end of art. Unlike the end proclaimed by Hegel, this end is not brought about by philosophy and the unifying movement of the dialectic, but, rather, by desire and its disruptive and dispersive movements and countermovements. The most powerful aspects of Lyotard's libidinal (para)esthetics, as the oxymoron constituted by the term itself indicates—an oxymoron because the libidinal cannot be accounted for by any form of aesthetics—is the way the limit of the aesthetic is approached, the way Lyotard's own critical strategy risks undermining itself in its critique of discourse and figure. Here art is approached at the moment of its dissipation, and critical discourse, in pursuing the libidinal through and beyond art, risks its own dissipation as well. For in pure libidinal formlessness, there is no place for art and no place for discourse either. Art and discourse can approach this limit, but are necessarily destroyed when they plunge into the abyss beyond it.

4. Libidinal Politics

An important question, however, remains unanswered at the end of *Discours, figure*: what are the political implications of such a libidinal paraesthetics? The "detour" through art "leading to the practical critique of ideology," which Lyotard claims this work constitutes, in fact terminates before it reaches its destination in politics. A critique of ideology is certainly implied in his overall critique of the limits of discourse (in the first part of the book) and in his critique of form and visibility in general (in the second), but it is not developed to any extent. Lyotard uses Freud to show a way beyond the aesthetic; in the works that follow *Discours, figure*, Freud also provides the way into and beyond politics, as Lyotard makes desire the fundamental and, it could be argued, absolute, exclusive principle of his entire critical enterprise.

Lyotard's reading of Freud stresses the way desire is unbounded—how it disorients, disrupts, transgresses, and transforms everything it touches, continually reversing directions and cathecting itself elsewhere and otherwise. With *Economie libidinale* and the numerous essays written at approximately the same time and collected in *Des dispositifs pulsionnels*, the detour through art does return to politics, and one can even sense an obvious impatience on Lyotard's part for the disruptive principle of desire to begin *to work* on theory, on society, and on, or, as politics. The problem will be how to think politics in terms of desire and desire in terms of politics—which, on the theoretical level, translates in Lyotard's approach into the problem of how to think Freud in terms of Marx and Marx in terms of Freud.

To make each a force of disruption and transformation rather than of conservation—which is what Lyotard considers all Freudianisms and Marxisms to be—Lyotard will attempt to play Marx and Freud off against each other, thereby undoing "everything by means of which the libidinal hides the political in Freud, or the political the libidinal in Marx" (*Dispositifs pulsionnels*, 12). But in order for such a confrontation to take place, each must be opened up to the possibility of transformation so that their linkage will not result in the domination of one over the other: that is, in either a psychoanalysis of politics or a political determination of psychoanalysis. At one point, Lyotard provocatively asserts that what is first needed before the meeting can take place is "a critique of Freud by Cézanne" and "of Marxist theorism, say, by

Pollock" (235). A certain practice of art, then, is still seen as an antidote to the limits of theory, a way of opening theories up to what they exclude or repress.

In his impatience to do away with the limitations of theory, Lyotard's critique of theory takes more and more the form of a diatribe against theory in general for not risking a confrontation with formlessness and libidinal excess. The central critical problem he faces is no longer the tension between theory and art, between form or system and excess or disruption. In his "libidinal texts," he speaks as if from the other side of the limit, as if he effectively occupied the space "beyond form and theory" indicated by a certain art and by certain aspects of Freud's work. With such a strategy, he has gained an unassailable, transcendent perspective on all other critical positions, but, he has also lost aspects of the conflict of form and formlessness, discourse and figure—aspects that the *struggle* to approach and exceed the limits of theory and art highlighted.

There is little evidence of critical modesty in *Economie libidinale*. The text, even though quite humorous, is also quite nasty, even arrogant, a blast at practically every contending theoretical and political position—especially those closest to Lyotard's own.[14] The book's reader is put in a difficult, if not impossible situation; unless he/she is willing to accept the position of the fool being ridiculed, he/she is coerced to join the strange "we" ("we, libidinal economists") that recurs throughout the book. On one level, this "we" is a parody of all philosophical and political "we's," the voice of a kind of libidinal *Ubermensch* (and the style and tone of the book are obviously Nietzschean), of a small (and totally fictive) community or clique of superior beings who laugh at the false superiority of all right-thinking individuals, a "we" defined in opposition to "them." The "we" is, in particular, a parody of the proletarian "we" of Marxism, a "we" that laughs at the universalist pretensions of its counterpart and predecessor. As the "we" of desire and not of labor, it is fragmented, heterogeneous, dispersive, and, in each instance, specific: impossible as a "we," the "we" of the dispersion and destruction of all "we's."

But in speaking as this impossible "we" and drawing its own authority from that of desire, *Economie libidinale* is nevertheless quite intimidating (perhaps one could say in the vocabulary of the recent work of Lyotard, dogmatic or even terroristic), in its attacks on dogmatism and terror. As Jean-Loup Thébaud suggests at the beginning of *Just Gaming* (translated by Wlad Godzich [Minneapolis: University of Minnesota Press, 1985])—a book written in dialogue form with a completely different tone and from a more modest, more critical perspective—it does not allow for any "negotiation," but was written "to be taken or left." In the same work, Lyotard himself admits that *Economie libidinale*, "insofar as it does not lend itself to dialogue, . . . perpetuates a kind of violence" (3–4). Lyotard also claims that one should not be intimidated by the book because of all its theoretical inconsistencies (5). But *Econ-*

omie libidinale does everything it can to intimidate and silence all possible critical responses to it, especially those that might point out any inconsistencies on the theoretical level. The book sets up a rhetorical situation such that the reader is either with the libidinal "we" or against it; but if he is against the "we," he is against desire and thus either impotent, cowardly, religious, repressive, or foolish, or all of them together.[15]

At the very end of the book, a "non-we" does ask a number of pertinent critical questions, the precise sort of questions that Lyotard himself will ask in his next works; the door to dialogue would seem to be opening. The questions are the following: "What is this discourse? How does it legitimate itself? Where does it place itself? What is its function? What authorizes you to speak this way? . . . Is not your whole enterprise nothing but imagination and rhetoric? Are you looking for truth? Do you pretend to say it, to have said it? . . . In truth, it's on your part a purely imaginary fabrication, . . . as you would say, a form of aestheticism, elitism" (*Economie*, 287). But the response of the libidinal "we" is not to answer these questions. Instead, it throws them back at the imaginary interlocutor, thereby ending any possibility for critical dialogue:

> And your own theoretical discourse, what is it? All your questions are supported by the reference to this discourse, by the reference to the word of truth. We will not let ourselves be intimidated by this reference, for you know nothing of the truth and will never know anything. We know that it is the arm of paranoia and power, the claw of unity-totality in the space of words, the return of terror. (287)

The pretense that one knows the truth may be as intimidating and terroristic as Lyotard claims. But what this work reveals—that the knowledge that the truth is "the arm of paranoia and power" and the way this second form of knowledge can silence all critical questions—is equally "terroristic."

In *Just Gaming*, even if Lyotard does not defend the libidinal position taken in *Economie libidinale*, he does still attempt to justify the mode of "argumentation" of the work (if it can be called that), by claiming that it is pure rhetoric—that is, literary rather than philosophical or political in nature. This is one way to excuse, at least in part, its violence:

> This book has been written in a scandalous fashion. What is scandalous about it is that it is all rhetoric; it works entirely on the level of persuasion, . . . and even if all its twists and turns were not controlled (for the most part they were not), nevertheless, it is certain that the effect that was "anticipated" (and not controlled) was certainly not pedagogical, and not even dialectical. It was much more poetic or literary, but in a rather odd sense of these words. It is a

book that belongs more to the arts of discourse than to philosophical writing, including dialectics. (*Just Gaming*, 4, t.m.)

But even if *Economie libidinale* is read as a rhetorical exercise—as a strange form of literature whose purpose is to affect its reader and not teach him but move (anger) or persuade him—this does not mean that its rhetoric should not be evaluated critically, or that the way it moves and persuades not opened to challenge. It does not go without saying that all "coups" that disturb or scandalize can be justified in terms of their "aesthetic" qualities and that their theoretical-political effects should be ignored. One could justify just about anything in this way; moreover, Lyotard's own work demonstrates why the rhetorical, the literary, and the aesthetic should not be taken as ends in themselves and why no "we" can claim to master them or speak for them, why the aesthetic and the libidinal are not territories to be occupied by any subject or group of subjects, fictional or real. If "we" know what desire is and how it works, if "we" know what art is and how it works or moves, then a science or philosophy of desire and art becomes possible and each loses its potential disruptive, critical dimensions.

I believe Lyotard's parody of the Marxist "we" resembles the "we" being parodied more closely than he, in fact, calculated. In many ways, it is simply a reversal of the Marxist "we," its mirror image. Given that his *différend* with Marxism throughout his political life has, in part, been over the lethal effects of positing a universal, proletarian subject as the subject of history,[16] doesn't a "libidinal we" in whose name one speaks against such repression nevertheless still, in some way, participate in it? Shouldn't the critique of the Marxist "we" also extend to the libidinal one opposed to it? Can the parody of such a "we" really be considered free of all the limitations of the "we" being parodied? It seems to me that the powerful critique of orthodox Marxism that this book contains is thwarted more than helped by such a parody.

In *Economie libidinale*, the chapter entitled "The Desire Named Marx" has as one of its chief purposes to unravel the universal "we" of Marxism. In it, Lyotard attacks this universality by treating Marx, not as a master theorist, but as a writer like any other—which means as an "author, full of affects, his text taken not as theory but as folly. . . . Marx's desire interests us not for itself but insomuch as it informs the themes of his writing which are transformed into themes of social and political 'practices'" (117). Lyotard's purpose in treating Marx in this way—besides scandalizing orthodox Marxists—is to avoid what he feels is the trap awaiting any *critique*, which is "to remain within the field of the thing criticized and within the dogmatic, even paranoid relation to knowledge" (117). Treating Marx as a writer or poet, dealing with his theoretical work as if it were a "'work of art'" (118), opens up the possibility of pushing Marx's texts beyond the limitations of the theoretical-political field as it has heretofore been constituted by Marxists and non-Marxists alike.

Treating Marx as "a work of art" does not mean, however, that critical judgment should not be used to evaluate his texts. It does mean that the theoretical frame will be forced open, that theory will be inscribed within what, for lack of a better term, could be called an (para)esthetics of affects. In using a libidinal-aesthetic approach to read Marx rather than a political-theoretical approach, Lyotard has, as his goal, the uncovering of what in Marx moves, displaces, affects, etc.—what is not theorizable as such and, thus, what for Lyotard is "political" in a more radical sense. To treat Marxist theory as art in Lyotard's terms is to posit a desacralized, non-teleological, non-religious Marx within and at odds with the orthodox Marx.

Others, of course, (and the Frankfurt School certainly comes first to mind), have attempted to approach Marx in a similar fashion, to read him against himself in order to overcome the theoretical and political dogmatism associated with orthodox Marxism, to find a more radical level of Marxist thinking underneath or to the side of the sacralized Marx. But it has undoubtedly never been done so outlandishly as here, and never in the name of libidinal drives. And until the libidinal "we" takes over and becomes *the alternative* to the political "we," the strategy has important critical effects—especially as concerns the nature, place, and role of theory within Marx's writing and the relation of theory to his "art" and critical practice in general. For Lyotard, a libidinal reading of Marx reveals the unresolved contradictions within his theory and the forces that resist being sytematized and totalized within the dialectic.

For example, Lyotard criticizes the Althusserian notion of a radical break between the young, Hegelian, humanist, unscientific Marx and the wise, old, theoretical-scientific Marx—not only because the break is far from certain, but also because of the way it elevates theory to a dominant position and mystifies science. Lyotard caricaturizes this position by describing the two figures constituting "Marx" as a young woman and an old man. The first is the lover of organic humanity who hates capitalism and demands that "this industrial and industrious crap stop," who desires "the return of the (in)organic body." The second is the old, bearded theoretician, "who establishes the thesis that *it cannot not stop* and who places in evidence, as the lawyer of the suffering masses, . . . his revolutionary conclusions" (121). In Lyotard's version (fiction) of Marx, it is the intercourse and not the divorce between the two figures that dominates Marxist theory; out of their union is born the promise of the proletariat as the universal subject and a particular concept of socialism as *the form* of organic unity.

Unity remains just a promise, however, and the pleasure taken in it is the pleasure of deferred pleasure, argues Lyotard. Thus, in opposing the sterility of capital, its incapacity to give birth to an organic social totality or to satisfy

47

the desire for such a body, Marx ends up repeating the form of this deferral: "Thus even if in the content of his work, he is still searching for the lovable body that he-she desires, the form of this search contains the denial and the impossibility of such a body" (121). Lyotard thus highlights the irreducible tension or conflict of forces and desires in the work of Marx—a tension or conflict which has the effect of keeping his theory unfinished, unfulfilled (unscientific) in spite of itself and in spite of its teleological, redemptive characteristics. Lyotard finds in Marx not just a movement towards closure, towards totalization and unification, but also a countermovement of additions and accumulations, of bits and pieces of strategies and theories that are needed to compensate for the deferral of desire and are evidence of a flight from the realization of social unification and the fulfillment of this political desire. Lyotard considers this process of deferral to be structurally and practically infinite. The gap between desire and fulfillment, theory and practice, is for him never overcome in Marx—which means that in the political realm, just as in the aesthetic, desire remains unfulfilled, destructive of the social unities already formed or to be formed, and, is, in general, at war with unification and totalization.

Lyotard claims that Marx considers this non-synchronization at the heart of his work—what Lyotard calls "dischrony"—to be a sign of failure: "What Marx perceives as a failure . . . is the mark on his work of a situation that is precisely that of capital and that produces just as many strange achievements as horrible misery: his work cannot be integral, a corpus [*faire corps*], just as capital cannot" (125). In stressing the elements of Marxist theory that do not lead to unification or constitute a corpus, Lyotard situates Marx's critical achievements in the very place he claims Marx locates his own failure. Lyotard is interested in the tension between unifying and fragmenting forces, between what he calls the "insane patchwork" he finds characteristic of certain aspects of the form of Marx's writing and of the teleological narrative schema that is put in place to regularize and rationalize the "insanity": to negate and overcome fragmentation, contradiction, and all other "inorganic" elements whose presence continues to defer the coming of the organic social totality.[17] If Althusser considers Marx's later texts to represent the theoretical-scientific in its purest and most developed form, Lyotard reads Marx's early and later texts in terms of their paratheoretical elements, that is, the libidinal-aesthetic elements that move his text beyond the limitations of the theoretical.

Beyond the polemics, the critical project of *Economie libidinale* is to challenge and undermine, in as many ways as possible—through ridicule, parody, hyperbole, sarcasm, etc.—the seriousness and assumed superiority of theory, not only Marxist theory, but theory in general. Lyotard aims to force theory to abandon the dominant "virile position" (146) and accept the consequences of being not a unified, totalized system, but, instead the "patchwork" that he considers Marx's texts, and all other theoretical texts (including his own), to be. Lyotard focuses on the complex of libidinal forces in Marx's theory that resist theorization and, in their name, demands a clean break with theory. As its mirror image, this position curiously resembles Althusser's argument that there exists between Marx's early and late texts an epistemological break with humanism, a break which guarantees the scientificity and theoretical purity of his later work. Lyotard's defense of the theoretical *impurity* of the libidinal constitutes not just an anti-Althusserianism, but, more importantly, an anti-theorism—which like all reversals of theory has important theoretical implications. While Marx may have been "libidinized" in the course of *Economie libidinale*, Freud and the libidinal-aesthetics postulated in his name have not really been politicized in the same way; the libidinal has, thus, been given an unquestioned privilege in the relation between theory and desire, politics and art. It has been constituted as *the* alternative to the theoretical.

In this work and others of the period, Lyotard considers all forms of *criticism* to be ultimately inadequate and impotent because they must necessarily remain negative—at best, a form of negative theology or critical theory without any affirmative, disruptive force. I would argue, however, that the libidinal—no matter how affirmative it is claimed to be—could also be considered another, perhaps more radical form of negative theology inasmuch as Lyotard treats it as the negation of all theorization, as the true form of theorization. With the libidinal, Lyotard attempts to jump beyond all theoretical limitations. But by doing so, he covers over the conflict of theoretical and libidinal-aesthetic forces which persists within the libidinal itself.

Negative theology is precisely the term Lyotard uses to characterize the work of Adorno (in an essay from this period entitled "Adorno come Diavolo"); and by doing so, he opposes his own approach to that of Adorno. Given that so many of the same issues are to be found in their works—and none more important than the central place each assigns to art—Lyotard's critique of Adorno is of utmost importance for understanding Lyotard's rejection of critical theory during this period, or, to put it more precisely, his rejection in fact of the critical and the theoretical in general:

> Adorno, like Marx, considers the dissipation of subjectivity in and by kapitalism [sic] to be a defeat. He is only able to overcome this pessimism by making of this life a negative moment in a dialectic of emancipation, of the conquest of creativity. But this dialectic is no less theological than the nihilism of the loss of the subject-creator; it is its therapeutic resolution in the frame of a religion, here religion of history. . . . Art is a kind of Christ in its denunciatory function. As for effective redemption, it is even further removed in chronology, and it must be this way because art is not a regenerator; its force is to place itself in nihilism, assume it, and thus manifest it. (*Des dispositifs pulsionnels*, 109–10)

49

By fully assuming, manifesting, and remaining within the negative, art for Adorno denounces all positivity and keeps all reconciliation, all transcendence of negativity at a distance: it is the support for a *critical theory*. What Lyotard objects to the most in this configuration is that art continues to denounce only in order all the better to "save."

Art, when it is considered—as it is by Adorno—as the manifestation of critical thinking, may be the sign of a loss or failure in terms of the criteria and values of traditional art, but it is also the indication that this loss will eventually be compensated for. Lyotard considers Adorno's aesthetics to be "tragic," but he demands that this loss be conceived affirmatively and not tragically, with no implication of possible reconciliation. The libidinal side of art is, for Lyotard, the affirmation of what in Adorno remains negative: the arbitrary, the fragmented, the irrational, and the non-dialectical. Libidinal aesthetics thus constitutes the reversal of critical theory and aesthetics, the affirmation of what is negative—not as if it were negative—but as if the negative were really the affirmative and of no need of reconciliation or redemption. Taken to the extremes that Lyotard takes it here, the libidinal in its radically affirmative nature is a mirror reflection of an extreme negative theology. Arbitrary, irrational, and non-dialectical, it is the negative of the necessary, rational, and dialectical characteristics of Adorno's negative dialectics.

Adorno does represent for Lyotard the most radical possibility of critical theory, "the culmination of criticism, its bouquet, its revelation as a kind of fireworks" (*Des dispositifs,* 114). He says this, however, not just to praise Adorno but also to criticize him for remaining within the critical, for being content to be the "devil" in a world without true gods:

> The totality is missing = there is no god to conciliate = all conciliation can be present only in its impossibility, that is, parodied = this is the devil's work. But you have replaced god with the devil in vain; . . . you remain in the same theological apparatus. You pass simply from shameful nihilism to proclaimed nihilism. . . . The devil is the nostalgia for god, an impossible god, thus possible precisely as god. (118)

As Lyotard also admits, the place of the devil is not always a bad place to occupy, for when the gods are those of fascism and Stalinist communism, it is better to be on the side of the devils of critical theory: "When creation raves, it is the devil who is probably right" (124).

Lyotard demands more than any critical devil, more than any form of theory, can offer. In the twilight of the gods of totality, he is impatient to move beyond good and evil, right and wrong, gods and devils, and theorisms and aestheticisms. At times, because of his insistent attacks on the limits of theory, even in its most critical form, he gives the impression that it is possible to move, that he, in fact, has effectively moved beyond the limitations of all forms of criticism or outside the restrictions of the theoretical in general. And yet, I would argue that what is most powerful in all of his texts, *Economie libidinale* included, is the struggle with and against theory and not the proposed resolution or transcendence of the struggle. For not only do the devils of critical theory still remain within the same theoretical-theological apparatus of the absolute, but the more clever, libidinal devil or jokester who positions himself in such a way to be untouched by the theoretical and the theological also owes more to this apparatus than he realizes.

The endless nature of the critical task may often seem frustrating, and impatience may be necessary at times to keep theory critical—to undermine the ends it sets for itself and move beyond them—but the endless character of the critical process (without nostalgia or the promise of reconciliation) remains, in my mind, its strongest justification. Lyotard's libidinal aesthetics may end up by presenting itself as anti- or trans-theoretical rather than as critically or para-theoretical—that is, as an aesthetics of drives purified of all contamination by theory, rather than a paraesthetics that crosses over into the theoretical and constantly does battle with it and extends its boundaries. At the very least, it must constantly refer to the limitations of other positions in order to distinguish itself from them. If I have attempted to save a notion of the critical and the theoretical from Lyotard's attacks, it is in order to combat the effects of the generalization of the libidinal, a generalization which constitutes a kind of radical aestheticism—something that the totality of Lyotard's work continually argues against.

In *Discours, figure* and *Economie libidinale*, we thus confront both the critical advantages and risks of using art as a weapon against theoretical closure. If the first text argues that it is impossible for the discursive (even in its theoretical form) to eliminate effectively the figural from within it, I have argued that it is equally impossible to eliminate the theoretical from the libidinal, to postulate, as the second text implies, a realm totally "beyond theory." I have also shown that curiously enough, Lyotard, in the name of libidinal drives and tensions, moves closer in his libidinal texts than anywhere else in his work to eliminating the tensions and antagonisms between discourse and figure, theory and art—ones which he himself has argued constitute the critical force of art, and what I call paraesthetics.

But the most powerful aspect of Lyotard's overall work on the questions of art and theory consists in dramatically demonstrating that no critical aesthetics, no critical theory, can be satisfied with being critical; it must constantly be made to confront the limitations of the critical and the theoretical. At the same time, however (and this is what some of his statements concerning the libidinal perhaps obscure), no position can pretend that it has reached the culmination point of criticism or already transcended the critical—for the critical condition must be one of constant dissatisfaction and

51

unfulfillment. To transpose Lyotard's statement about Adorno, when the gods of theoretical or aesthetic closure rage, it is the various critical devils who constantly do battle with the gods of closure who undoubtedly do the most damage to them and have the best chance of offering the greatest variety of critical alternatives to closure.

C H A P T E R T H R E E
SELF-REFLEXIVITY AND CRITICAL THEORY

F O U C A U L T

The critical ontology of ourselves has to be considered not, certainly, as a theory, a doctrine, nor even as a permanent body of knowledge that is accumulating; it has to be conceived as an attitude, an ethos, a philosophical life in which the critique of what we are is at one and the same time the historical analysis of the limits that are imposed on us and an experiment with the possibility of going beyond them.
> —Michel Foucault, "What is Enlightenment?"

1. The *Mise en abyme* of Historical Representation

One of the important characteristics of certain tendencies of contemporary theory is their emphasis on the critical significance of the phenomenon of self-reflexivity in art and literature. It seems undeniable that certain texts and paintings are self-reflexive, that they represent or mirror their own image of themselves and explicitly reflect how they are constructed and how they function. Less clear is whether this mechanism of self-reflection (the *mise en abyme*)—which suggests an infinite process of doubling and regression up to and into the "abyss"—has metaphysical, aestheticist, or critical implications.

To take an obvious example, the debates between American deconstructionists and their opponents were, for a certain period at least, centered on this issue. In France, much attention was paid to this phenomenon by structuralist-formalist critics intent on making the *mise en abyme* the defining characteristic of all literature and art.[1] Critics who have emphasized the centrality of the *mise en abyme* in literature have, for the most part, claimed that the literariness of literature is best ensured when a literary text stages itself as literature and explicitly displays its own formal properties, when it encloses itself within its own textual frame and cuts itself off from extra-textual relations (the extra-textual being defined as everything that is not reflected in the mirrors constructed by the text itself). For these reasons, the *mise en abyme* has largely been considered a tool of formalist critics used to ensure the purity of the literary and to exclude the extra-literary from having any significant impact on literary texts. In other words, in contemporary theory, the *mise en abyme* has almost always been the sign of literary or aesthetic closure and a denial of the impact of the historical, socio-political, and philosophical contexts of literature and art.

In the debates over the importance to be given to the *mise en abyme*, Michel Foucault's interest in self-reflexive texts and paintings has largely been ignored. Perhaps this is because many of those who deplore the use and abuse of this concept in criticism and theory are militantly anti-formalist and consider Foucault to be an ally in their fight against inflated notions of textuality—notions which, they argue, obscure the workings of history and neutralize all political implications of literature and art. But, as an analysis of Foucault's use of self-reflexivity will show, a critical approach to the *mise en abyme* can, in fact, be of assistance in challenging both traditional notions of history as well as some of the sterile alternatives that still dominate so much of contemporary theory—the alternatives of text *or* context, art and literature *or* history, anti-representation *or* represention.

The best known of Foucault's analyses of self-reflexivity in art is to be found in the first chapter of *The Order of Things*.[2] His treatment of Diego Velázquez's *Las Meninas* is a kind of *mise en scène* of the entire book, a curtain raiser for the "Archaeology of the Human Sciences" (the subtitle he gives to the work) that will follow. One characteristic of all of Foucault's major works is undoubtedly the way he stages in miniature their major problematic in the opening chapters, thus delineating a space that he will attempt to saturate in the course of his analyses. The initial staging of the field also indicates the sites within the field as a whole where the archaeologist can "dig" to uncover traces of how the field is constructed and what kinds of activities are possible within it—in the case of *The Order of Things*, sites where the different "epistemes" governing the ordering of words and things are to be found. Much can be learned about Foucault's critical perspective by paying close attention to these opening scenes—the mirrors Foucault places at the beginning of his works to reflect his works back upon themselves, revealing both their principal assumptions and the critical strategies they will be using.

Foucault argues that *Las Meninas* dramatizes the entire process of representation in the Classical period. Since representation is posited by Foucault as the episteme of this period, the principle of its mechanism of ordering, the painting can be said to represent Representation itself. It is the fullest realization, the culmination of representation in the Classical age: "the manifest essence" of representation (16). To represent the principle and process of representation in a period where representation is *the* principle of ordering would be in a dialectical context to finalize representation, to contain it within a metarepresentation that is the ultimate word or the ultimate context or scene of representation, its end. Nothing seems to escape representation when representation itself is represented.

Foucault's analyses, here and in the chapters to follow, are not free of such totalizing resonances, but, as if to counter them, Foucault at the same time emphasizes the existence of a number of openings in the Classical space of representation—both at its center and on its borders—that lead outside the space of representation and complicate its culmination or finalization in the representation of representation. The mirroring of representation in a particular representation serves both to reflect representation back on itself and to open it up to what it is not—to make it conscious of itself and, in doing so, to indicate the limitations of this consciousness, the gaps or empty spaces within it. Thus for Foucault, self-representation is apparently not limited to what it represents itself to be.

This curtain raiser to *The Order of Things* itself follows a prologue in which Foucault indicates that the birthplace of the entire book could be considered to be a "passage in Borges," specifically, the strange taxonomy of animals it quotes from "a certain Chinese encyclopedia." The series of animals listed by Borges is an example, Foucault claims, of "the exotic charm of another system of thought," one that indicates "the limitation of our own, the stark impossibility of thinking *that*" (xv). Such a radically alien "logic" defamiliarizes our own logic and way of thinking and upsets our sense of identity: "it shatters . . . all the familiar landmarks of thought—of *our* thought, that of our age and geography— . . . disturbing and shaking up for some time our age-old use of the distinction between the Same and the Other" (xv, t.m.). I would argue that Foucault is giving his reader here much more than an introduction to the specific problem of the order of words and things; he is, in fact, presenting his prerequisites for critical thought in general.

Without such disturbance and defamiliarization, the familiar aspects of thought would continue to be taken for universal truths, the Other kept in a relation of dependency or derivation in terms of the Same. When the familiar is made unfamiliar, thought is forced to question itself and confront alternatives to itself; it loses its self-certainty and begins to have trouble recognizing itself in the mirror it holds up in order to send back a reassuring image. For Foucault, critical thought begins in non-recognition, as a result of the distorted mirror in which the confrontation with radical alterity forces it to see itself.

Foucault considers Borges's "Chinese taxonomy" to be a case of radical "illogic," but not primarily because of the improbability of the series of animals and the impossibility of finding a coherent thread to link one category to the next. Rather, its radical alterity is rooted in the category that falls in the sequence between "stray dogs" and animals that "run around like crazy": the self-reflexive category of animals "included in the present classification." Like two other categories that follow later in the sequence—"innumerable" and "*et cetera*"—this category concerns the system of classification itself more than it does the nature or activities of the animals being classified. But unlike the subsequent two categories (both of which have to do with empirical exhaustivity, the inclusion of all remaining animals in two grab-bag sets), the set of animals "included in the present classification" folds the system back onto itself; it presents a problem of classification more difficult to resolve than the requirement of empirical exhaustivity. This set undermines the very foundation of any "logic" that might be used to justify the classification— any ideal, empirical, or even fantastic basis for its existence—by rooting the entire system in or on itself.

The problem of the set of all sets is a basic one for logic, for how can a category remain one category among others, and, at the same time, include all other categories, including itself, within it? How can it be simultaneously one among many and all-encompassing? Foucault states the problem in the following terms:

> The central category of animals "included in the present classifica-tion," with its explicit reference to paradoxes we are familiar with, is indication enough that we shall never succeed in defining a stable relation of contained to container between each of these categories and that which includes them all: if all the animals classified here can be placed without exception in one of the divisions of this list, then aren't all the other divisions to be found in that one division too? And then again, in what space would that single, inclusive di-vision reside? The absurdity of this destroys the *and* of the enumer-ation by making impossible the *in* where the things enumerated would be classified. (xvii, t.m.)

Space is turned inside out, and the category of all categories or the space of all spaces is empty at its core, impossible insomuch as it is all-encompassing. The ground in which it could be rooted is undercut through the very process of self-inclusiveness. This paradox, and the instability it produces, fascinate the archaeologist of *The Order of Things*—an archaeologist looking for any sign that the ultimate foundation of order is not in itself or any metaprinciple, but in the instability or disorder inherent in all order. If the first step for the archaeologist is to understand the rules of each epistemological "game," then the next step, the critical step, is to approach the point where Order itself— rather than any particular order—is in question, the point where the various orders break down and open onto alternative possibilities. The paradox of self-inclusiveness indicates that the order of all orders is also the point of disintegration of order.

At the point where the different orders break down (though that point can never be made present in itself), what is at stake is the "raw being of order" (xxi, t.m.). Such a fundamental form of "being" can never be the object of perception of an "already encoded eye," claims Foucault—hence the necessity for a critical process of decoding. The being of order is not captured by a "reflexive consciousness," one that discovers the arbitrary nature of all codes; it is located in a more fundamental space, a space that flees the theorist as he approaches it, a space that all theories and forms of reflexivity distort and obscure in their attempts to reveal its form and meaning:

> Thus between the already encoded eye and reflexive knowledge there is a middle region in which order itself is rendered. . . . This "middle" region, then, in so far as it makes manifest the modes of being of order, can be posited as the most fundamental of all: anterior to words, perceptions, and gestures, which are then taken to be more or less exact, more or less felicitous translations of it (which is why this experience of order in its massive and primary state always plays a critical role); more solid, more archaic, less dubious, always more "true" than the theories that attempt to give the modes of being an explicit form, an exhaustive application or a philosophical foundation. Thus, in every culture, between the use of what one might call ordering codes and reflections upon order itself, there is the pure [naked, undisguised—*nue*] experience of order and its modes of being. (xxi, t.m.)

Borges's text leads Foucault to this "experience" by means of an outlandish taxonomy and the logical paradox it contains. The "experience itself" is indicated in the "laughter" (xv) its reading provokes, an ironic laughter that acknowledges the limits, not only of order, but of the experience of its being as well. The kind of "experience" in question in the laughter, is not directly of the "raw being of order," but, rather, of the inadequacy of the "familiar landmarks of thought."[3]

This is only one of many indications that *The Order of Things* can be read in two very different ways. The first is the way it is usually read—as an analysis of the "deep structure" of thought in the modern period, an attempt to delineate the fundamental epistemes or rules of the game in terms of which thought was possible in each of the periods treated: a radical attempt to periodize the human sciences without relying on traditional historicist concepts or strategies of periodization. Read in this way, the book constitutes a reversal of the evolutionary theories of periodization and the historicist assumptions supporting those theories (assumptions it mercilessly attacks). It gives historical thinking a new foundation in an alternate form of periodization insomuch as it replaces historical continuity with a discontinuous series of epistemological breaks, each defining a separate but integral time and space. The reader is thus reassured that history remains the foundation for thought, in spite of the series of radical breaks constituting history, and in spite of the lack of explanation as to why those breaks occurred when they occurred. He/she is reassured even in the face of Foucault's many provocative attacks on the traditional mainstays of history—for example, Foucault's claim that "man" is a recent phenomenon and destined to "be erased" in the same way that other phenomena in previous systems of thought were erased when the systems making them possible "crumbled" (387). The reader is reassured because the book—no matter how critical of previous attempts to map out and account for periods of thought—gives him/her the sense of finally getting the mapping right and mastering the rules of the various games, the most fundamental principles of order of each epistemological period. Read in this way, *The Order of Things* is perhaps a more daring form of intellectual history than previous forms, but, it remains *a form* nonetheless.[4]

But *The Order of Things* tells at the same time another, much less familiar, less reassuring story, one more closely related to the "experience" produced by reading Borges's text than to the rearrangement of historical periods. This second story is found between, or, at the limits of, the discontinuous narrative of epistemological events, at the limits or just outside each period and system of thought. At the moment and in the space where one episteme gives way to another—in the space of absolute difference between orders—Foucault locates paintings and texts that do not fit into any of the orders and which demand a radically different "theory" and critical strategy of analysis. In these instances, Foucault's analyses are grounded not in any particular epistemological order but are oriented toward indicating, no matter how indirectly, what is at stake in all orders and principles of ordering: a fundamental disorder or absence.

There is little or no security to be found in these paintings and texts, for they provide no principle or rules in terms of which one can evaluate and explain them. Analysis itself is at risk when confronted with them, threatened by the disorder, illogic, or even madness they are "rooted in." I would even argue that Foucault's "Archaeology of the Human Sciences" has its obscure center in such limit texts—this is undoubtedly what he means when he says that the book was born in the laughter provoked by reading Borges—rather than in the theses supporting his notion of the episteme or the analyses designed to convince us of the unity of each epistemological space. This does not mean that the content of these analyses is without interest or importance, but, rather that another, and I would claim, more critical side of the book will be missed or treated too lightly if one concentrates too intently and exclusively on the explicit analyses of each episteme and the discursive configurations determined by them.

As much as it reveals its "manifest essence," Foucault's analysis of *Las Meninas* indicates the instability at the heart of representation and the representation of representation—unless, of course, that instability could be shown to be part of its essence itself. Foucault's analysis emphasizes the complex and unstable set of relations among the various functions of the subject—subject-viewer, subject-creator, subject-model—within the space of representation (that is, specifically within the painting, but also within the entire epistemological space of the Classical era). This complexity and instability are largely due to the intricate play of absence and presence figured in the painting and at the heart of its representational space; they originate in and are accounted for by representation, but, at the same time, indicate the limits of representation.

The painter is represented within the painting at work on a painting that cannot be seen by the viewer, and he is looking out at his model and thus at the same time at all viewers of the painting who look back at him. A visual space of cross-reference is established in which every spectator is also spectacle and every spectacle also spectator. The model to be represented is outside the scene of representation itself, never directly presented as either an "original" or copy and only dimly visible in a mirror which those represented in the scene cannot see. The spectator, the origin of the gaze that would ideally, encompass the entire scene of representation and thus understand its "essence," is also drawn into the relations established by the painting (by virtue of being the object of the painter's gaze)—even if the viewer's presence is indicated only by his absence. The painting is presented by Foucault as a kind of labyrinth of representation—is this the essence of representation, one could already ask?—from which there seems to be no escape, where the outside (all subjects and spaces in front of or behind the space of representation) is brought inside and the inside is projected outside. Representation thus dominates not only its own space but also the space it projects outside itself. There seems to be no alternative to representation possible, for it, too, would have to be *represented* either as absent or as present.

Each epistemological space, like the space of Classical representation represented in the painting, is closed, argues Foucault time and time again, and no discourse from one space can be understood if it is interpreted in terms of principles specific to another. For example, Foucault's controversial statements on the absence or death of man should certainly be understood in this context. In arguing against all evolutionary forms of historiography (all historiography?), Foucault never claims that a concept of man did not exist before the nineteenth century—such an argument would be absurd in the face of a long humanist tradition—but rather that man is not "born" as an

59

original, fundamental "positivity," as an episteme, until then. Before the epistemological break between the eighteenth and nineteenth centuries, Foucault considers man as a derived, surface concept, a function in an order or "game" organized according to other principles: in other words, man had the status that the figure of the painter (present in the painting but dependent on the complex set of relations established in it) or the model (dimly reflected in a mirror no one looks at) or the spectator (absent as a figure but whose place is indicated) has in *Las Meninas*. But in the Classical age, man did not yet determine an epistemological space; "he" was only a visitor in a space determined by other rules.

For Foucault, man is born as an object of knowledge in "his" own right only at the end of the Classical period and only as a result of the increasing reflexivity of the space of representation:

> But as things become increasingly reflexive [literally, wind back on themselves], seeking the principle of their own intelligibility only in their own development and abandoning the space of representation, man enters the field of Western knowledge in his turn and for the first time. Strangely enough, man—the knowledge of whom is supposed by the naïve to be the oldest form of research, dating from Socrates—is probably no more than a kind of rift in the order of things, or, in any case, a configuration sketched out in terms of the new place he has so recently assumed in the field of knowledge. . . .
> It is comforting, however, and a source of profound relief to think that man is only a recent invention, a figure not yet two centuries old, a mere wrinkle in our knowledge, and that he will disappear as soon as knowledge has taken on a new form. (xxiii, t.m.)

Foucault's analysis of *Las Meninas* shows, among other things, how man as such is an insignificant element of the Classical space of representation compared to the complexity of the process of representation itself, how his place is neither original nor determining. Foucault demands that interpretation respect the Classical space for what it is and read it in terms of *its* rules rather than those of another space that has not yet taken form. This is, in fact, the dominant argument of *The Order of Things,* one continually evoked against all interpretations that posit or assume continuity or evolution from one period to the next.

For Foucault, there can be only one episteme in play for each period, one and only one set of rules for each game: "In any given culture and at any given moment, there is always only one *episteme* that defines the conditions of possibility of all knowledge, whether expressed in a theory or silently invested in a practice" (168). The uniqueness and unity of each episteme determines a space, which, no matter how internally complex and divided it may appear to be, is always unified in terms of its episteme and is always contemporaneous or present to itself—the closed context and frame of all thought. "The history of knowledge can be written only on the basis of what was contemporaneous with it, and certainly not in terms of reciprocal influence, but in terms of conditions and *a prioris* established in time. It is in this sense that archaeology can . . . delineate a space without cracks, one in which the history of the sciences, the history of ideas, and the history of opinions can, if they wish, romp" (208, t.m.).

The first step in Foucault's archaeological approach, therefore, is to define "systems of simultaneity." Once done, then and only then does he proceed to deal with "the series of mutations necessary and sufficient to circumscribe the threshold of a new positivity" (xxiii). This is why Foucault is so polemical in defending his archaeology against all theories that argue that thought evolves from period to period; his notion of the episteme depends on the simultaneity of the space it delineates. But having established the existence of the episteme, he himself then goes on to disturb the unity and simultaneity of each epistemological space, to indicate openings within it and at its limits. Thought in general may be possible for him only because of the unity of each epistemological space. What I would call critical thought is possible only at the limits of the archaeology delineating such a space—in the cracks that do appear in it after a system of thought has been made possible and at the moment (from the beginning?) it turns back to reflect on how it was made possible.

The closure constituted by each period determines that all concepts have one and only one "life," that they are born and die in their own period and do not continue on in any form from one period to the next. Even though more attention has been paid to statements concerning the birth and death of man in *The Order of Things* than to any other aspect of the book, man is only one of a long list of concepts whose apearance and disappearance are charted by Foucault. At the end of the sixteenth century, for example, resemblance disappears as the governing episteme: "We must pause here for a while, at this moment in time when resemblance was about to relinquish its relation with knowledge and disappear, in part at least, from the horizon of cognition" (17, t.m.). Foucault even claims that language does not exist within the epistemological space determined by representation:

In the seventeenth century, it is the massive and intriguing existence of language that is eliminated. It no longer appears hidden in the enigma of the mark; it does not yet appear explicitly in the theory of signification. From an extreme point of view, one might say that language in the Classical era does not exist. But that it functions: its whole existence is located in its representational role, is limited to performing it with exactitude, and ends up by being used up by it. (78–79, t.m.)

In order to convince us that his periodization is legitimate and the frame constituted by each episteme closed, Foucault must deny the importance (and even the existence) of a heritage concepts such as man, representation, language, life, nature, etc. bring with them at birth, as well as the legacy they leave after their declared death.

In his desire to establish his archaeology as a radical alternative to historicism—which remains for him *the sign* of the failure to think critically—Foucault is led to frame his own argument in terms of the birth and death, that is, the full presence or radical absence of concepts in one period or another. At least he "almost" or "in part" does, qualifiers he himself uses when he analyzes the appearance or disappearence of a concept and leaves open the possibility that the closed space he is in the process of defending so energetically against historicists or dialectical historians will be undone—undone not from "outside" by the general movement of history but from within by the activity of the episteme itself as it saturates its space and as the fragile base on which it rests is reflected in the mirror it holds up to itself. Foucault in *The Order of Things* charts both the closure of the different epistemological spaces and the openings within each that are indications of alternate spaces organized according to completely different rules.

The first phase of Foucault's analysis of *Las Meninas* concerns the position the painting itself assigns to the spectator and the spectator's relation both to the painting represented in the painting and to painting (representation) in general. The place of the spectator is determined by representation in both these senses, but a certain play of absence and presence is possible in spite of, or really because of, the particular form of this determination. The painting captures the painter on the border between visibility and invisibility, at a moment when he can still be seen looking out at his model and just before he moves behind his painting in order to paint his model and is hidden from view: "Now he can be seen, caught at a moment when he is immobile, at the neutral center of this oscillation . . . half-way between the visible and the invisible" (3, t.m.). His visibility in the painting renders the visibility of his own painting invisible to him (and to his model and us as well): "As though the painter could not at the same time be seen on the painting where he is represented and also see the one upon which he is representing something. He rules on the threshold of these two incompatible visibilities" (4). Foucault is interested in all such thresholds, for the threshold indicates the fragility of any perspective on the visible, including Foucault's own. The painter is said to "*rule* on the threshold," but, in fact, the threshold is precisely the fine line where no one and no one thing rules, where all sovereignty is undermined, where incompatibile spaces, epistemes, and modes of discourse struggle for dominance.[5]

The positioning of the painter on the threshold of different modes of visibility undercuts the stability of the spectator's perspective as well.

> He is staring at a point to which, even though it is invisible, we, the spectators can easily assign an object, since we, ourselves, are that point: our body, our face, our eyes. The spectacle he is observing is thus doubly invisible: first, because it is not represented within the space of the painting, and, second, because it is situated precisely in that blind point, in that essential hiding-place where our own gaze slips away from us at the very moment we look. And yet, how could we fail to see that invisibility, there in front of our eyes, since it has its own perceptible equivalent in the painting itself? (4, t.m.)[6]

One effect of self-reflexivity on "our own gaze" is that it "slips away from us" in the very same process that makes it "ours"; it never quite meets itself except in and as a visible absence. Foucault's analysis returns constantly to these pockets of invisibility and slippage, these gaps or cracks in the visible universe of the painting. In positioning his own gaze on them, and determining and then displacing his perspective in terms of them, his strategy is to enter into the complex system of relations constructed by the painting and treat it "on its own terms"—while at the same time to avoid being totally determined by the dominant episteme, representation, which is claimed to regulate both the visibility and invisibility of the painting and the Classical space in general.[7]

The mirror on the wall of the studio may be the only form of representation represented in the painting to function, as Foucault says, "in all honesty," to offer "at last that enchantment of the double that until now has been denied us, not only by the distant paintings but also by the light in the foreground with its ironic canvas" (7). But the mirror does not effectively close off the scene of representation by turning it back on itself or limit the process of referentiality to what is actually represented. On the contrary, it repeats and extends the oscillation between visibility and invisibility at the heart of re-presentation—first of all, because no one in the scene represented in the painting is looking at the mirror, and, secondly, because "it reflects nothing, in fact, of what is in the same space as itself: neither the painter whose back is turned to it, nor the figures in the centre of the room. . . . Here the mirror says nothing that has already been said before" (7). The double reflected in the mirror is not the scene depicted in the painting (as was, for instance, the convention in Dutch painting), but what is outside the scene, invisible within it. The scene of representation is turned inside out by the mirror, the outside doubled within it. But once again the two visibilities do not complete each other, for a gap continues to exist between them that neither can fill.

Only well into his analysis does Foucault name the models being painted, Philip IV and his wife Maria Ana, who are absent from the scene except in this distant mirror. An "honest" representation, no matter how faint, evokes names and identities, and with them the representational dynamics of the scene appear to have a particular purpose and end outside themselves. Re-presentation, no matter how circuitous its path, would thus appear to culminate in the models outside the scene (in their names and identities)—even if the painting being painted within the painting remains invisible. Here Foucault intervenes forcefully from offstage to assert that this is not the case; the support for such an assertion is not provided by the painting itself, but by a general principle: language and painting, because they come from totally different spheres, are irreducible to each other.

> It is in vain that we say what we see; what we see never resides in what we say. And it is in vain that we attempt to show by the use of images, metaphors, or similes, what we are in the process of saying; the space where they shine is not that deployed by our eyes but that defined by the sequential elements of syntax. And the proper name, in this particular context, is merely an artifice: it allows us to identify things [literally, point things out], in other words, to pass surreptitiously from the space where one speaks to the space where one looks; in other words, to close one space comfortably back onto the other as if they were equivalent. (9, t.m.)[8]

The principle of a radical discontinuity between visual and discursive spaces is evoked here by Foucault for a very particular purpose: to indicate the potentially infinite play of representation within the painting, a process which would be seriously truncated by saying (naming) what is shown and collapsing one realm into the other.

Since his own discourse on the painting cannot claim to overcome this incompatibility, Foucault insists that such incompatibility does not prohibit all relations between discursive and visual realms. Rather, it means that the two spaces can only be related in terms of what differentiates them, that their relation is open, a relation of nonrelation: "But if one wishes to keep the relation of language to the visible open, if one wishes to speak not in opposition to their incompatibility but starting out from it, so as to stay as close as possible to each one, then one must erase those proper names and persevere in the infinity of the task" (9–10, t.m.). It is as if this perseverance were, for Foucault, the critical task itself and the overcoming of this radical incompatibility—no matter how and for what purposes it is done—the sign that the task had been abandoned. Even if it means that proper names must be erased or that we must "pretend not to know who is reflected in the depths of the mirror," the main task is to "question that reflection on the level of its existence" (10, t.m.) and not on the level of its identity or name.

This procedure of forgetting or pretending not to know the identities of the figures represented in the painting may seem even more scandalous to historians of art and philosophers of history than are Foucault's statements concerning the disappearance of man—for facts, dates, names, etc. are the raw matter and foundation of history. And yet if the full impact of representation is to be understood (in history as well as in the painting), the historian, Foucault seems to be saying, must proceed *as if* he did not know the names. For the immediate imposition of the knowledge of the names has severely limiting consequences for the analysis. An "active forgetting" of names makes it possible to understand representation on its own terms, to understand how what names represent is represented.

But there is still a problem in this willed ignorance. Even if their names are erased and we concentrate on their place in the painting and their relation to a general network of representation, the figures remain sovereign, although now in a different sense from the sovereignty given them by their names. Their representational sovereignty, if I can call it that, does not come from any material qualities their images possess either. In fact, of all the figures represented, they are "the palest, the most unreal, the most compromised. . . . In so far as they are visible, they are the frailest and the most distant form of all reality" (14). But it is precisely from this lack of substantial, material visibility that their ideal, sovereign status in the painting comes; by being the least visible of all images, they are, paradoxically, the most completely dependent on representation, the most fully representational.

These two almost invisible images are sovereign for Foucault in various ways. First of all, they "order around themselves the entire representation," and because "the entire arrangement of the painting" is organized in terms of their gaze, they constitute the "true centre of the composition" (14, t.m.). If we are able to forget who they are, we can then see all the better the place they occupy:

> In the realm of anecdote, this centre is symbolically sovereign . . .
> but it is so above all because of the triple function it fulfills in relation
> to the painting. For in it come to be exactly superimposed the model's
> gaze at the moment it is being painted, the spectator's as he con-
> templates the scene, and the painter's as he composes his painting.
> These three "perceiving" functions come together in a point exterior
> to the painting: that is, a point that is ideal in relation to what is
> represented but perfectly real since the representation becomes pos-
> sible with it as a starting-point. Within this reality itself, it cannot not
> be invisible. And yet this reality is projected within the painting—

projected and diffracted in three forms which correspond to the three
functions of that ideal and real point. (14–15, t.m.)

This point possesses all the characteristics (and contradictions, I might add),
of transcendence: outside and inside at the same time, ideal and yet determining reality, it is the origin and center without which the space of representation cannot function. It remains sovereign as long as it remains almost
without substance, a nearly empty space at the intersection of all other
spaces.

This "spectacle-en-regard," as Foucault calls it, this painting which in its
entirety "is looking at a scene for which it, in its turn, is a scene" constitutes
a "condition of pure reciprocity manifested by the mirror looking and being
looked at" (14, t.m.). In principle, then, everything in the space constituted
by self-reflexivity exists only as representation, that is to say, everything is
reflected back onto itself within the closed space constituted by the mirror
reflecting the outside in and the inside out. And yet, even when the cycle of
representation is perfect—as Foucault claims it is in this painting—the cycle
is at the same time not perfect, nor is representation complete. Because
spectator and spectacle and painter and model cannot be present in the same
space at the same time, there are always insurmontable gaps between them
and the spaces in which they are located: "The double relation of the representation to its model and to its sovereign, to its author as well as to the
person to whom it is being offered, this relation is necessarily interrupted.
It can never be present without some remainder, even in a representation
that offers itself as a spectacle" (16, t.m.). Representation, even in its "pure,"
complete form, always lacks something at its core for which it compensates
with a remainder that further complicates the representational space and
prolongs the process of representation.

At the heart of the self-reflexive space, at the very core of the cycle of
representation and supporting it, there is, Foucault asserts, "an essential void:
the necessary disappearance of that which is its foundation—of the person
it resembles and the person in whose eyes it is only resemblance. This subject
itself—which is the same—has been elided. And representation, freed finally
from the relation that was enchaining it, can present itself as pure representation" (16, t.m.). "Pure representation," then, reaches a limit as it approaches
the void on which it rests; in order to be itself and only itself, representation
has had to displace any subject that could serve as its foundation or referent.
In order to be only itself, it constantly risks being nothing.

Throughout *The Order of Things,* Foucault's analyses of the various epistemological spaces terminate with them being put into question at the very
moment when their cycle is complete, when the possibilities of the episteme
have been most fully realized through a process of self-reflection. At the very
moment of completeness or perfection a gap or void is revealed at the core

of the space, a gap basic to the space and to the process of self-reflexivity itself. This is also the moment when a new episteme is anticipated or begins to take form.[9] In his analyses of each period, Foucault charts a kind of dialectical process that follows the episteme from its birth, through the realization of its multiple possibilities, and finally to the moment of self-fulfillment and self-awareness and its death. What is undialectical about the process—and Foucault always presented the book as profoundly undialectical—is that the process terminates, in each case, in the awareness of a fundamental incompleteness at the heart of this completeness and self-fulfillment—meaning that the next stage is not a retention and transcendence of the previous stage, but a radical break with and rearrangement of the epistemological field and the rules of the game.

Foucault repeatedly returns to the void and the heart of the order of words and things, a void that no epistemological order or historical series effectively compensates for or overcomes. His position is not, as some have argued, a form of nihilism, however; the death of man (and other concepts), the absence of universal values, the disorder at the heart of order, the irrationality at the core of rationality, etc., are not presented by him as negative truths to replace those being disputed. Rather, the repeated return to the point where the different orders break down is an attempt to indicate the possibility of transgressive, critical perspectives on any order or process of ordering. These perspectives are always situated by Foucault in terms of what he calls the "essential void," but they are not equivalent to the void. To be equivalent would make them negative absolutes and make the archaeology of the human sciences a negative theology or metaphysics. In Foucault's work, they emerge out of the void, link up with it, and return repeatedly to it. In each case, the way to the void is indicated by self-reflexive paintings and literature, and, most often, by the "mad" philosophers, painters, or poets who dare pursue the self-reflexivity of language up to and even into the void—the place from which all orders emerge and in which they break apart. It is the place to which Foucault's own critical discourse repeatedly returns, not in order to occupy this place, but in order to (de)position itself in terms of it.

2. A Poetics of Absence

If *The Order of Things* were to be considered apart from the rest of Foucault's work, it might be possible to argue that the problem of the absence of any solid foundation—not only for representation but, more importantly, for each of the epistemological orders—was never more than a marginal concern for him. Since most of the book is devoted to analyzing the way knowledge is produced in each period in terms of a particular episteme, the question of what Foucault calls the "being of order" is barely addressed at all. But in essays devoted to such writers as Sade, Klossowski, Bataille, Blan-

67

chot, and especially in his book on Raymond Roussel (all of whom are evoked in *The Order of Things* as limit cases whose "thought" belongs to no particular episteme), Foucault pursues this problem at much greater length—at such great length, in fact, that it would not be an exaggeration to speak of the existence of a Foucauldian poetics of self-reflexivity or absence in terms of these texts. Influenced most definitely by Blanchot, especially the Blanchot of *L'Espace littéraire* (Paris: Gallimard, 1955), Foucault in all these essays investigates what he calls the "absence d'oeuvre" (the absence of the work), a concept which echos Blanchot's notion of *désoeuvrement*.[10] With all the interest literary critics and theorists have taken in Foucault's work, it is surprising that so little attention has been paid to these texts in which Foucault has the most to say about literature and language, for in them he develops to a fuller extent than anywhere else a notion of self-reflexivity crucial to his entire critical project.

In the very lyrical beginning to his inaugural lecture at the Collège de France entitled *L'Ordre du discours* (translated by Rupert Swyer as *The Discourse on Language*, a title from which the problem of order has unfortunately been dropped),[11] Foucault refers to the status of his own discourse and the difficulty any discourse has in justifying its own beginnings.[12] He emphasizes the anxiety and uncertainty of the moment when silence is broken and a discourse must not only say something but legitimate itself in terms of the mass of discourses that precedes and surrounds it. In the face of this anxiety, not of influence but of beginning, he expresses the following impossible wish: that on this, the most visible of all Parisian intellectual stages, his discourse might go unnoticed and simply disappear into the discourses that precede it, that his beginning not constitute a beginning or a continuation or a culmination, but be consumed by discourse in general, that is, find its place in the spaces left open in and by discourse:

> Rather than begin speaking, I would have preferred to be enveloped by speech, borne away beyond all possible beginnings. I would have liked to become conscious of the fact that at the moment of speaking a nameless voice had long been leading me: in this situation it would have been sufficient for me to make links with it, to continue its phrase, and to lodge myself, without anyone really paying attention, in its gaps as if it had paused an instant, in suspense, to beckon me. There would have thus been no beginning, and instead of being someone from whom discourse comes, I would be instead a miniscule lack in its haphazard development, the space of its possible disappearance. (215, t.m.)

This impossible wish written in the past conditional reveals at least two important aspects of Foucault's notion of his own critical discourse: first, that in spite of a wish not to, he is forced by the very nature of discourse to begin not once but repeatedly; he is thus in the position of having to justify each beginning in terms of the discourses with which his own is linked. And second, the place he assigns to critical discourse—even if it may never actually occupy it fully—is not a transcendent position outside or above the discourses that it comments on or with which it is linked, but rather within them. For Foucault, critical discourse is located not at the place(s) where a discourse most fully realizes itself and closes itself off to other discourses, but rather in the gaps within every discourse where it is not itself but separated from itself, where it is threatened with its own disappearance, its fusion into other discourses, or its return to silence.[13]

If institutions obscure the difficulties of beginning by holding onto traditions such as inaugural lectures, and if rhetoric, linguistics, philosophy, logic, literary criticism, etc., all regulate in their own way the uncertainties of discourse by providing it with rules and enforcing prohibitions, critical discourse, for Foucault, must attempt to highlight its own uneasiness against all attempts to make discourse seem natural, universal, rational, logical: in other words, necessary and unproblematical. Foucault's work on such institutions as the prison and the asylum and his critique of the confining and distorting effects of the dominant institutional discourses on insanity, punishment, and sexuality are obvious examples of his attempt to challenge the foundations of dominant forms of discourse. Less well known, or at least less often studied with much care, are his essays on literature in which he pursues in great detail the problem of the origin of language, or more accurately, the problem of the lack of substantial foundation for language and the unsettling effects on all discourse of this lack at (of) the origin.

The question of whether Foucault has a "theory of language" is not an easy one to answer; in his various works, different aspects of language are emphasized and his own approach to language differs greatly from his early works to his late ones. It would be safe to say, however, that from *The Archaeology of Knowledge* on, the question he investigates in depth in his earlier essays on literature—the question of the "origin of language"—is abandoned as an explicit question. His later work situates all discourse on the surface of a power-knowledge network and treats discourse predominately as a form of action, as a movement within a field of forces. The question of the origin or foundation (or lack of) of discourse seems to have little relevance when the principal questions being asked of discourse are how it performs and what its effects are.

Some theorists see Foucault's abandonment of his mode of questioning the origin of language through a reading of self-reflexive literary texts as a sign of his critical development—Foucault freeing himself from the metaphysical concerns of his earlier work in order to proceed to more concrete sociopolitical analyses.[14] Perhaps even Foucault, influenced in part by those making this argument, came to see his own work this way. Be that as it may, while the abandonment of a question such as the origin of language may permit a different kind of research to be carried out, this does not mean that nothing from his work on literature is retained in his later form of "discourse analysis," that his "genealogies" have no relation to his "archaeologies." It seems to me that early and late works are related in much more complicated ways than any theory either, on the one hand, charting progress or decline from one to the other, or, on the other, proclaiming a radical break between them, can account for. An understanding of Foucault's dogged pursuit of a question like that of the origin of language in an entire series of texts cannot be considered irrelevant as concerns his later works—even if that question is no longer specifically addressed by them. At the very least, it seems safe to say that Foucault's analyses of certain complex self-reflexive literary texts in terms of the problem of language are not without their own critical force.

It is no secret that Foucault hated to be considered a structuralist and often mocked the naïveté, if not the stupidity, of those who lumped him together with Lévi-Strauss, Lacan, Barthes, and others as the inheritors of a Saussurian model of language.[15] Foucault was obviously right to claim that his work did not fit into this category, for he always treated structuralist linguistics as only one theory of language among many others and never privileged it as *the* model for the study of language. Throughout his work, he stresses the way all linguistics and all philosophies of language are linked to specific, rather than universal epistemological conditions; it could be concluded that for Foucault "the linguistic turn" associated with structuralism is critically significant insomuch as it encourages a critical reevaluation of the discourses of the "human sciences"—but not because it can be accepted as a general model for all discourse, as militant structuralists sometimes argue. Foucault's strategy, then, is not just to distance himself from structuralism, but also to undermine and relativize all *theories* of language as such.

The problem for Foucault seems to be how to maintain this critical distance, not only *on* language but also *in* language, without postulating another totalized theory of language. In *The Archaeology of Knowledge,* Foucault attacks all historical and linguistic totalities and replaces them with a modified speech act theory that stresses the performative aspects of discourse and the multiple series with which any "discursive event" intersects. But even here, in his most developed theoretical statement on discourse, the perspective from which discourse can be considered to be constituted entirely as action—that is, the perspective of the archaeologist defining the different units of discourse and measuring its effects in different contexts—is left for the most part uninvestigated.

The discourse of the archaeologist has the decided privilege of dominating the discursive field, of being extra- or trans-discursive in its ability to describe the way discourse works and distinguish among the different levels and categories of discourse. But nowhere in this text does Foucault pursue how this is possible if no totalization or systemization of discourse is permitted. If *The Archaeology* was written, as Foucault claims in his introduction, in part to supply the "methodological guidelines" missing from *The Order of Things* and thus to correct the "impression that [his] analyses were being conducted in terms of cultural totalities" (16, t.m.), by not subjecting the discourse of the archaeologist to critical scrutiny (no matter how diversified the discursive field is argued to be), the perspective of the archaeologist ends up totalizing the very discursive diversity it has as its purpose to defend.[16]

I would argue that it is in his numerous essays on literature that Foucault, in a complicated and indirect way, situates his own critical discourse in relation to language or discourse in general more carefully than in *The Archaeology* or anywhere else in his work. In these essays, Foucault focuses on how certain writers, in their practice as writers and not through some generalized theory of language, push against and transgress the boundaries of language—whether language is defined by philosophy, linguistics, or literature—to such a degree that they approach the very "origin" of language itself. This relentless pursuit of an impossible origin becomes a kind of model for the critical theorist. It reveals the limitations involved in any finalization of the process of questioning and the necessity of undermining any perspective that attempts to transcend the process or remove itself from that process by giving itself a solid foundation outside of language.

The critical theorist is, in a sense, made positionless by these texts, forced to link his own discourse to them on "their terms" rather than his own. He cannot flee the issue of the legitimation of his own discourse, but is forced to confront it over and over again because no response can be more than temporary or situational and must be transgressed in its turn. As Foucault argues (in "What is an Author?"), "writing in our day has freed itself from the necessity of 'expression'" and instead "implies an action that is always testing the limits of its regularity, transgressing and reversing an order that it accepts and manipulates. Writing unfolds like a game that inevitably moves beyond its own rules and finally leaves them behind" (*Language, Counter-Memory, Practice,* edited by Donald F. Bouchard [Ithaca: Cornell University Press, 1977], 116). The task he implicitly assigns to the critical thinker—whether, in his terms, an archaeologist or genealogist—is, I would argue, practically the same: to test the limits of regularity and reverse the orders being manipulated in order to move beyond its own rules (and those of language) and leave them behind.

Foucault's book on Raymond Roussel[17] constitutes an extended analysis of a radical form of self-reflexivity in literature and, at the same time, an important statement on the place of critical discourse in general. Foucault's interest in Roussel and in the complicated formal techniques to be found in his writing is slightly different from that of formalist critics who have also rediscovered this writer who was first championed by the Surrealists.[18] Foucault's interest can be explained, first of all, by the fact that Roussel could be included in the list of "mad poets" (like Rousseau, Hölderlin, Nietzsche, and Artaud) whose work Foucault assigns a special place in his "history of madness," at the very limits of thought. Foucault's *Raymond Roussel* could thus be considered to be an extension of *Madness and Civilization*—an elaboration of *Madness and Civilization's* scattered pages devoted to the relation between madness and writing, an attempt to understand better the place or nonplace of madness in a certain form of radically self-reflexive literature.[19] For Foucault, the question of "madness" has to do with Roussel's practice of writing itself, his confrontation with language on its deepest and most unstable level, the proximity of his work to the absent origin out of which Foucault claims all writing emerges.

Like formalist structuralist critics, Foucault focuses mainly on the problem of *dédoublement* in Roussel's work—the various ways his writing reflects and doubles back on itself. Foucault's reading, however, does not follow the pattern of the work of the great majority of theorists interested in the same phenomenon (the phenomenon of the *mise en abyme*): that is, to argue that the process of doubling or self-reflection in literature leads inevitably to a concept of the literary text as a self-sufficient, integral entity. In fact, Foucault's reading of Roussel leads to a very different notion of the literary text and has radically different, perhaps even opposite theoretical implications from those of the formalist reading of the *mise en abyme*. Foucault is more interested in the deconstitution of the literary text than its constitution, in the way such a literature reveals in its mirrors of itself that it has no solid foundation in itself or in any other origin.

In an attempt to account for their formal complexity, critics have frequently categorized Roussel's figurative use of language and rhetorical techniques in classical tropological terms, but Foucault insists that all rhetorical systematization seriously reduces the critical, disruptive force of his language. For Foucault, Roussel's writing is more anti-rhetoric than rhetoric:

> The "tropological space" . . . is not considered as the birthplace of canonical figures of speech but as a blank space in language that opens up inside the word its insidious, arid, and booby-trapped emptiness. . . . Roussel takes [this game] for what it is, as a lack to be extended as far as possible and to be measured meticulously. He senses in it not merely the semi-freedoms of expression but an absolute void of being that one has to invest in, master, and fill with pure invention. . . . He does not want to duplicate the world with another world but in the spontaneous doublings of language *discover* an unsuspected space and *cover* it with things never before said. (24–25)

For Foucault, Roussel's fantastic inventions and turns of phrase are "coverings" for the void lying under them. The void cannot be presented in itself, but is uncovered in its self-reflexive coverings. The proliferation of figures and images in Roussel's texts thus arises out of, and indirectly points back to, the lack at the foundation of language disseminated throughout language.

Foucault is arguing that the most radical forms of poetics—if we can still call Roussel's writing practice a poetics—reach their limit and culminate in their own annihilation. The moments of greatest inventiveness always take place over a void and are thus also the moments of greatest risk. The space separating poetry from the void on which it rests is incredibly slight, a "tightrope" holding only the most agile of poets (and theorists): "Roussel's narratives roam . . . as if on a tightrope over the void" (29). The problem of how to relate to or take a position in terms of the void is an especially difficult problem, then, for the critic or theorist; the natural tendency is to load the surfaces of the texts to be interpreted with as much meaning as possible. Here the tightrope is so fragile, however, it holds almost no weight at all. If the critic or theorist is not just to remain silent before such texts or simply recite them verbatum—for if he does, he is no longer fulfilling a critical function—he must find a way of walking the tightrope without adding too much weight to it. If Roussel's texts, and others like his, constitute a poetic and critical limit of some sort, it is not a limit the critic approaches easily.

Foucault finds numerous examples in Roussel's work of scenes "which show that they show but not what in them is shown" (68), of a "reversible system" of narrative "that repeats the [linguistic] machine which in turn repeats the narrative" (70), of "machines that enclose the procedures in which they are enclosed" and that constitute "in themselves their own space" (85). As varied and interesting as these procedures and machines are, there is something overly predictable about Foucault's analysis: they all lead back to the *abyme* of the *mise en abyme*. "Here language is arranged in a circle inside itself, hiding what it makes visible, dissimulating from each look what it proposes to offer it, and falling at a vertiginous speed into the invisible cavity where there is no access to things and where it disappears in their mad pursuit" (172). Because, in this text and in others devoted to literature, Foucault never seems to grow tired of describing this movement of language toward its own disappearance, one could conclude that much is at stake for his own theoretical position in this movement.

In Roussel's case, the proliferation of fantastic figures, the incredible language machines, and the bizarre narratives and tropes all point to instability and disorder at the heart of language and indicate the limit situation of language, the place where language breaks apart: "As if things followed one after the other into the void. . . . At each instance words are born in an absence of being, flowing one against the other. . . . A somber machine . . . gives birth to repetition and through it digs out a void where being wastes away, where

73

words hurry off in pursuit of things, and where language falls apart indefinitely into this central absence" (175). Roussel's work, as well as that of the other "mad poets," is of no particular order but floats freely in the disorder that underlies all order. Its "limitlessness" or disorder indicates both the possibilities and limits of all other orders that do not partake—one is tempted to say do not dare partake—of this "freedom."

It should now be possible to describe more clearly the relationship between Foucault's archaeological project and the excessive or transgressive discourses of "mad writers" (such as Roussel) that Foucault relies upon to provide a perspective on order from outside—at the origin of—order. The archaeologist focuses on the systems of opposition, classification, and analogy that arise to cover over the dissipation of being, the void at the origin of language. He digs beneath the surface in order to discover the rules which make possible and regulate the different orders of words and things, the knowledge that is produced in spite of (or is it not, rather, because of?) the abyss at the heart of the "being of order." His desire is to understand each set of rules on its own terms and thus to relativize all knowledge, to force us to see that the regularities making knowledge possible in the various periods have no more profundity than a set of rules in a game, that knowledge itself is merely the product of moves which these rules make possible.

The poet of the abyss is never reassured by any of these games or any of those he invents or practices himself, for he has another project: if "language flees from within itself, it is of this flight and against this flight that it is necessary to speak, and thus it is necessary to hurl verses in this void not at things (now lost along with being) but in pursuit of language and in order to rehabilitate it and form a barrier covering this opening—a barrier which is at the same time a closed threshold and new opening" (176). The barrier cannot hold, of course, because it too is constructed out of language; thus, the poet's task is infinite, the opening needing to be constantly covered over again. The rehabilitation of language and thought is never completed, and a self-reflexive discursive practice such as Roussel's continually manifests the lack of solid foundation for language and thought by refusing to accept either the abyss or any form of discourse that covers it over as conclusive. In Foucault's work, self-reflexivity, if pushed far enough, leads inevitably to the void; but the void itself is not an origin or end for discourse. It is the place from which discourse is repeatedly regenerated, where what has not yet been said or figured takes form.

Madness—as the other of reason, as an alterity that cannot be spoken or figured in the discourse of reason—is for Foucault intimately connected to the void manifested in self-reflexive literature and art. Madness and self-reflexive literature are linked to each other in Foucault's work because of the way each relates to the void at the origin of discourse. But they are connected to each other and to the void through separation rather than fusion. In other

74

words, no literature, no matter how "mad," self-reflexive, or transgressive, can ever be equated with the void or be seen as a means of occupying it or filling it in:

> Nothing can ever fill in the central hollow. Artaud wanted to approach this void in his work but never stopped being separated from it: separated by it from his work but also separated by his work from it. He ceaselessly hurled his language at this medullary ruin, excavating from it a work that is the absence of the work. This void is paradoxically for Roussel the sun. . . . But what can the solar hollow be except the negation of madness by the work? And of the work by madness? . . . This solar hollow is neither the psychological condition of the work (an idea that makes no sense) nor a theme that it would have in common with the illness. It is the space of language of Roussel, the void out of which he speaks, the absence through which work and madness communicate with and exclude each other. (207)

Separated from itself and the madness to which it gives form—and which by being given form is negated—the "mad" literary work is considered by Foucault to be, really, an absence of the work, a poetic practice that is the absence of the poem as such. Work and madness communicate with, and exclude each other in, and through, the void.

For Foucault, madness constitutes the ultimate challenge to and limit of discourse in general; a certain poetic practice reaches this limit by approaching the abyss separating discourse and madness. But Foucault is equally careful to stress that madness is not found *in* literary-poetic works. For him, no form of psychoanalysis has been able to articulate the links between madness and literature—because the psychoanalysis of literature in its various forms has sought to locate madness "in" or "under" the work as its original or ultimate sense or truth, as the source of its thematic or formal unity. Psychoanalysis tries to make madness speak, to have it make sense.

A poetics of the absence of the work (in Foucault's sense) imposes a certain silence on critical discourse as it approaches the point where the work reaches its limits and is itself silent: "Nietzsche's last cry . . . is not on the border of reason and unreason, on the path of the work's flight. . . . It is rather the very annihilation of the work, that point where it becomes impossible and where it must be silent. . . . Madness is the absolute break with the work" (*Madness and Civilization,* 287, t.m.). As Foucault repeatedly states in all of his work having to do with madness, *"where there is a work, there is no madness"* (*Madness,* 289, t.m.). A "mad" poetics cannot be defined, then, in terms of works, but only in terms of the transgression of the limits of works—

75

there where the work becomes impossible in terms of an absence or void it may indicate, but is not able to master or make its own.

The role of critical discourse in terms of such a poetics of absence, of "unworkness," is not to attempt to identify madness by treating it as a theme or form, but, rather, to question itself in terms of this radical absence or extreme limit it cannot attain: "By the madness which interrupts it, a work opens a void, a moment of silence, a question without answer, provokes a breach without reconciliation where the world is forced to question itself" (288, t.m.). Such a (un)work destabilizes the orders of discourse and provides a perspective in terms of which nothing really holds. For Foucault, any form of critical discourse, which attempts to master this instability or disorder is immediately confronted with its own limitations and forced to situate itself in terms of what it cannot master or measure: "The world that thought to measure and justify madness through psychology must justify itself before madness, since in its struggles and debates it measures itself by the excess of works like those of Nietzsche, of Van Gogh, of Artaud. And nothing in it, especially not what it can know of madness, assures the world that it is justified by such works of madness" (289, t.m.). Critical discourse is thus left the task of measuring itself in terms of the immeasurable, but without measuring and therefore limiting the immeasurable itself.

The immeasurable makes demands on the world, therefore; the most obvious is that all limits be continually recognized, transformed, and transgressed. And in spite of the risk that this might in fact be a way of measuring and limiting the immeasurable, Foucault does derive a certain sense of possible alternative futures from the "(non)perspective" of the immeasurable. For example, madness, which he claims is for us today undefinable and immeasurable, will someday, he hypothesizes, become the measure of ourselves and no longer an undecipherable sign of radical alterity:

> Perhaps someday we will no longer know very well what madness could have been. Its figure will have so closed in on itself as no longer to allow the traces that it will have left behind to be deciphered. At best, they will be among the configurations that we today would not be able to draw, but which in the future will be indispensable grills for interpreting us and our culture. Artaud will then belong to the grounds of our culture and no longer to the break with it; neurotics, to the constitutive forms (and not to the deviations) of our society. Everything that we experience today in the form of a limit or as foreign or insupportable, will have taken on the serene characteristics of what is positive. And what for us today designates this Exterior risks one day designating us. ("La folie, l'absence d'oeuvre," in *Histoire de la folie,* 575)

Prophetic statements such as these are quite common in Foucault's work. Even though the future he proposes is always qualified by a "perhaps" or postulated in the form of an "as if," and therefore uncertain in its exact form, Foucault does seem to be certain that exterior and interior, same and other, identity and alterity, the measurable and the immeasurable, will not have the same form or content or the same relation to each other in the future.[20]

One reason for Foucault's confidence that the links with alterity will not remain constant is his argument that anonymous and formal transformation on the epistemological level can be anticipated because such changes have occurred before. But he is arguing even more strongly that such links *must not* remain constant, that the limits of thought, language, discourse, etc. must continue to be confronted and transgressed—as they are in the poetics (and politics) he champions—in order to bring about the next form of these relations and a new set of limits. The "mad," self-reflexive text constitutes for Foucault a model of transgressive critical activity. Its self-reflexivity is thus not the means it uses to ensure its own integrity, but, on the contrary, a strategy that opens it to a radical form of alterity or exteriority.

3. Thinking the Outside

The problem remains as to how to evaluate the importance and limitations of such a critical strategy in terms of Foucault's overall work. The vast majority of Foucault commentators simply ignore the existence of a transgressive aesthetics or poetics of self-reflexivity in his work. Those who refer to it at all rarely do more than mention it in passing, judging Foucault's interest in literature and art to be peripheral to whatever they consider his major critical project to be. In a recent book, *Michel Foucault: The Freedom of Philosophy* (New York: Columbia University Press, 1985), John Rajchman devotes one chapter to Foucault's early work on literature and the question of language in order to argue that it is not as critically sophisticated as his later work, and, more specifically, that Foucault's interest in the question of language and a certain radical form of literature constitutes a search for a "romantic alternative to a culture obsessed with the principle of systematic reason and the idea of a foundational humanism." Rajchman concludes that it is because Foucault "could not sustain this vision" that he "abandoned his early romanticism. In freeing himself from it, Foucault disowned the theory of language as a basis for his skeptical tropes, and the question 'what is language' as the center of his history" (6).

Since this is one of the few works on Foucault to take this aspect of his work at all seriously,[21] it seems to me important to address the accusation that Foucault's interest in the problem of the "origin" or "being" of language and in the transgressive literature he claims best approaches it constitutes a naïve romanticism which he abandons when he moves beyond a "modernist" aesthetics. There may very well be aspects of Foucault's approach to self-reflexive literature and language that are naïve. But it may be even more naïve and shortsighted to claim that his approach to the problem of the origin of language is without positive critical effects throughout his work or to equate it with an early romanticism from which Foucault eventually freed himself.

This is an especially important issue since Rajchman feels that Foucault's "delusions" were those of an entire movement—he includes Barthes, Lacan, Derrida, Leiris, Blanchot, Bataille, Beckett, some of the new novelists, and Julia Kristeva and the journal *Tel Quel* in this movement, which he claims was "fighting for the privileges of a political culture by theorizing about writing" and promoting "a revolution emerging from avant-garde writing" (11). He also claims that it is the very same "relentless theorization of writing" that "was to resurface in the American university in the 1970's and is still very much a topic of debate" (10), and with consequences that he obviously feels were and are regrettable. Rajchman's reading of Foucault is, thus, also an indictment of "deconstructionist" and "poststructuralist" forms of literary theory which make the question of writing a central concern. If Foucault saw the error of his ways, he seems to be saying, why haven't all those who continue this movement done likewise?

Rajchman is obviously not wrong to claim that something like a "relentless theorization of writing" (Foucault's term) had an important place in France for a certain period and is still prominent in America today. What is less sure is that the various names he lists ever constituted a "movement" (it is an incredibly eclectic list) or that "la révolution du langage poétique" proclaimed by Kristeva represents, as Rajchman claims, "a great summation of the movement" (11). In retrospect, it probably represents nothing more than a slogan characterizing the aesthetic and political interests of *Tel Quel* for a certain period. What is even less sure in Foucault's case, or in the case of others on the list, is that the theorization of writing or an interest in self-reflexivity in literature and art inevitably "leads one to a politics of the supremacy of the literary and of the writer" (30). It can lead, and in certain instances (*Tel Quel* being the most blatant case in France and a certain form of "literary deconstruction," the obvious example in the United States), it has led to an acritical privileging of literature as such, but in other cases it has not. Rajchman's judgments here are much too sweeping. He is much too eager to use Foucault in order to proclaim the "swan song of literary theory" to do justice to the problem of the place of literature in Foucault's various critical strategies and in the other theoretical positions he would like to dismiss as being dead and buried.[22]

My differences with Rajchman, thus, have to do with whether a theorization (relentless or not) of writing or a concern with the self-reflexive or transgressive discursive elements of certain forms of literature is naïvely romantic in and of itself. I would agree that there is a naïve, acritical, and even perhaps "romantic" side to some of Foucault's remarks concerning madness and transgression—evident especially when he describes as supremely heroic the "experience" of confronting absence and writing in the abyss characteristic of "the poetics of absence." But I would also argue that Foucault's texts in which he addresses this issue are, for the most part, more than a simple *éloge* of the heroic, mad writer; thus it cannot be considered a totally positive move when he "abandons" the question of the (non)being or lack of foundation of language—which is not exactly the same question that Rajchman sees him abandoning, that is, the question of what language is.

Rather than dismiss this aspect of Foucault's work for not being critically vigilant enough, I have, on the contrary, tried to understand its critical force— how Foucault attempts to link his critical perspective to certain transgressive, self-reflexive, "mad" literary practices in order to do precisely what Rajchman claims Foucault's later work does: constitute itself as a *"critique* which does not attempt to fix the foundations for knowledge, to provide theory with a justification, or to defend Reason, but to occasion new ways of thinking. . . . Foucault's philosophy is thus . . . occasion, spark, challenge. It is risk; it is not guaranteed, backed-up, or assured: it always remains without an end" (123). As we have seen, Foucault's readings of self-reflexive literary texts do not, as most theories of self-reflexivity do, assign literature and, thus, criticism an end in literature; his strategy is to show how self-reflexivity reveals a lack at the origin of language and forces literature and thought outside themselves. "The thinking of the outside,"[23] the very possibility of a philosophy as *critique*, as being without an end, first takes form and must be rooted in Foucault's analyses of literature. That he finds other ways to articulate this critique does not cancel out the importance of his "early" strategy—which, in fact, can be found, as I shall show in Chapter 5, in his later work as well. It is still much too early to declare the "swan song" of the theorization of writing or of literary theory in general. And it is also important to see that the one cannot be equated with the other, even if important links exist between them. Certainly, as I have shown, much more is at stake in Foucault's self-reflexive 'poetics of absence' than a defense of literature.

C H A P T E R F O U R
DECONSTRUCTION AND THE QUESTION
O F L I T E R A T U R E

━━━━━━━━━━━━━

D   E   R   R   I   D   A

Writing is one of the representatives of the trace in general; it
is not the trace itself. *The trace itself does not exist.*

The graphic and the political thus refer to one another according to complex laws.

—Jacques Derrida, *Of Grammatology*

1. Writing and the Priority of Literature

Even though the words writing (*écriture*) and textuality are clearly associated with the work of Jacques Derrida, there is probably more controversy
and confusion over their meaning than there is over the term deconstruction
itself. In a note at the beginning of "The Double Session," Derrida acknowledges the existence of interpretations of his work that misunderstand his
notion of writing; he insists here that his position on writing can in no way
be considered to be *against* speech or a defense of writing in the traditional
sense of the term:

> For those who, lacking the ability to read, would be simple and hasty
> enough to content themselves with such an objection, let us very
> briefly go back over this: what is being pursued . . . is a certain dis-
> placement of writing, a systematic transformation and generalization
> of its "concept." The old opposition between speech and writing no
> longer has any pertinence as a way of testing a text [Mallarmé's *Mi-*

81

mique] that deliberately deconstructs that opposition. Such a text is
no more "spoken" than it is "written," no more *against* speech than
for writing, in the metaphysical sense of these words. (*Dissemination,*
translated by Barbara Johnson [Chicago: University of Chicago Press,
1981], 181)

Too often—in spite of abundant evidence in all of Derrida's work to the
contrary, as well as explicit caveats like the above—Derrida's notion of writing is still being equated by many with the everyday sense of writing (as the
opposite of the everyday sense of speech), and his position thus considered
to be the simple reversal of positions that privilege voice over writing. If such
confusion does still persist, it undoubtedly is not due to hasty readings alone;
certain benefits are derived from this form of simplification of Derrida's
work—and curiously enough, the benefits are shared equally by "deconstructionists" and "anti-deconstructionists" alike.

One form of this confusion or simplification benefits "deconstructionists"
by allowing them to use Derrida's work and the term deconstruction to "save
the [literary] text" through what Rodolphe Gasché has called the "illicit application of the Derridean notion of *écriture* to all forms of discourse" ("Deconstruction as Criticism," *Glyph,* no. 6 [1979], 179). The reduction of textuality to the properties of particular literary texts, however, is not only the
basis of the literary appropriation of Derrida's work, of the reduction of deconstruction to a form of literary criticism, as Gasché has forcefully argued.
It is also the basis of many of the harshest critiques of Derrida's work. These
take him to task for overemphasizing the "inner workings" of texts at the
expense of the "world," history or politics, for not investigating the way in
which forms of writing are determined by social praxis, for privileging writing
at the expense of speech and action. If American "deconstructionists" have,
as Gasché claims, turned Derridean deconstruction into a "newer form of new
criticism," then anti-deconstructionists have accepted this version of Derrida's work in order to attack it for being a literary formalism. But it is only
when writing has been equated with (the form of) literature and textuality
with specific literary texts that "deconstruction" (as criticism) is open to such
attacks. Even if literature has an important strategic place in his work, Derrida
is very careful not to make such an equation.[1]

The debates over Derrida's work remain highly charged, often polemical;
like all polemics, they have too often consisted of partial and partisan readings, if not pure and simple misreadings, on both sides.[2] But underneath, or
to the side of, the polemics and obscured by them, there is a question still
waiting to be investigated: it is the question of the place and function of
literature in Derrida's work, the relation of literature, on the one hand, to
such terms as writing, textuality, dissemination, and, on the other, to terms
supposedly designating the "outside" or the "hors texte"—that is, to those

concerns Derrida is sometimes attacked for neglecting: the world, society, history, politics, etc. It is certainly clear that "literature" has an important strategic function in Derrida's overall critical project. But before deciding, as some have done, that this necessarily makes him a formalist or an aestheticist, it will be important to study with some precision how he approaches the question of literature and why this question has such an important place in his work.

In "The Time of a Thesis: Punctuations," Derrida reminds his thesis committee that literature has always been an important concern for him, his "first concern": "For I have to remind you, somewhat bluntly and simply, that my most constant interest, coming even before my philosophical interest I should say, if this is possible, has been directed towards literature, towards that writing called literature" (*Philosophy in France Today,* edited by Alan Montefiore [Cambridge: Cambridge University Press, 1983], 37). If literature is "first" in the hierarchy of Derrida's interests, it is primarily because the question of what literature is brings the general problem of writing to the forefront and leads to a reinvestigation of the fields to which literature is in some way related:

> What is literature? And first of all, what is it "to write?" How is it that the fact of writing can disturb the very question "what is?" and even "what does it mean?" To say this in other words, . . . when and how does an inscription become literature and what takes place when it does? To what and whom is this due? What takes place between philosophy and literature, science and literature, politics and literature, theology and literature, psychoanalysis and literature? . . . . The question was doubtless inspired in me by a desire which was related also to a certain uneasiness: why finally does the inscription so fascinate me, preoccupy me, precede me? Why am I so fascinated by the literary ruse of the inscription? (37–38)

As the above quotation clearly indicates, literature is not for Derrida a field that encompasses or defines writing in general; rather it is one in which writing is an unresolved issue that is constantly being pursued in a multiplicity of forms. Literature comes "before philosophy" in the hierarchy of Derrida's concerns—not because it is a higher or more essential form of philosophy that knows its own truth and that of philosophy, but rather because it does not, because what "it is" remains in question.

Because the question of the specificity of literature is so intimately entwined for Derrida with the problem of inscription in general, literature is a kind of privileged entryway into writing—an entryway that also leads into science, philosophy, politics, psychoanalysis, etc., and provides critical perspectives on these fields as well. The uneasiness he expresses over his own fascination with the literary inscription has to do, I would argue, with the difficulties involved in delineating this entryway, and, most importantly, with the difficulties in keeping such fascination from leading to an equation of literature with writing—as many have done in his name. When writing is equated with literature, the entryway provided by literature opens only onto itself: that is to say, the entryway is immediately closed off when the question of what literature is (and what writing is) is definitively answered.[3]

Gasché insists on the double nature of Derrida's strategy of deconstruction in order to distinguish it from "deconstruction-as-criticism" and to differentiate between Derrida's notion of writing and the normal, everyday concept. As Gasché argues:

> Two moments are thus characteristic of deconstruction: a *reversal* of the traditional hierarchy between conceptual oppositions . . . and a *reinscription* of the newly privileged term. . . . The deconstructed term, however, as a result of a reinscription of the negative image of absolute exteriority and otherness . . . is no longer identical with the inferior term of the initial dyad. . . . Although it uses the same name as its negative image, the deconstructed term will never have been given in the conceptual opposition it deconstructs. ("Deconstruction as Criticism," 192–93)[4]

In other words, to put it as succinctly as possible, *writing* is not writing, textuality is not the property of any single text or group of texts. Not to understand this is to miss one of the most basic elements of Derrida's work. But even in understanding this, terms such as *writing* and *text* remain elusive, difficult to define and manipulate critically. For there is no immediate access to these terms, no way to present them directly as concepts, no definite methodology or system that can be derived from them. This does not mean, however, that they are ineffable, transcendental, or ideal terms—for they are related to the "everyday sense" given them, insomuch as they constitute the critical reversal *and* reinscription of this sense.

Gasché indicts deconstructive literary criticism for what I would call *believing (in) the text,* that is, believing that individual literary texts know better what they are and how they function than do all theories of literature. While deconstructive critics are ferocious when it comes to attacking the philosophical naïveté of all other theories, they take "the information and knowledge explicitly or implicitly displayed by a text for granted" and "the reflections a text confers about itself literally" (Gasché, 179). This not only has the effect of isolating the individual text from any context or intertextual network, but also leads to a dependence on certain privileged texts to tell us, to show us, and even to perform for us what writing and textuality really are. Here

84

the theory of literature has been collapsed into literature and leads nowhere, that is, nowhere except to its own image of itself.

Derrida uses the word "disguise" to describe the relation between concepts of language and writing. The same could be said of the relation between literature and writing, or even between *writing* (arche-writing) and writing: "It is as if the Western concept of language [literature] . . . were revealed today as the guise or disguise of a primary writing" (*Of Grammatology,* translated by Gayatri Chakravorty Spivak [Baltimore: Johns Hopkins University, 1976], 7). Derrida insists that a concept of writing has often been privileged in the history of philosophy, but that any privilege granted one form of writing has always been at the expense of another form of writing: "As was the case with the Platonic writing of the truth in the soul, in the Middle Ages too it is a writing understood in the metaphorical sense, that is to say a natural, eternal, and universal writing, the system of signified truth, which is recognized in its dignity. As in the *Phaedrus,* a certain fallen writing continues to be opposed to it" (15). In this way, a concept of writing represses another form of writing, disguises itself as writing in general in its highest form to enclose, master, situate, or simply dismiss all lower, "fallen" forms.

What Derrida refers to as the notion of the book is an outgrowth of such a concept of eternal or universal writing: "The good writing has therefore always been *comprehended.* Comprehended as that which had to be comprehended: within a nature or a natural law, created or not, but first thought within an eternal presence. Comprehended, therefore, within a totality and enveloped in a volume or a book. The idea of the book is the idea of a totality, finite or infinite, of the signifier. . . . The idea of the book, which always refers to a natural totality, is profoundly alien to the sense of writing" (18). It could also be shown that certain contemporary notions of the text, some claiming to be derived from Derrida himself, continue this tradition of the book—not in the form of the book of nature, the book of god, or even the book of the self, but rather with a notion of the text as book, the "text-book," that is, the text as a closed, self-contained totality. This notion of the text is, I would argue, also "profoundly alien to the sense of writing" evoked above by Derrida—its presentation of itself as text constituting a disguise of textuality all the more difficult to penetrate insomuch as it pretends to be a direct presentation of textuality.

It is important to stress, therefore, that there is no way to strip off all the disguises imposed on writing in order to approach it in itself; it is possible to approach writing only in its disguises. In *Of Grammatology,* Derrida insists that the task of freeing such notions as the *graphie* and trace from the heritage that "disguises" them is unending: "My efforts will now be directed toward slowly detaching these two concepts from the classical discourse from which I necessarily borrow them. The effort will be laborious, and we know a priori that its effectiveness will never be pure and absolute" (46). An equation of writing with literature certainly makes the process less laborious, but it also makes writing too easy a concept to manipulate and in this way assigns the critical process a definite destination in literature. It may even end up collapsing criticism into literature and erasing the distinctions between them. Destroyed in such an equation is the critical potential of literature itself, as well as the complexity of the question of writing.

As Derrida indicates in *Positions* (translated by Alan Bass [Chicago: University of Chicago Press, 1981]), there is always a risk, when the problem of the specificity of literature is pursued, of "isolating, in order to shelter it, a formal specificity of the literary which would have its own proper essence and truth and which would no longer have to be articulated with other theoretical or practical fields" (70). Throughout his work, Derrida warns against this formalization of the question of literature; a sure sign that a critical strategy has become too pure or absolute, its effectiveness too predictable, is that it ends up consistently in the same place and produces the same effects time after time. The problem is, therefore, how literature can be considered an entryway into writing without being treated as the undisguised and therefore true version of writing. In other words, how can the pursuit of the problem of the formal specificity of the literary be articulated with problems associated with other fields, rather than kept tightly wrapped within itself? How can a concern with the question of literary specificity affect the delineation of the various practical and theoretical fields to which literature is linked?

In *Of Grammatology*, Derrida analyzes how literature is linked by both Rousseau and Saussure to the question of writing as part of the process—denounced by both of them—of the violent usurpation of an "original," "innocent" language by writing. Derrida quotes Saussure, who, he claims, "anagrammatizes Rousseau" when he says that "literary language adds to the undeserved importance of writing" (37). Within contexts such as these in which writing is denounced—one could think of other contexts in which a certain notion of literature is given a privileged status and thus in which a different strategy would be needed—Derrida shows how literature plays a key role for Saussure (and Rousseau) in what is claimed to be the fall from original language and the presence of the spoken word. Denounced by Saussure as the ally of writing, literature is treated by Derrida as an important factor in the reversal and reinscription of writing. These allies, though not identical to each other, are for him inextricably linked, for better and for worse.

Literature is also a central element of Derrida's discussion of the Copenhagen School of linguistics, which, like Derrida, works both with and against Saussure and gives literature an important place in its attempt to define the specificity of writing:

By recognizing the specificity of *writing*, glossematics did not merely provide itself with the means of describing the *graphic* element. It also indicated the path to the *literary* element, to what in literature is constituted as an irreducibly graphic text linking the *play of form* to a substance of determined expression. If there is something in literature which does not allow itself to be reduced to the voice, to epos or poetry, it can be recovered only by rigorously isolating this link of the *play of form* with the substance of determined expression. (By the same token, it will be seen that "pure literature," thus respected in its irreducibility, also risks limiting or binding up play. The desire to do so is, moreover, irrepressible.) (59, t.m.)

Derrida thus recognizes the contributions made by the Copenhagen School towards the study of literature in terms of its "written" aspects; he praises it for overcoming "the Rousseauist and Saussurian distrust of the literary arts" and for radicalizing "the efforts of the Russian formalists, . . . who in their attentiveness to the being-literary of literature perhaps privileged and phonological instance and thus the literary models dominated by it. Notably poetry" (59, t.m.). But Derrida is, at the same time, warning that a respect for literature in itself, for poetry as the form of "pure literature," is also a way of restricting the play of the written aspects of literature. This is what is usually not seen by readers of Derrida.

What makes the critical task so difficult in this area is that the boundary separating a respect for literature that limits play and a respect for the written aspects of literature that does not is never clearly marked—especially in a modernity that defines itself, at least in part, in terms of a certain literary radicality. In terms of literary specificity, one is inevitably working on a very fragile borderline where one has to have enough respect for the written characteristics of literature, for its specificity—but not so much that literature is restricted to itself and its own essence or truth. It may be impossible to maintain, in all instances, the critical vigilance necessary to walk the fine line separating the "enough" and the "too much," and, thus, here too "effectiveness will never be pure and absolute."

Theory generally has functioned to restrict the play of writing—for the desire to do so, argues Derrida, is "irrepressible" and evident, as we have seen, even in those approaches to literature that are concerned with the question of its "literarity":

> The natural tendency of *theory*—of what unites philosophy and science in the *epistémè*—is rather to move toward filling in the breach than toward breaking through the closure. It was normal that the breakthrough has been more definitive and penetrating with literature and poetic writing: normal also that, just as with Nietzsche, it has

disturbed and destabilized the transcendental authority and dominant category of the *epistémè:* being. (92, t.m.)

The words "natural" and "normal," at first glance, might seem to contradict
what I have been saying about Derrida's relation to literature; they suggest
that he is attributing a nature to literature that allows it to break completely
with the devaluation of writing he argues is at the basis of the entire Western
philosophical tradition. They seem to suggest that literature, for him, is by
its very nature outside that tradition.

And yet it is clear from his overall argument, and especially from passages
previously cited, that literature is not simply outside the closure instituted
by theory: the "natural tendency of *theory*" and the "normality" of the breakthrough of a certain literary practice (Derrida refers explicitly to Pound and
Mallarmé and their "graphic poetics") are "natural" and "normal" only given
the very particular form of the traditional relation between theory and literature. And even given that relation, literature does not in all instances and
contexts disturb and destabilize the "transcendental authority and dominant
category of the *epistémè:* being." In most instances, literature has been one
of the strongest supports of that authority—and Derrida also suggests that
this is even true when literature is considered in terms of a formal specificity
or integrity. Literature does have strategic, critical value for Derrida. But like
writing in general, it cannot be taken as *the alternative* to theory or philosophy: the way literature serves as a support for transcendental authority
is just as important as how, in certain contexts, it disturbs and destabilizes
it.

One example from *Of Grammatology* where literature supports, rather than
menaces, philosophical authority is found in Derrida's discussion of Rousseau. In its history, literature, as much as philosophy, has had the project of
denying or effacing its written or textual characteristics:

> For example, the philosophical text, although it is in fact always writ-
> ten, requires, precisely as its philosophical specificity, the following
> project: that it efface itself before the signified content it transports
> and in general teaches. All reading should be aware of this project,
> even if, in the last analysis, it intends to expose the project's failure.
> The entire history of texts, and within it the history of literary forms
> in the West, should be studied from this point of view. With the
> exception of those instances when literature achieves a point of ad-
> vance or a point of resistance [*une pointe ou un point de résistance*],
> something that has been recognized as such only very late in its
> history, literary writing has, almost always and almost everywhere,
> according to very diverse modes and in very different historical pe-
> riods, lent itself to this *transcedent* reading, to that search for the

signified we have been putting into question here, not to annul it but to understand it within a system to which such a reading is blind. (160, t.m.)

Literature, as much as philosophy, then, lends itself to "transcendent readings." If the aim of philosophy could be said to be the effacement of its written, textual characteristics before the signified it wants to convey, the same could be said for literature and literary theory—at least in the great majority of cases. It is clear from what I have already argued that Derrida's stated critical project is certainly to push both philosophy and literature beyond their traditional delimitations and to rework their relations with each other through the transformation of each. From his perspective, any *theory* of literature that does not work towards this double transformation is limiting the critical impact of deconstruction by making it a defense of literature. And, it should be added, any treatment of deconstruction as primarily a model or methodology for reading literary (or philosophical) texts is certain to have these restrictive effects—even if it initially challenges and disturbs more conventional forms of literary criticism and techniques of reading.

In a number of texts that analyze literary texts or problems of literary criticism, Derrida pursues the question of writing as it relates to the problem of literary inscription. In general, however, the same obstacles to a critical investigation of writing appear within the "field" of literature as within philosophy. Even if literature and literary criticism may often claim to have nothing to do with philosophical speculation, this claim itself is supported by assumptions and arguments that are fundamentally philosophical in nature. No form of criticism, no form of literary theory, no form even of reading or textual analysis—no matter how close to the literary text it might claim to stay—is ever really *purely literary*. Each, as Derrida argues is the case for structuralist literary criticism, "has already been determined, knowingly or not, as the philosophy of literature" (*Writing and Difference,* translated by Alan Bass [Chicago: University of Chicago Press, 1978], 28). The problem for a critical theory of and approach to literature, then, is never really how to stay within literature or be "faithful" to it; it is, rather, how to exceed the philosophical determination not only of the concept of literature itself, but also of the strategies used to interpret it. This is, of course, exactly the same problem faced by critical or deconstructive philosophy in terms of the determination of philosophy.

2. The Trials of Philosophy

Nevertheless, claims Derrida, it is in literature rather than philosophy that a point of resistance and excess has finally been recognized. Literature creates openings through which critical philosophy can also move in order to do battle with philosophical authority and the various forms of closure it imposes. Derrida claims in *Positions* that "certain texts classed as 'literary'"—for example, those of Artaud, Bataille, and Mallarmé—have always seemed to him "to operate breaches or infractions at the most advanced points" of theory—not just because they present particularly difficult problems for philosophical conceptualization by challenging it directly, but also because they lead us to "suspect the denomination 'literature,'" "which subjects the concept to belles-lettres, to the arts, to poetry, to rhetoric, and to philosophy" (69). In terms of these texts, Derrida goes on to argue, "one can best reread, without retrospective teleology, the law of previous fissures" (69). He is certainly not claiming here that literature alone is capable of such resistance and excess, or that the strategies necessary to achieve them are essentially "literary" in nature. Rather, he is arguing only that due to specific historical factors, a certain kind of breakthrough was *recognized* first in literature, and from the perspective of such a break both literature and philosophy can both be reevaluated critically—that is, without predetermining the end of the critical process or assigning a specific nature or form to either literature or philosophy.

If Derrida refuses to attribute a specific "nature" to literature and differentiate it in this way from philosophy, this does not mean that he approaches literary texts in all instances in exactly the same way as he does philosophical or theoretical texts. In his critical strategy vis-a-vis each, the effects of his interest in the problem of literary inscription become evident; here also, is where the points of excess and resistance to transcedent readings which he claims a certain literature has achieved are exploited. For example, in *Writing and Difference* (a collection of essays devoted to both "literary" and "philosophical" texts) it would be possible to discern differences of emphasis and strategy in Derrida's reading of texts of Artaud, Bataille, and Jabès on the one hand and those of Husserl, Lévi-Strauss, Foucault, and Rousset on the other. It is not that the former are treated in entirely positive, and the latter in entirely negative, terms. Nor is it that the former are considered representative of literature—in fact, Derrida for the most part treats Artaud's and Bataille's "theoretical" texts—and the latter representative of philosophy. It is, rather, that less deconstructive work seems to be needed to read the former critically and isolate a problematic of writing within them than in the case of the latter—where such a problematic is more repressed than explicit and is made evident only by working against the dominant arguments of these texts.[5]

It seems possible to argue that in *Writing and Difference* and in his other work as well, Derrida—even if this doesn't amount to an "essential difference" in his methodology—allows the more "literary" of the texts he treats (for example, texts by Mallarmé, Sollers, Ponge, Genet, and, more recently, Blanchot) to determine his approach to them; that is, he allows their language, strategies, and style, to infiltrate his own text to a much greater degree than is the case for the theoretical and philosophical texts. By comparing his approach to the two kinds of texts and the way he uses each, one might even be tempted to conclude that, for Derrida, the radical literary texts he chooses to work on have no need of being deconstructed, while all theoretical-philosophical texts and all forms of literary criticism do.[6]

Such a conclusion would be a bit hasty in this instance, however (and, I would argue, in general), for it would ignore in *Writing and Difference,* for example, the place of, say, Freud and Lévinas (especially in terms of a discussion of the trace), both of whose texts, even though not "literary," make important contributions—as do all the other texts—to the pursuit of the question of writing. It would also ignore that all of the texts analyzed in the volume—whether normally classified as literary or philosophical, and regardless of whether they explicitly repress or actively pursue the question of writing—are involved in the question in both "positive and "negative" ways. To claim that literary texts have no need of being deconstructed or that they function in Derrida's work only as "tutors" would also be to assume that one knows already that literature is and what distinguishes it from theory or philosophy; at least in the case of Artaud and Bataille on the one side and Foucault and Lévi-Strauss on the other, whose texts are certainly as "theoretical" as they are "literary," such an assumption would be difficult to sustain. The differences in strategy that one finds in Derrida's work, then, are undoubtedly significant. But it would be a mistake to conclude that these differences reflect fixed assumptions about the nature of either literature or philosophy—or, for that matter, about the essential difference between deconstruction and so-called "applied grammatology."

The nature of literary and philosophical inscriptions and of the inscription in general is precisely what is at stake in these analyses; it is in no way a question that can be assumed to have been already resolved by historically determined generic distinctions. In fact, as Derrida argues in "La loi du genre,"[7] generic distinctions (even or especially the distinction between literature and non-literature) and, in particular, the law that dictates that "genres are not to be mixed" (202), are more of an impediment to the critical investigation of writing than an aid. And what if, he speculates, "it were impossible not to mix genres? What if there were lodged within the heart of the law itself, a law of impurity or a principle of contamination" (204)? Such a counter-law to the law of genre within the law itself would make all texts in some sense hybrid. It would also make the question of literature not one that can be resolved by assuming that formal or generic distinctions between the literary and non-literary hold in the face of critical scrutiny or that "literature" or literary theory can or should respect them. If the law of genre is not, for Derrida, a guarantee of the specificity of literature, the problem remains as to where and how he locates its specificity.

91

In *Margins of Philosophy,* there is only one chapter devoted to a "literary" author—in this case, Paul Valéry—and thus it could be concluded that the question of literature has a very small place in the entire volume. But Valéry is described, at least in terms of one crucial philosophical problem, as being a better philosopher than two of the giants of philosophy, for he "recognized the immense bearing of this autonomous circuit of 'hearing-oneself-speak' . . . and he did so better, without a doubt, than any traditional philosopher, better than Husserl and better than Hegel" (*Margins,* 287). And if Valéry seems already to have the same critical position on the problem of voice that Derrida himself develops in *Speech and Phenomena* (translated by David Allison [Evanston: Northwestern University Press, 1973]) and *Of Grammatology,* this becomes even more evident when Derrida describes Valéry's challenge to philosophy: "Valéry reminds the philosopher that philosophy is written. And that the philosopher is a philosopher to the extent that he forgets this" (291). But where does this leave the philosopher after he has been reminded, first by Valéry and then repeatedly by Derrida, of the written nature of philosophy—especially if because of these reminders he is subsequently unable to forget it? Where does this leave Derrida himself? Because of his "good memory" hasn't he excluded himself from the ranks of (forgetful) philosophers. And by equating philosophy with bad memory hasn't he determined that philosophy will never be critical, will never achieve the breakthroughs that, he claims, literature has already achieved?

By statements such as these, Derrida appears to make any philosopher who no longer forgets less of a philosopher and more of a poet or writer of literature—especially if literature is defined as that form of writing that does not forget it is writing. But, Derrida will argue, literature does forget; it just is not as massively dominated by the *project* to forget as is philosophy. And the writings of even traditional philosophers, perhaps in spite of the project governing them, do not always forget. Here, too, the line between philosophy and literature—even if it should never be ignored or completely erased—is not as firmly drawn as Derrida's statement on Valéry, taken on its own and out of context, might lead one to believe.[8] In other words, neither forgetting nor remembering is conclusive when it comes to literature or philosophy and the problem of writing basic to each. Valéry's "reminder" is nothing more than a starting point, an entryway into a problem; it should in no way be considered a definition of literature or a sufficient explanation of the critical place given literature in Derrida's overall work.

But "literature" can be found in at least one other place in *Margins—* precisely in the margins of its beginning. The introduction to the entire collection is entitled "Tympan," an essay which discusses the issue of the margins of philosophy and whose slender right-hand column consists of excerpts from Michel Leiris's *Biffures* (Paris: Gallimard, 1948). Themes from *Biffures,* cross over the margin separating it from Derrida's text and enter, as a dis-

92

ruptive force, into the body of the "philosophical" analysis of margins. Derrida, however, gives no direct analysis of Leiris's text itself, but lets it stand on its own—as if it had no need of commentary, as if it commented on philosophy and philosophical analysis simply by being located where it is, as if it provided all the material necessary for the deconstruction of philosophy because of its marginal location. It stands as a graphic reminder that philosophy has margins, that it is always inscribed in particular contexts and is, thus, always in relation with other texts—texts that it may attempt to marginalize, but that it cannot effectively neutralize.[9]

Is the role of literature for Derrida, one could logically ask, to stand for and act as the marginal, to represent what philosophy defines itself against but what it cannot effectively neutralize? And, if so, must literature in order to disrupt philosophical closure be left without commentary or analysis—as is the case for Leiris's text here? Is Derrida's position that we must let literature *perform* its deconstructive activities on its own and that the only role left for critical discourse is to mime literature and become literary in its turn? If this were, in fact, the case, Derrida's work would imply an "applied grammatology," as Ulmer has argued. A case should not be made based on this one instance, however, for the marginal is not as "purely performative," as purely "literary," as such a position would imply. As I shall show, the lines of margins hold no better in Derrida's work than the previously mentioned "law of genre."

In *Glas* (Paris: Galilée, 1974), all this comes to a head with Jean Genet's texts answering and outdistancing Hegel's at each step of the way. If both Hegel and Genet are quoted, paraphrased, and mimed at great length in their respective columns, the miming of Genet is done in the spirit of Genet while the miming of Hegel is also done in the spirit of Genet and aimed at undermining the absolute spirit of Hegel. It might even appear that Derrida considers Genet's texts, when situated next to and made to interfere with Hegel's texts, to be capable on their own of bringing down the sacred, the absolute spirit, and the dialectic—given their irreverant, scatological nature. The Genet side of *Glas* would, of course, have less critical force without the Hegel side to provide it with material for mockery. But it is in each instance Genet's texts that have the last and deciding word—or at least the last laugh.[10] For how can Hegel be taken seriously after being brought down by Genet? How can philosophy in general be taken seriously any longer if it can be undermined by such a "low" form of literature? Or, as Derrida puts it more graphically, "How can ontology take possession of a fart" (69)? But is it enough to remind philosophy that it is inscribed within a general intertextual network where the "low" and the "base" are interconnected with the "high" and the "spiritual?" Is it enough to ridicule philosophy when it forgets this?

Laughter and ridicule certainly have a place in Derrida's assault on philosophy, but they are not the only weapons he uses. In "Tympan," he refers to Nietzsche's expression, "to philosophize with a hammer," and what he calls "tympanizing philosophy"[11] could be considered to be a particularly aggressive form of this hammering carried out with the assistance of certain forms of literature. But ridicule obviously is not enough; the blows scored by the hammer of literature are ultimately easily absorbed by philosophy and used for its own ends if they are only oppositional in nature and if they come from a locatable place outside, an exteriority already mapped out by philosophy (or literature) as the other *of* philosophy. If philosophy has always "believed that it controls the margin of its volume and that it thinks its other," as Derrida argues, if it "has always insisted upon this" (x), then it certainly has defenses against all hammers and ways of explaining, conceptualizing, turning aside or turning back on literature the ridicule literature directs at it. It would even possibly gain from undergoing this test of its strength and absorbing the blows directed at it.

Derrida insists in this prefatory essay and elsewhere that the threat of reappropriation is constant—especially when the question of the other of philosophy is raised directly. "In thinking it [the other] *as such,* in recognizing it, one misses it. One reappropriates it, or rather one misses (the) missing (of) it, which, as concerns the other, always amounts to the same" (*Margins,* xi–xii). As concerns literature, this means that one should be careful not to posit literature, either explicitly or implicitly, as *the* space of alterity, as the "nonphilosophical place, a place of exteriority or alterity from which one might still treat *of philosophy,*" because "this space, will it not have always been occupied by (with) philosophy in advance?" (xii, translation completed). In making literature *the other* of philosophy one misses the alterity one has supposedly located there by recognizing it, naming its place, and presupposing in advance that one knows how this place is constructed and how it functions. Literature, then, cannot be considered *the* margin of philosophy, but only one of the margins; if the margins of philosophy are, in fact, many and varied, then the concept of "*a* philosophy, *the* philosophy" (xvi) cannot be sustained—and neither can, I would insist, the concept of *a* literature or *the* literature.

I would argue, therefore, that *Glas* does not represent the victory of literature over philosophy, writing over theory, grammatology over deconstruction—or the contrary. It is, rather, an experiment in playing one type of text off against a radically different type, one kind of discursive style, logic, and "reasoning" off against a form of discourse that not only does not obey the rules and logic determined by dialectical thought but, even more, does not conform to any sense of decorum at all. The form, rules, and logic of such an experiment cannot, therefore, be given in advance. And, as Derrida admits near the beginning of the Hegel side of *Glas,* "It is the trial itself (*épreuve*) that interests [him] and not success or failure" (26).

The goal of the double strategy that dominates Derrida's work at this time (see also "The Double Session" in *Dissemination*) is to make the trial of philosophy and literature interminable, without resolution: "Why write at least two texts at the same time? What scene is one playing? What does one desire? In other words, what is one afraid of? One wants of course to make writing impregnable. When you have your head here, you are reminded that the law of the text is in the other text, and so on and so forth without end" (76). To make writing impregnable is clearly not to make it "literary" in any conceivable literary or philosophical sense, but, rather, to emphasize the hybrid nature of all writing and the way the "face-à-face" of literature and philosophy is as much within as between each.

In Derrida's critical strategy, it could be argued that Genet's texts need Hegel's texts—not just in order to be played off against them, but also in order to be submitted to the test of dialectical logic—as much as Hegel's need Genet's in order to be opened up, desacralized, and displaced by them.[12] Some of the techniques of disruption and displacement Derrida uses in *Glas* are philosophically "serious" and respect the "rules" of philosophical discourse; others are "frivolous" or even "vulgar" and respect no rules whatsoever. Derrida insists that the results of such "experimentation" with form and logic are not predictable and cannot be predetermined: "The operation must each time remain singular and uniquely take its chances" (191–92).[13] Taking its chances means that the critical operation or experiment could just as well result in literature "losing" as "winning" the battle, in literature just as much as philosophy "running amok."[14]

3. The Crisis of Literature and the Displacement of Theory

Literature, for Derrida, is certainly not determined by philosophy. But it cannot simply be opposed to philosophy either. Philosophical assumptions govern the various concepts of literature and thus limit all literary practices and critical approaches to literature—even when their project is to break with or destroy all previous concepts and forms of literature (as is the case with all literary and critical "avant-gardes"). The foreknowledge of what literature is limits the critical enterprise—not only when literature is treated as an alternative to philosophy and a higher, more complex form of discourse, but also when literature is being opposed in the name of a supposedly more historical or political form of discourse, or even in the name of a more radical form of literature itself:

> Why should 'literature' still designate that which already breaks away from literature—away from what has always been conceived and signified under that name—or that which, not merely escaping literature, implacably destroys it? (Posed in these terms, the question

95

would already be caught in the assurance of a certain foreknowledge: can 'what has always been conceived and signified under that name' be considered fundamentally homogeneous, univocal, or non-conflictual?) ("Outwork," *Dissemination,* 3–4)

If the homogeneity of literature is a problem, as Derrida's questions imply it is, not only does it become difficult if not impossible to continue to argue that the integrity of literature must be respected, but, also, all declared breaks with literature, all movements outside the field it is assumed to constitute, must be more carefully articulated in terms of an open, heterogeneous, conflictual field whose boundaries are in question rather than given.

Not only does the question of "literature" become more complicated, but the relation between literature and the "outside" must, Derrida argues, also be rethought in terms of this complexity:

This is the protocol indispensable to any reelaboration of the problem of "ideology," of the specific inscription of each text . . . within the fields commonly referred to as fields of "real" causality (history, economics, politics, sexuality, etc.). The *theoretical* elaboration . . . ought to suspend or at any rate to complicate, with great caution, the naïve opening that once linked the text to *its* thing, referent, or reality, or even to some last conceptual of semantic instance. Every time that, in order to hook writing precipitously up with some reassuring outside or in order to make a hasty break with idealism, one might be brought to ignore certain recent theoretical attainments, . . . one would all the more surely regress into idealism, with all of what . . . cannot but link up with it, singularly in the figures of empiricism and formalism. (43–44).

For Derrida, then, the most common attacks on the aesthetic or literary idealism governing formalist or textual theories of literature fall back into the idealism they denounce—not only by ignoring the complex heterogeneity of literary texts, but also by simplifying the historical, economic, political or sexual realities they link literature with. In their haste, they tend to reduce both terms of the relation by not analyzing the complexity of the relation itself.

The question of literature cannot, for Derrida, be separated from the ongoing transformation of the notion of the text in general. In *Of Grammatology,* Derrida's claim, that there is "nothing outside the text," caused some theorists and critics mistakenly to take this as a defense of the interiority of the text (and, by extension, of the interiority of literature) to the exclusion of the outside. Responding to their reaction, Derrida in "Outwork" takes up this question again in the following terms:

> To allege that there is no absolute outside of the text is not to pos-
> tulate some ideal immanence, the incessant reconstitution of writ-
> ing's relation to itself. . . . If there is nothing outside the text, this
> implies, with the transformation of the concept of text in general,
> that the text is no longer the snug airtight inside of an interiority or
> an identity-to-itself . . . but rather a different placement of the effects
> of opening and closing. (35–36)[15]

The problem for Derrida is not whether or not the literary text opens onto
the so-called outside (the "world" or whatever else it is called). For him, the
text does open onto the outside because the outside is not completely outside.
Rather, the problem is how what he calls in various places the general text
encompasses both the openings and closings of any particular text. The implication is that the question of literature can never be raised entirely in itself;
it can only be raised within the general context of literature's relations with
the multiple forms of the "non-literary" that it both opens onto and is closed
off from.

For example, it can be raised in terms of literature's relation with philosophy. In "The Double Session" Derrida turns to the question of literature as
part of his discussion of the general problem of mimesis; he pursues the
question on a stage inaugurated, structured, and dominated by Plato. But
Derrida attempts to approach literature on this stage *as a question,* that is,
without the foreknowledge of what literature is. This doesn't mean, however,
that for him literature escapes from philosophical determination and remains
untouched by the mimetic tradition. Rather, it means, among other things,
that the long tradition which tells us what literature is or what it does—the
tradition inaugurated as a result of literature having been brought onto the
philosophical stage in the first place—has to be confronted and undermined
at each step of the way.[16]

Derrida's investigation of the place of literature on this stage has as its
purpose to challenge even the form of the question "what is?":

> The double session . . . about which I don't quite have the gall or the
> self-assurance to say that it is reserved for the question *what is lit-
> erature,* this question being henceforth properly considered a quo-
> tation already, in which the place of the *what is* would lend itself to
> careful scrutiny, along with the presumed authority under which one
> submits anything whatever and particularly literature, to the form of
> its inquisition—this double session, about which I will never have
> the militant innocence to announce that it is concerned with the
> question *what is literature,* will find its corner *BETWEEN* literature
> and truth, between literature and what the question *what is?* demands
> as a response. (177, t.m.)

To know what literature is and to use this knowledge against philosophy and its form of knowledge is to pit one truth against another; it is to remain within the philosophical determination of the truth even if literature is given the upper hand in the struggle for dominance. By situating his investigation "between" literature and truth—in terms of a relation in which neither term is determined as such—Derrida is attempting to undermine the authority of the *what is?* as it concerns not only literature but philosophical truth as well.

Though Derrida considers knowledge of the type demanded by the question "what is?" to be "inquisitional," he defends a form of critical knowledge or at least know-how. For if Plato did not know (or forgot) what he knew when he pretended to know *what is,* Mallarmé, on the contrary, did know enough to know when not to know and not to decide: "Mallarmé knew this. Indeed, he had constructed this question [of the title], or rather undone it with a bifad answer, separating the question from itself, displacing it toward an essential *indecision* that leaves its very titles up in the air" (177). This strange form of knowledge—which is not the knowledge of what is or what should be, but a critical knowledge of how to postpone and displace knowledge—is not a knowledge *of literature* or one that necessarily comes from literature. It, rather, consists of the knowledge that the *what is* is precisely the problem and is rooted in the know-how necessary to circumvent this problem.

Derrida argues that the critical project of the displacement of the truth cannot be identified with literature in general or with any particular form of literature or any event within the history of literature. "This displacement does not take place, has not taken place once, as an *event.* It does not occupy a simple place. It does not take place *in* any particular writing. This dislocation (is what) writes (is written)" (193, t.m.). And yet, in the long history of the relation between truth and literature from Plato to the present, along comes Mallarmé and something crucial nevertheless seems to occur with him.

It cannot be denied that Derrida treats Mallarmé's texts as exemplars of this displacement of the truth. But at the very same time, he also challenges the notion of exemplarity: "This redoubling of the mark, which is at once a formal break and a formal generalization, *is exemplified* by the text of Mallarmé, and singularly by the 'sheet' you have before your eyes [*Mimique*] (but obviously every word of this last proposition must by the same token be displaced or placed under suspicion)" (193–94). This passage (perhaps better, or at least more economically, than any other) highlights the difficulty of the problem of the critical place and function of literature in Derrida's work. Mallarmé's text is exemplary in that it works to dislocate truth, reinscribe the relation of literature and truth, and transform both literature and truth in the same process. At the same time, Mallarmé's text cannot be taken as exemplary because this would make a particular form of literary displacement into an event that could serve as a model and thus be repeated in the same form afterwards.[17] Exemplary and yet at the same time questioning the notion of exemplarity, the place of Mallarmé (critical literature) in Derrida's work is overtly contradictory; it should be clear by now that Derrida is in no hurry to resolve this contradiction. On the contrary, he attempts to maintain and even intensify it as much as possible.[18]

Derrida claims that between Plato and Mallarmé "a whole history has taken place," a history "governed in its entirety by the value of truth," a history which "was also a history of literature" (183). The point of Derrida's analysis is not to overturn Platonism with Mallarméism, but rather to read each with one eye turned to the other so that the paradoxical status of mimesis is highlighted not just in Mallarmé but in Plato as well. In Derrida's text, it is as if Plato is reading and writing over Mallarmé's shoulder as much as Mallarmé is reading and writing over Plato's.[19]

Already in Plato, Derrida argues, "it is impossible to pin *mimesis* down to a binary classification or, more precisely, to assign a single place to the *techne mimetike* within the division set forth in the *Sophist. . . . The mimetic form is both* one of the three forms of 'productive or creative art' *. . . and . . .* nonproductive, nonpoetic" (186). The Platonic project, as Derrida sees it, is "to separate good *mimesis* (which reproduces faithfully and truly yet is already threatened by the simple fact of its duplication) from bad, which must be contained like madness . . . and (harmful) play" (186–87), to decide in each instance what serves and does not serve the truth. Derrida questions the grounds for any distinction between good and bad mimesis, or, I would add, between mimesis and antimimesis, given the paradoxical "logic" of mimesis that makes any decision concerning its truth relative and partial.[20]

Derrida focuses on the irresolvable contradictions within Plato's presentation of mimesis and then proceeds to analyze the effects of these contradictions in the work of Mallarmé, where they are pushed to an extreme limit. Even if some consider Mallarmé to have broken definitively with the mimetic tradition, this is not Derrida's position; he argues that no form of literature or philosophy is free of mimetic contradictions, regardless of whether mimesis is opposed or championed (or, as is perhaps most often the case, both opposed and championed at the same time). Derrida's analysis of Mallarmé's *Mimique* is, first of all, aimed at showing how the reference to the truth in the name of which "*mimesis* is judged, proscribed or prescribed" is "discretely but absolutely displaced in the workings of a certain syntax" (193). But he also argues that Mallarmé's attempt to resist, undermine, and moved beyond mimetic truth takes the form, not of anti-mimesis, but, rather, of a generalization of mimesis and a miming of the mimetic process itself.

In Mallarmé, according to Derrida's interpretation, it is not a question of eliminating imitation, but, rather, of achieving some form of inaugural imitation, a miming without referent or precedent. In *Mimique* a mime is on stage with no text to follow and no model to guide him:

There is no imitation. The mime imitates nothing, and to begin with, he doesn't imitate. There is nothing prior to the writing of his gestures. Nothing is prescribed for him. No present has preceded or supervised the tracing of his writing. His movements form a figure that no speech anticipates or accompanies. . . . The mime *follows* no preestablished script, no program obtained elsewhere. Not that he improvises or commits himself to spontaneity: he simply does not obey any verbal order. . . . The mime inaugurates, he broaches a white page. (194–95, t.m.)

The mime performs for the first time something that exists only in and with his performance; the "originality" of the performance seems once and for all to abolish all forms of mimesis and be nothing but itself: pure performance or writing, one might argue, maybe even pure literature. We seem as far removed here from Platonic mimetic views as could be imagined, far outside philosophy and at the extreme limits of literature as pure performance.

And yet if the mime really imitates nothing and his performance is without any predetermined links to any outside (any "hors scène" or "hors texte"), then the performance of the mime and the mime himself constitute a self-sufficient, self-reflexive version of the truth,—of a "literary truth" perhaps, of the truth as literary—of a truth defined in terms of unveiling, production, and performance, rather than expression, reproduction, adequation. As Derrida puts it:

One can here foresee an objection: since the mime imitates nothing, reproduces nothing, broaches in its origin the very thing he is tracing out, presenting or producing, he must be at the very moment of truth. Not, of course, truth in the form of adequation between representation and the present of the thing itself, or between the imitator and the imitated, but truth as the present unveiling of the present: monstration, manifestation, production, *aletheia*. The mime produces, that is to say makes appear *in praesentia,* manifests the very meaning of what he is presently writing: of what he *performs*. He enables the thing to be perceived in person, in its true face. If one follows the thread of this objection, one would go back, beyond imitation, toward a more "originary" sense of *aletheia* and of *mimeisthai*. One would thus come up with one of the most typical and tempting metaphysical reappropriations of writing, one that can always crop up in the most divergent contexts. (205–6)

Performance theories and theories of literary production may break with one form of mimesis, therefore, and this is not without importance. But they do so, one could conclude from what Derrida argues here, only to reinstitute another form. "Pure literature" would thus be just another reappropriation of writing, a reversal of, rather than an undermining and complication of, the truth and the mimetic tradition supporting it.

If "such is not the case" with Mallarmé, Derrida claims, "it is because, *there is* mimicry, . . . a mimicry imitating nothing, . . . a double that doubles no simple, a double that nothing anticipates, nothing at least that is not itself already double. There is no simple reference" (206). Mimesis is not abolished or opposed, but, rather, pushed to an extreme and generalized; as a result, reference is complicated, the doubling process shown to be indigenous even to the model or original in which mimesis is meant to be grounded. In such a situation, mimesis has no simple referent but continues nevertheless to *refer,* to produce a "reference without a referent."[21]

As his reading of Mallarmé shows, Derrida's strategy for dealing with the contradictory status of mimesis—although closer in a certain sense to the "anti-mimetic" tendencies of the more formalist side of contemporary theory than to their supposed alternatives—in no way constitutes a rejection of mimesis. In general, Derrida's analyses have, as one of their purposes, to show that there are always, in all situations, other texts and contexts "at the origin" of any text—that no origin is ever truly original or inaugural. A text, for Derrida, is always at a distance from and other than its model or precedent, but never, however, self-contained or its own origin. One sense of his notion of the general text or *arche-writing* is that in terms of it no particular text can ever be considered to be only *itself.* Even if a text can never be shown to refer directly or immediately to its referent, no text—even the most radically self-reflexive text—can be said to eliminate or transcend reference either.

In other words, Derrida's analysis of *Mimique* shows that even when a literary text refers to or mirrors itself, it necessarily also refers outside itself. This indicates that self-referentiality is not, for Derrida, as it was not for Foucault (see Chapter 3), the means by which a text guarantees its own integrity. On the contrary, as important as self-referentiality is in Derrida's critical strategy as a means for undoing the most naïve forms of mimesis and the referential theories supporting them, it is just a means or a moment in a more complicated critical process, not an end in itself. The aim of Derrida's analyses is not to close the text back in on itself, but to understand how, by referring to itself, it refers to other texts: "A writing that refers back only to itself carries us *at the same time,* indefinitely and systematically, to some other writing. At the same time: this is what we must account for. . . . It is necessary that while referring each time to another text, to another determinate system, each organism only refer to *itself* as a determinate structure; a structure that is open and closed *at the same time*" (202). If the outside of a text is always indicated inside, the inside in the same process is inevitably drawn outside as well. For Derrida, this is not, however, an exclusive characteristic of literature, but a property of textuality in general. If *Mimique* is considered by him at one point to be "nothing other than the space of writing" (208), then it is a space turned inside-out as well as outside-in.

In "The Double Session," then, an essay that could be taken as Derrida's most developed "treatise" on literature, the question of literature is far from resolved. All of the formalist, aestheticist theses that have been associated by some literary critics with his work are, in fact, complicated and under-mined in his reading of Mallarmé: namely, literature as a self-reflexive, self-contained text, literature as a pure form of fiction that by admitting its fictive status radically cuts itself off from all outsides, and, finally, literature as a model for nonreferentiality or anti-mimesis and thus an antidote to philo-sophical or historical truth. In Derrida's reading, "the pure medium, of fiction" sought by Mallarmé is paradoxically a medium contaminated from the start by the mimetic contradictions constituting it.

Derrida does claim that *Mimique* could be taken as Mallarmé's "handbook of literature." But if we "learn something" from Derrida and his analysis of Mallarmé, it is to be suspicious of the term literature itself. The lessons of this handbook do not tell us what literature is, but make the *what is* more difficult to determine:

> If this handbook of literature meant to *say* something, which we now have some reason to doubt, it would proclaim first of all that there is no—or hardly any, ever so little—literature; that in any event there is no essence of literature, no truth of literature, no literary being or being-literary of literature. . . . All this, of course, should not prevent us—on the contrary—from attempting to find out what has been represented and determined under that name—"literature"—and why. (223)

Derrida persistently insists that the question of literature in Mallarmé leads somewhere other than back to itself, or, rather, that when it does lead back to itself it really leads elsewhere. For the "itself" in question is so very little, almost nothing, a difference within discourse in general, and, more specifi-cally, within what has been represented and determined under the name literature.

The self-reflexivity of a certain form of literature is not for Derrida, then, a sign of the triumph of literature, but, rather, an indication of a profound crisis—one in which literature is as much threatened as reassured. As he argues near the end of "The Double Session" as part of his analysis of Mal-larmé's "Crise de vers": "The crisis of verse (of 'rhythm,' as Mallarmé also puts it) thus involves all of literature. . . . It solicits the very bases of literature, depriving it, in its exercise, of any foundation outside itself. Literature is at once reassured and threatened by the fact of depending only on itself, standing in the air, all alone, aside from Being" (279–80). We have probably just passed through (or perhaps are still passing through) an age that overemphasized the sense of security and well-being attributed to literature when it attempts to stand on its own and cut itself off from all foundations—an age that, as a consequence, underplayed the crisis provoked by such a strategy by giving it a resolution in (as) literature.[22] The critical dimension of self-reflexivity emerges precisely at the point where the crisis provoked cannot be resolved by the self-reflexive text itself, where the deprivation of any foundation outside itself entails a rethinking of literature as well as those concepts and theories traditionally thought to found it.

Derrida's strategy in reading Mallarmé is to maintain the crisis, to extend it as far as he can within literature in order better to "remark" its historical implications: "All this intimate space, however, seals itself off only so as to remark a certain historical storm—the crisis—the final inanity of that of which there will never again be quite so much" (282).[23] The critical force of literature derives not from its inflation, but its deflation, when it is reduced to almost nothing: "The crisis of literature takes place when nothing takes place but the place, in the instance where there is no one there to know" (285). This minimalist notion of literature situates literature in a (non)space "between—in this essay Derrida argues this point in terms of Mallarmé's use of the paradoxical figure of the *hymen*—and treats it as a relational rather than substantial entity. When literature is almost nothing in itself, it paradoxically reveals the most about itself and the crisis located both inside and outside itself.

The history of literature and theory certainly contains no shortage of proclamations of crises. But for the most part, these are surface crises that are proclaimed only in order to be resolved in the literature and theory proposed by those declaring the crisis. If the crisis of literature and theory Derrida uncovers in Mallarmé is any different from other crises, it is because it affects the very foundations of literature and theory and demands extreme critical vigilance in order to be understood on this level. But it is also a crisis of (in) critical vigilance, which now no longer has a fixed site either inside or outside literature from which to survey and evaluate the constant movement or displacement of literature.[24]

For Derrida, a literature in crisis is "insupportable," by which he also means "without the slightest support" (*La carte postale,* 135). And yet, "insupportability" can never be declared as a general principle, but must be argued each time in terms of the specific supports, boundaries, frames, locations, and destinations that theory assigns literature or that literature assigns itself. The "internal drift" of literature, which, Derrida argues, is inherent in its open structure—that is to say, the structural possibility of all writing "possibly-not-arriving" at a destination (517), which a certain form of literature makes explicit—indicates that the critical function of literature, for him, is not to constitute a specific *literary* place but to undermine or displace all such fixed literary or theoretical sites.[25] Literature, in this sense, is an important critical weapon Derrida uses to displace theory from the site it establishes and move it elsewhere. Such a displacement is possible only because the site of literature itself is not fixed but continually in question.

Today, deconstruction in the hands of many of its proponents has undoubtedly established still another fixed theoretical site. But this has come to pass only because the caveats Derrida himself gives concerning this term have been ignored. As he explicitly argues more than once, deconstruction should not be used to characterize his entire work—because it is just one in a long list of critical terms or strategies he uses and has no privileged status over the others.[26] But even granted that it has an important, though not unique place in his work, deconstruction should not be equated with literary criticism. It is not, strictly speaking, a literary strategy, nor does it provide a model or methodology for reading literary texts. Finally, and most importantly, even in terms of the "priority" Derrida gives to the question of literature within his overall critical strategy, literature has priority only insomuch as it questions itself and makes possible the critical investigation of the extra- or para-literary as well, that is, only insomuch as it remains in crisis.

For Derrida, maintaining the crisis of literature and theory means pushing reading or interpretation to the point where it is blocked by contradictions it is unable to resolve. His general strategy of reading literary texts in terms of, and, in a certain sense, counter to, particular theoretical or philosophical texts and the issues they raise invariably leads to such blockage. Derrida calls this blockage either undecidability, when the grounds for any choice of one alternative over another ("good mimesis" over "bad mimesis" or mimesis over anti-mimesis, for example) have been undercut, or unreadability, when reading reaches an absolute impasse and is thwarted in its attempt to uncover, produce, or transmit the meaning of the text being read.

Certain literary deconstructionists have been known to use the terms undecidability and unreadability to provide a resolution for the contradictions of reading and interpretation and indicate the superiority of literature over theory—inasmuch as they claim that literature is "by nature" undecidable. For Derrida, however, the reading process does not end in undecidability or unreadability, but, rather, the blockage these terms indicate constitutes the precondition for starting reading going again. These terms are not concepts that can be evoked in order to *decide* what literature is, for they make deciding a much more difficult task. For example, in "Living On/Border Lines" (translated by James Hulbert, in *Deconstruction and Criticism* [New York: Seabury Press, 1979]), Derrida argues:

If reading means making accessible a meaning that can be transmitted as such, in its own unequivocal, translatable identity, then this title [Blanchot's *L'arrêt de mort*] is unreadable. But this unreadability does not arrest reading, does not leave it paralyzed in the face of an opaque surface: rather, it starts reading and writing and translation moving again. The unreadable is not the opposite of the readable but rather the ridge [*arête*] that also gives it momentum, movement, sets it in motion. (116)

In other words, a certain form of blockage occurring when reading reaches its limits forces the critic or theorist to develop alternate strategies for setting reading in motion again; and thus, by being stopped, reading gains critical force. The confrontation with the impasse of unreadability—which Derrida is arguing should not be (cannot be) simply negated or *overcome*—suggests the possibility of forms of reading beyond reading and interpretation in the traditional sense of these terms. Undecidability and unreadability can, in no way, then, be considered to encourage a passive acceptance of limits, as some theorists have argued.[27] The function of these terms is, rather, to promote dynamic critical strategies for working with and persistently displacing the limits of art, literature, and theory.

The crisis of literature and theory—the crisis into which literature leads theory and itself—is not resolved in Derrida's work because its resolution and the theoretical site that would be instituted "after" the crisis was resolved would lead to a continuation of the condition "before" the crisis. In other words, such a resolution would perpetuate the separation of theory and literature and the predetermination of the sites of each. As Derrida indicates in his introduction to *Parages* (Paris: Galilée, 1986), it is the *partage* (both separation and sharing) between philosophy and literature that must be constantly confronted—not in order to collapse one term into the other, but rather to develop "new and rigorous distinctions, an entire redistribution of their spaces" (10). For it is only in those limit cases where "the criteria of decidability"—in this case, those that allow one to separate and distinguish philosophy from literature—"cease being assured [that] a decision can finally be risked" (10). The crisis of literature and theory and the impasse to which it leads thus create the need for renewed critical activism and *decisive* critical strategies which, in the face of a fundamental undecidability, counter the limits of theory. Theory is, in this way, continually displaced outside or beside itself through its confrontation with a form of literature that is itself in crisis and more and/or less than what it is determined and what it determines itself to be.

CHAPTER FIVE
DISRUPTIVE DISCOURSE AND CRITICAL POWER

FOUCAULT

The sovereignty of these experiences [those of Bataille, Blanchot, and Klossowski] must surely be recognized some day, and we must try to assimilate them: not to reveal their truth—a ridiculous pretension with respect to words that form our limits—but to serve as the basis for finally liberating our language. But our task for today is to direct our attention to this nondiscursive language, this language which, for almost two centuries, has stubbornly maintained its disruptive existence in our culture; it will be enough to examine its nature, to explore the source of this language that is neither complete nor fully in control of itself, even though it is sovereign for us and hangs over us.

—Michel Foucault, "A Preface to Transgression"

1. Madness and Literature

Michel Foucault has, from the very beginning, directed his impressive critical powers against traditional philosophical and historical systems of analysis and classification in order to open up areas of investigation and posit objects of analysis forgotton, ignored, or exluded by the history of thought. Whether it is the "silence of madness" in *Madness and Civilization,* or the individual "epistemes" underlying and making possible the "human sciences" in each of the various periods delineated in *The Order of Things,* or the relations of power-knowledge inherent in all discourse in *Discipline and Pun-*

ish as well as *The History of Sexuality*,[1] the "object" of Foucault's critical gaze in each case owes its specificity—its critical difference from the objects of previous historical and philosophical investigation—to the "new," radical perspective from which it is described and analyzed. In this way, his work claims for itself the power to situate all previous historical and philosophical methodologies and systems and denounce their reductive strategies of analysis and exclusion. His own critical perspective is posited in such a way as to be so marginal, so disrespectful of tradition, that it cannot be situated, in its turn, by anything—by any history, ideology, or language—by anything, that is, but itself and the "disruptive discourses" with which it identifies itself and from which it takes its bearings.

What interests me is the source of Foucault's critical power, the underlying conditions of his archaeologies and genealogies. In other words, what permits Foucault to see so clearly when others before him have seen so poorly? Any analysis of the conditions of Foucault's critical perspective must inevitably confront the problem of a certain "sovereign form of discourse" in his work— the disruptive, excessive, transgressive role he assigns to a certain poetic or fictional practice of writing and with which he identifies his own critical perspective and, even, it could be argued, his "politics." To some, this might seem to be a rather frivolous, "literary," aestheticist approach to serious philosophical, historical, and political issues. But it is precisely the critical and even, at times, "transcendent" perspective—one he claims a certain subversive, disruptive form of literature or fiction provides—that situates and defines the political, the historical, and the philosophical for Foucault, at least in their critical forms. And, as I shall show, this is not just a characteristic of his "early work," but a fundamental component of his entire critical production.

In his "Foreword" to the collection of documents and essays published under the general title of the memoir central to the collection, *I, Pierre Rivière, having slaughtered my mother, my sister and my brother . . . ,*[2] Foucault claims that the primary reason his seminar spent a year studying these documents and decided to publish them was not their historical value, but "simply the beauty of Rivière's memoir. The utter astonishment it produced in us was the starting point" (x).[3] He goes on to add—in his own contribution to the volume, "Tales of Murder" (a more literal translation of his title would be "Murders that are narrated")—that "its beauty alone is sufficient justification for it today" (199). Is Foucault really proposing an aesthetics of violence or murder and equating beauty with the most violent forms of transgression, as the above quotations seem to imply? Is there really a place in his critical strategy for a concept of beauty, and, if there is, what concept of beauty is he implying by such statements? What are its socio-historical and political implications?

Foucault is obviously not an aestheticist, and so, the claim that Rivière's memoir is beautiful should not be too quickly linked to traditional concepts of beauty. If this memoir is judged to be beautiful by Foucault, and if he is demanding that it be taken to be such by all others, it is certainly not in the sense that it conforms to some ideal form of beauty or expresses any eternal truth. It is obviously not beautiful in the sense that it possesses a harmonious or organic form, or that it uplifts the spirit due to its high moral purpose. Nor can it be said to be beautiful because it has no purpose outside itself, because its only purpose is a "purposiveness without purpose." Its beauty conforms to none of the major tenants of either the pre- or post-Kantian aesthetic traditions.

And yet Kant is really not that far away either. For the beauty of Rivière's text lies in the fact that it cannot be judged according to any existing rules, that no concept is adequate to it, no form of knowledge able to measure up to it. What Foucault finds significant about the beauty he attributes to the memoir is that it can be used to reveal the inadequacies of all traditional philosophical, political, historical, moral, medical, psychological, and aesthetic categories that might be used to interpret it. It opens up a "new space" of analysis or judgment demanding different categories, rules, and strategies of interpretation. It offers a privileged vantage point from which to analyze the forms of discursive practice that do not measure up to it.

The special status Foucault gives to Rivière's memoir is not unique in his work. This text forms a series with other texts that could be classified under such categories as madness, deviance, violence, transgression, marginality, etc., and, as we have already seen in Chapter 3, a radical form of "literary" or "poetic" self-reflexivity. Throughout his work, texts fitting into one, or, more often, into several or all of the above categories at once, have played a crucial role in his critique of traditional history and philosophy. They have served as weapons against the postulates of consciousness, reason, transcendence, continuity, totality, dialectics, subjectivity, authorship, etc.—testifying by their mere existence to the reductive, coercive effects of the systems of thought organized according to these concepts. Foucault's "paraesthetic" critical strategy, to a large extent, is aimed at giving these texts their due, allowing them to speak in their own terms and act according to their own strategies, that is, without any interference from discourses that would limit their force and conceptualize and thus destroy their beauty. The radical nature of Foucault's critique of philosophy and history and the alternative discursive strategies he proposes rest, to a surprisingly large degree, on the "beauty" of these disruptive discourses and the way he situates his own position in terms of it.

In spite of important changes in emphasis and strategy between Foucault's earliest work on madness and his more recent work on punishment and sexuality, a reliance on, and identification with, a certain form of art and fiction can be found in all of his works: in *Discipline and Punish* as well as *Madness and Civilization,* in *The History of Sexuality* as well as *The Order of Things.* In *Madness and Civilization,* for example, art and fiction testify to and even preserve the existence of a madness existing outside or below the history of reason. The relation, or, rather, the non-relation or silence existing between reason and madness that Foucault analyzes in this work does not constitute a metahistorical, transcendent, eternal structure, but, rather, is part of a history with a very long duration. It reaches back into the most distant past and forward as far as, or perhaps even beyond, what one can imagine. A certain form of literature and art indicate the extent of this historical series: "The Reason-Madness nexus constitutes for Western culture one of the dimensions of its originality, it already accompanied the culture long before Hieronymus Bosch, and will follow it long after Nietzsche and Artaud" (xi). Literature and art, therefore, cannot be considered the origin and end of this nexus, but they are privileged signs of it, of a silence that exceeds the limits of discourse and a non-relation that pushes history beyond itself.

First of all, in order not to write just another history of madness from the perspective of reason and thus perpetuate the forced silence of madness, and, second, unable to write a history in which madness would speak directly in its own voice (for this would no longer be history at all, and not madness either, but a mystification of madness), Foucault's "archaeology of silence," as he calls it, focuses on and takes its own perspective from the "constant verticality which confronts European culture with what it is not, establishes its range by its own derangement, . . . a realm where what is in question is the limits rather than the identity of a culture" (xi). *Madness and Civilization* will do justice to madness and will neither exclude nor confine it if it is able to keep this "verticality" in sight at all times and make it, rather than any principle of history or reason, its (non)foundation. To do so, it must take on the perspectives provided by a certain transgressive art and literature.

It is not that all art and literature are rooted in this radical absence or alterity; there are basically two forms of madness to be found in literature since the sixteenth century and two very different forms of literature depending on which madness they "relate" to. There is, first, what Foucault calls the "tragic or cosmic experience of madness" of a limited number of privileged texts, and there is, secondly, the critical, moral experience of the great majority of texts. These two forms could, respectively, be called high and low madness: the high form of madness escaping rational discourse and the low form serving it. For Foucault, the high, tragic form of madness is, by definition, fundamentally non- or extra-discursive—which means that the "tragic experience" of madness in literature is an experience that exceeds the boundaries of discourse itself. It is an experience that Foucault—following a schema that can be found in *The Order of Things* as well—feels is found more easily in literature before the classical period, that is, before the rules of rational discourse radically exclude it from literature. The problem will be how the experience is kept alive when it has been excluded in such a way from literature.

For example, if in the classical period, and even before, *all* discourse as such is considered to be cut off from madness—philosophy excluding madness and literature standing at a distance from it and judging it in the name of reason—a certain form of painting, at least for a brief moment, may still be said to approach it, to locate itself in the proximity of madness and death. "Whereas Bosch, Brueghel, and Dürer were terribly earthbound spectators, implicated in the madness they saw surging around them, Erasmus observes it from far enough away to be out of danger; he observes it from the heights of his Olympus" (28). Erasmus, therefore, like Descartes (who in the next chapter will be held responsible for the radical exclusion of madness from philosophy),[4] is accused of eliminating the cosmic form of madness from discourse: "Whatever obscure cosmic manifestation there was in madness as seen by Bosch is wiped out in Erasmus" (26). At this moment, literary as well as philosophical discourse is claimed to be part of the process of confinement and exclusion. Madness and literature have no relation, except one of exclusion and silence.

This is the moment when the opposition is born that will structure the history Foucault narrates, a history consisting of the continual increase in the distance between the high and low forms of madness, between discourse and madness:

> The division [*partage*] has already been made: between these two forms of experience of madness, the distance will not cease to increase. The figures of the cosmic vision and the movements of moral reflexion, the *tragic* element and the *critical* element, will go their own way from this moment on, separating themselves from each other to an ever increasing extent, and opening in the profound unity of madness a void [*béance*] that will never more be closed.[5]

Without such a void and the division that creates the profound difference between the two forms of madness, *Madness and Civilization* would either be redundant—that is, like all other histories of madness, a *treatment* of madness—or impossible, taking on a subject that history, even in a radical critical form, could not or even should not touch. The division within art and literature and, for a certain period, the division between art and literature, are thus crucial for the entire critical project of the book.

Foucault's sympathies are obviously with painting and its non- or extra-discursive powers, and *Madness and Civilization* will attempt to assume the perspective of certain paintings outside the realm of discourse, will attempt to say in words what words cannot say anymore. For, if "with Erasmus, with the whole humanist tradition, madness is caught in the universe of discourse"

(*Histoire de la folie,* 39), in certain paintings, something very different is happening:

> On one side Bosch, Brueghel, Thierry Bouts, Dürer, and the entire silence of images. It is in the space of pure vision that madness extends its powers. Phantasms and menaces, pure appearances and the secret destiny of the world—madness possesses there a primitive force of revelation: the revelation that the dream-state is real, that the fragile surface opens onto an undeniable profundity . . . and the reverse but equally painful revelation that the entire reality of the world will someday be reabsorbed into the fantastic Image, in this moment between being and nothingness which is the delirium of pure destruction. The world is already no more, but silence and the night are not yet entirely closed in on it. . . . This entire network of appearance and the secretive, of the immediate image and the hidden enigma, is depicted in the painting of the fifteenth century as *the tragic madness of the world.* (38, Foucault's emphasis)

This is only one of the many forceful and incredibly lyrical descriptions Foucault gives of the powers of madness in these paintings, descriptions which constitute what Derrida has called the *pathos* of the book.[6] The mere existence of such descriptions indicates that Foucault feels that it is still (or again) possible "in language" to evoke the "silence of images" without "catching madness in the universe of discourse," still possible to return, in some sense, to this "space of pure vision" characteristic of certain paintings at *the moment* of the division itself. One must wonder how this can be done when the terminology, categories, rules, logic, and rhetoric of the discursive universe of the period "after-the-division" is all that is available in language. In other words, precisely how "pure a vision" of madness is possible within such a "fallen" form of discourse?

The archaeology of silence *written* by Foucault must take, for its perspective on madness, and follow as closely as possible the lead of the "non-discursive" practices of painting. But this leap of discourse beyond discourse isn't as great as it might at first seem—because the way has been indicated by poets, writers of fiction, and even certain "mad" philosophers who have repeatedly exceeded the universe of discourse, not by painting, but through certain radical discursive practices. These are the models for Foucault's impossible project, and they guarantee that such a project can be realized in its very impossibility. Their names reverberate not just in this text, but throughout Foucault's entire work: not only Sade, Nietzsche, Hölderlin, Roussel, Artaud, Bataille, but also Cervantes, Shakespeare, Nerval, and Diderot. They keep alive within discourse, but outside and beyond it at the same time, the possibility of alternatives to the discourse capturing and controlling madness.

112

They refuse to depict, judge, analyze, or interpret madness from the safe distance established by reason. They are situated *outside*, at and beyond the limits of discourse, and *in* the void in which madness is rooted and in which they too, before Foucault, silently speak or "paint" its forceful, disruptive silence.

For example, if the Renaissance silenced the high or tragic form of madness by "highlighting the critical consciousness of madness," by "making madness an experience in the field of language," the extra-discursive, tragic experience is nevertheless kept alive in a few disruptive texts and paintings:

> Alone, several pages of Sade and the work of Goya witness that this disappearance is not a total destruction; but obscurely, this tragic experience subsists in the nights of thoughts and dreams. . . . Underneath the critical consciousness of madness and its philosophical and scientific, moral or medical forms, a hidden, tragic consciousness never ceased being vigilant. This is what the last words of Nietzsche and the last visions of Van Gogh rewoke. . . . It is this experience, this consciousness, finally, that came to be expressed in the work of Artaud. . . . *It is these extreme discoveries, and these alone,* that permit us today to determine, therefore, that the experience of madness which extends from the sixteenth century up to the present owes its particular figure and the origin of its sense, to this absence, to this night and to everything that constitutes it. (*Histoire de la folie,* 39–40, my emphasis)

The "History of Madness" narrated by Foucault would then be the culmination of this series of fictions (texts and paintings) that remain vigilant in darkness, that resist the obscuring clarity of rational philosophical discourse. In other words, the darkness of the night, the silence of the unsayable in which these fictions (and *Madness and Civilization* after them) are rooted, is the source of their critical clarity and discursive power. This is how they are able to describe both sides of the division, to participate, at the same time, in the extra-discursive silence of madness and the confining discursiveness of *logos.*

All of these texts and paintings are, in some sense, also "beyond history," then: not only because they cannot be contained or silenced by the languages, institutions, ideologies, and discursive practices of their own historical period—or by any other period—and not only because they cross over or transcend all archaeological divisions, but also, and more importantly, because they communicate with each other directly across history and establish a kind of original, extra-, or parahistorical continuity, one which is radically different from both the assumed continuity of evolutionary or dialectical history and the discontinuities posited by the archaeological enterprise itself.[7] Shakespeare and Cervantes, for example, have direct links to a past which is irretrievably lost to their contemporaries and to us, except through them: "Both testify more to a tragic experience of madness appearing in the fifteenth century, than to a critical and moral experience of Unreason developing in their own epoch. Outside of time, they establish a link with a meaning about to be lost and whose continuity will no longer survive except in darkness" (*Madness and Civilization,* 31). Capturing, in some sense, the "lost time" of madness, these texts also link up with a future not yet "in time." They thus help constitute a kind of eternal, transhistorical present of Unreason. Past, present, and future are all linked together in the invisible, unsayable "present" constituted outside of history by these disruptive, nondiscursive discourses.

The *Neveu de Rameau* is perhaps the best example of the trans-historical continuity established by these disruptive texts. Foucault asks:

> What is the significance of this unreasonable existence which Rameau's nephew figures in a manner that remains a secret for his contemporaries but which is decisive for our retrospective perspective? It is an existence which is rooted very far back in time . . . and announcing also the most modern forms of unreason, those which are contemporaneous with Nerval, Nietzsche, and Antonin Artaud. To interrogate the paradox of the existence of Rameau's nephew, which is so visible to us and yet which remained invisible to the eighteenth century, is to place oneself slightly in retreat from the chronicle of evolution. But it is at the same time to allow oneself to perceive in their general form, the vast structures of unreason—those which lay dormant in Western Culture, a little underneath the time of historians. . . . It is necessary to investigate it [*Le Neveu*] as a condensed paradigm of history. Because, for the flash of an instant, it sketches the great broken line that goes from the ship of fools to the last words of Nietzsche and perhaps even up to the cries of Artaud. . . . The history that we will have to write in this last part installs itself in the space opened by the discourse of the Nephew. (*Histoire de la folie,* 364)

Texts such as *Le Neveu* serve as paradigms for Foucault's critical-historical project because they open up the discursive space that traditional history and philosophy have closed—a space that *Madness and Civilization,* in its turn, will attempt to reopen. In a flash, *Le Neveu* is already what Foucault's "history of madness" wants to be; in a flash, the meaning of madness emerges out of the darkness surrounding it and links up with all the other figures and extra-discursive "cries" of madness yet to come.

As I indicated in Chapter 3, in *The Order of Things,* a similar role is assigned to certain texts that escape categorization and contextualization and remain the only discursive elements not dependent on the episteme of their period.

They provide Foucault with a perspective outside each episteme, a perspective from which the episteme that is about to disappear and the one that is about to take over can be described and their "productions" analyzed. *Don Quixote,* for example, is used to mark the limits of the sixteenth-century episteme and anticipate the new, classical episteme, wandering between spaces and without a home in either:

> With all their twists and turns, Don Quixote's adventures trace out the limit: they mark the end of the old games of resemblance and of signs, and already in them new relations are set in place. (46, t.m.) *Don Quixote* sketches the negative of the world of the Renaissance; writing has ceased to be the prose of the world; resemblances and signs have dissolved their former alliance; similarities have become deceptive and head in the direction of visions or delirium. . . . Words wander off aimlessly, without content, without resemblance to fill them up. . . . Writing and things no longer resemble one another. And between them, Don Quixote wanders off aimlessly. (47–48, t.m.)

The archaeologist, following in the wake of Don Quixote's wandering, will attempt to situate himself in the (non)space or the interspace opened up by this aimless wandering—one of whose aims, nevertheless, is to trace out the limits of the different epistemological spaces wandered through.

At the limits of the classical period, the work of another figure, Sade, has the same function and the same position as *Don Quixote*: "Possibly *Justine* and *Juliette* are in the same position at the birth of modern culture as that occupied by *Don Quixote* between the Renaissance and Classicism. . . . Sade's characters respond to him [Don Quixote] at the other end of the Classical age, at the moment of its decline. . . . Sade attains the limit of Classical discourse and thought. He holds sway precisely at their limit" (210–11, t.m.). And, finally, Nietzsche, Mallarmé, and various twentieth-century poets and writers have a similar function in terms of the period still to come. They trace the limits of the nineteenth-century epistemological space and point to what Foucault's own "Archaeology of the Human Sciences" can anticipate with their help, but can't yet classify and define: the effects of the "end of man" and the emergence of a new episteme in the space opened up by "his" absence. They are already functioning in this not yet delineated space and according to rules that it is not yet possible to define.

Here is where the two principal transgressive terms of Foucault's "early work" come together: madness and the "being of language." As we have seen in Chapter 3, the self-reflexive pursuit of the origin of language leads to the repeated discovery of the lack of foundation of language, the "essential void" at its center, and, in this way, links up with madness. In "La folie, l'absence d'oeuvre," an appendix to the second edition of *Histoire de la folie,* Foucault writes:

> It is not a question of a ciphered language but of a language structurally esoteric. That is to say, it does not communicate a prohibited signification by hiding it; it rather installs itself from the start in an essential recess [*repli*] of discourse. A recess which hollows it out from within and perhaps to infinity. . . . It is this obscure and central liberation of discourse at the heart of itself, its uncontrollable flight towards a hearth which is always without light, this is what no culture can immediately accept. Not in its meaning, not in its verbal matter, but in its *play* [*jeu*] is such a discourse transgressive. (578)

The play of such a discourse respects no internal or external limits, and it sheds light—as it transgresses each and every limit—on their restrictive, coercive effects, as well as on the "obscure hearth" which can never be brought completely into the light without destroying its obscurity and critical power.

Surprisingly enough for this ferocious opponent of metaphysics, in this empty space at the origin of language the *being* of language is at stake. And it is, as we have seen, a certain literature that gives us access to being as well as madness:

> It is time to realize that the language of literature is neither defined by what it says, no more than it is by the structures which make it meaningful. But that it has a being and it is in terms of this being that it is necessary to question it. This being, what is it actually? Something without a doubt that has something to do with auto-implication, with the double, and with the emptiness that is hollowed out in it. In this sense the being of literature, such as it has become evident since Mallarmé and is still evident today, enters the region where since Freud the experience of madness takes place. (581)

The poet and the madman thus share the same dwelling and the same proximity to being in Foucault's work; they both dwell not so much "poetically in the house of language," as Heidegger would have it, but in or over the empty cellar or abyss under the house of language.[8]

The "tragic experience of madness" would have been totally lost had not certain painters and writers kept it alive in their work; similarly, the being of language would also have been lost in the Classical age and forever after had not a certain literature kept it alive:

> There is nothing now, either in our knowledge or in our reflexion,

116

that still recalls even the memory of that being. Nothing, except perhaps literature—and even then in a fashion more allusive and di-
agonal than direct. It may be said in a sense that "literature," as it
was constituted and designed as such on the threshold of the modern
age, manifests, at a time when it was least expected, the reappearance
of the living being of language. . . . Throughout the nineteenth century, and right up to our own day . . . literature was able to exist
autonomously and separate itself from every other language by a
profound scission only by forming a sort of "counter-discourse" and
by thusly making its way back from the representative or signifying
function of language to this raw being that had been forgotten since
the sixteenth century. (43–44, t.m.)

Literature at its most critical may constitute a "counter-discourse," as Foucault argues, and it may even constitue a kind of Nietzschean "counter-memory," as the title of a collection of his essays indicates.[9] But counter-discourse
and counter-memory still function here exactly as memory and discourse
have traditionally been thought to function: that is, to recover what has been
forgotten, to restore what has been lost, to make present again what is absent.
The difference is that what is to be recovered, restored, or made present is
not recoverable, restorable, or presentable as such. The being in question at
the origin of language and literature—"the discourse that holds onto this
being and frees it for its own sake is literature" (119, t.m.)—is non-being, a
radical transgression of being.

There is definitely a risk of mystifying literature by attributing to it too
great critical powers and by not turning back onto it the critical perspectives
it is claimed to provide for other forms of discourse. Foucault, it must be
admitted, in his haste to affirm transgression, often does not take enough
time to analyze critically the literature and art he posits as being transgressive. It is as if figures such as Sade, Nietzsche, Artaud, Bataille themselves
had already created such a transgressive space and that it was left to critical
discourse only the task of approaching this space and situating itself within
it in its turn.

The authentically transgressive writer—in this case Bataille, but such assertions are made of all of the above names—speaks, for Foucault, "in a
language stripped of dialectics," a language located "at the center of the
subject's disappearance. . . . It proceeds to the limit and to that opening
where its being surges forth, but where it is already completely lost, completely overflowing itself, emptied of itself to the point where it becomes an
absolute void" ("A Preface to Transgression," *Language, Counter-Memory,
Practice,* 41, 43). Such statements seem to indicate that there is no doubt in
Foucault's mind that such writers have already achieved absolute transgression (it would be possible to say, have already achieved a kind of negative

transcendence), that the liberation of thought and discourse has already occured and that the critical perspectives it provides can simply be assumed. The problem with his identification with all "those who have liberated their thought from all forms of dialectical language" (51) is the act of identification itself. It provides him, at times, with a perspective that serves to guarantee in advance, and without much work, his own critical power. It allows him to reap the spoils of victory from a battle fought and already won by others.

2. The Theaters of Power

Regardless of the many differences between his "early" and "late" works, Foucault's "late" works on discourse and power do, in fact, continue to give a certain transgressive literature an important place in the positioning and determination of his own critical perspective. For example, in the middle of volume I of *The History of Sexuality,* Foucault presents his project for the entire series,—a project that he changes drastically when he writes volumes II and III—and here, as at the beginning of *Madness and Civilization* and *The Order of Things,* he relies on a work of fiction to provide him with a perspective on his subject: "The aim of this series of studies? To transcribe into history the fable of *Les Bijoux indiscrets*" (77). For Foucault, the magical ring found in Diderot's fiction is the key to the whole history of sexuality, because it stands for all the mechanisms that coerce sex to speak (Foucault denies that speaking of sex per se can in any way be considered "liberating")—or, at least, coerce one sex to speak of the other, given that it is only women's sex organs that the Prince's magical ring forces to describe their experiences with men—a point conveniently ignored by Foucault.

> One day a certain mechanism, which was so elfin-like that it could make itself invisible, captured this sex and, in a game that combined pleasure with compulsion, and consent with inquisition, made it tell the truth about itself and others as well. For many years, we have all been living in the realm of Prince Mangogul: under the spell of an immense curiosity about sex, bent on questioning it, with an insatiable desire to hear it speak and be spoken about, quick to invent all sorts of magical rings that might force it to abandon its discretion. (77)

The ring(s) used to make one sex reveal the secrets it knows about itself and about the opposite sex is mute, however, when it comes to its own powers of coercion. The ring constitutes, for Foucault, a metaphor both for our desire to make sex loquacious and for all the mechanisms of power-knowledge involved in making sexuality discursive.

Foucault will use Diderot's fiction as a way of focusing on the problem of the mechanisms at work in all such discursive and discourse-inducing rings. But he will attempt to take Diderot's fiction one step further, by aiming all such "magical" rings at themselves to make them talk about themselves and reveal the source and nature of their power:

> Our problem is to know what marvelous ring confers a similar power on us, and on which master's finger it has been placed; what game of power it makes possible or presupposes, and how it is that each one of us has become a sort of attentive and imprudent sultan with respect to his own sex and that of others. It is this magical ring, this jewel which is so indiscreet when it comes to making others speak, but so ineloquent concerning its own mechanism, that we need to render loquacious in its turn; it is what we have to talk about. (79)

In revealing the games of power permeating the discourses of and on sex and the masters of these games, Foucault is, in one sense, repeating the sultan's actions by directing his own ring at the sultan's but remaining silent as to its own critical (coercive and/or liberating?) powers. But the critical, reflexive process can certainly not be terminated before it reaches Foucault—for his own critical power cannot be removed from the relations of power-knowledge he makes visible in other discourses and critical perspectives. To place Foucault's own critical discourse outside or above these relations would be a truly magical, mystical, fictitious solution to the problem of critical power. The ring that makes other rings loquacious needs to be investigated in the same way that it investigates the rings that make a sex speak in its own name.

The problem of power is, of course, central to the most important of Foucault's later texts and, at least implicitly, present in all his work. But the questions one is led to ask in reading Foucault in a critical way are the following: what permits Foucault to see, delimit, and thus criticize and undermine the configurations or theaters of power he focuses on in these texts without participating in and repeating the very mechanisms he is denouncing and attempting to transgress? From what site does he survey the scenes of surveillance and punishment without reenforcing them? Towards what ends is his critique oriented, and what, if any, alternatives to the surveillance and control of a certain configuration of the power-knowledge network does it propose? To answer these questions, it will be necessary to study closely the theatrical aspects of punishment in what Foucault calls disciplinary society and the alternate, transgressive theater he uses to oppose the disciplinary form of theater.

Discipline and Punish has much to say about vision as a form of power, that is, about the different political theaters that delimit and form vision—those places in which one sees and is seen, in which one becomes a subject and object of knowledge, where one is formed and kept in line. The principal

119

opposition that structures the entire book and gives form to Foucault's narrative and critical strategy is much like the opposition in *Madness and Civilization* between the high (tragic) and low forms of the presentation of madness, between a form of literature and art that allows madness to speak and one that confines and silences it. In *Discipline and Punish,* Foucault opposes the theater of *supplice* (of public, judicial torture and execution) to the theater of discipline and surveillance: the former openly displaying power at work, the latter hiding it under layers of moral-political, legal, and philosophical justifications and ideals. The first is described by Foucault as a "great, tragic theater," one taking place on the public square; the second consists of a series of petty, melodramatic theaters, located everywhere in society. Foucault describes the passage from one form of theater to the next in the following terms:

> The Shakespearean age when sovereignty confronted abomination in a single figure was finished; the everyday melodrama of police power and of the complicities that crime establishes with power was soon to begin. (283)
>
> The great terrifying ritual of public torture and execution gives way day after day, on street after street, to this serious theater with its multiple and persuasive scenes. . . . thousands of tiny theaters of punishment. (113)

With the passing of the theater of *supplice,* we move from high tragedy to low melodrama, from the central square to the back street, the workplace, the school, and even the home. Along with the "invention" of the panopticon, it is the turning point of the history narrated in this text. "It was an important moment. The old partners of the spectacle of punishment, the body and the blood, gave way. A new character came on the scene, masked. It was the end of a certain kind of tragedy; comedy now takes over, played by shadowy silhouettes, faceless voices, impalpable entities" (16–17, t.m.). The characters of this low comedy are all the more successful insomuch as they remain shadowy, faceless, impalpable—present everywhere and never letting their identity or their purposes be known.

Foucault even goes so far as to quote Vico in order to say that the old jurisprudence was an "entire poetics"—but what kind of poetics is at stake here? Even if Foucault claims that *supplice* constituted a form of "high tragedy," it was certainly not the tragedy of Aristotle's *Poetics.* Here, the tortured, dismembered, and sometimes already dead body is acted on, put on display, present at all times in open combat with the sovereign: in "hand to hand combat," says the translation quite accurately—but the French phrase "corps à corps" (literally, body to body) is more suggestive of Foucault's meaning.[10]

120

In scenes that often read like bloody sporting events when described by Foucault and that are referred to as duels, power is *visible:* it speaks, acts, and displays itself in its own name and wearing no disguises. As Foucault puts it: judicial torture (literally, "putting someone to the question") "was also the battle, this victory of one adversary over the other, that 'produced' truth according to a ritual. In torture employed to extract a confession, there was an element of the investigation; there was also an element of the duel" (41). In such a duel, power is exercised openly. But in doing so, it also risks itself. Battles, duels, and boxing matches are, in fact, sometimes, though not often, won by the less powerful, less well-armed combatants. An upset is always within the realm of possibilities. When power is on display—as it is here—and exercised openly, it opens itself up to the possibility that "truth" may not end up being on its side.

In a certain sense, the purpose of this book is to make power and the theater of discipline that structures power after the end of its "tragic," "poetic" phase as visible as that of the earlier age: that is, to make the private disciplinary theaters as public as those on the public square. When power is publically exercised—even when it is from the position of absolute authority, that of the sovereign—Foucault seems to feel that it can be better combated, resisted, and even more easily reversed, at least momentarily and marginally. There where it remains in shadows, invisible, in the disguises of education, knowledge, humanist ideology, judicial reform, etc., it reigns all the more absolutely and is all the less successfully combated.

Rather than the poetics of Aristotle, then, the poetics in question in the "great, tragic theater" of *supplice* is closer to that of Sade, Bataille, and, especially, Artaud. No matter how violent and inhumane the first form of judicial theater, the second is not considered by Foucault to be more progressive or even more humane. It simply punishes differently, in a disguised, more efficient, and, therefore, more effective and complete way. To distinguish between public torture and modern interrogations, Foucault uses terms that evoke Artaud's "theater of cruelty": "Judicial torture [putting someone to the question] was not a way of obtaining truth at any costs; it was not the unrestrained torture of modern interrogations; it was certainly cruel, but it was not savage. It was a regulated practice, obeying a well-defined procedure" (40). What is evident in such a form of interrogation—besides its cruelty—is its "theatricality," the fact that it is a *regulated practice.*

But there is more. In the high, tragic theater of *supplice,* the stage itself is absolute, a space of corporal presence in which the distinction between actor and spectator is broken down. All spectators are actors, participants in the cruelty and bloodshed, a part of the play of forces, and not outside it or silent witnesses to the drama. Thus the public is not able to dominate the stage from a safe moral and aesthetic distance—as it does both in a certain traditional theater and in disciplinary society. In fact, the crowd watching the

121

scenes of torture and execution are, in Foucault's words, "the main character whose real and immediate presence was required for the performance" (57). "The people claimed the right to witness executions and see who was being executed. The people also had the right to take part in it" (58). It was the only place the poor were given such a right, the only place "they could intervene, physically: enter by force into the primitive mechanism and redistribute its effects, take up in another sense the violence of the primitive rituals" (61). The poetics and power of this theater, then, are reversible: it is an "uncertain festival in which violence was instantly reversible" (63)— where, for as least as long as the ritual or festival continued, the class differences existing everywhere else in society are not so much suspended in a carnivalesque atmosphere of frivolous play as open to resistance and even reversal in the violence put on display in the "body-to-body" combat in which all participate and risk themselves.[11]

To conclude this section, Foucault gives examples of the two theaters. In Avignon at the end of the seventeenth century, the people drive the executioner off-stage and reverse the outcome—an upset, we would say today in the terminology of sports—saving the condemned man and condemning the executioner. In Paris in 1775, the army is placed between the stage and the public, ensuring by force that there will not be any public intervention or upset: that is, that the public will know its place as spectator and not participate, that each spectator will have an assigned seat and keep it. Watching the now neutralized spectacle while being watched and kept in place, the seeds of the modern theater of surveillance and discipline have already been planted.

The possibility of the panopticon—the extreme opposite of the high, tragic theater of cruelty—is already evident in the new form punishment takes in the late eighteenth century, when an "aesthetic space" is inserted between spectator and stage: "Contact was broken; it was a public execution but one in which the element of spectacle was neutralized, or rather reduced to abstract intimidation. Protected by the force of arms, in an empty square, justice quietly did its work. If it displayed the death that it dealt, it was from high and afar" (65). Visibility has begun to be the trap it will be in the panoptic theatrical space. The crowd is individualized and neutralized, as far as concerns participating in the action on stage—subjugated to relations of power that are automatic, uncorporal (having as their object the "soul" rather than the body), abstract, and absolute. The individual subject in its true sense is thus born as a subject of and subjected to power-knowledge.

Even though Foucault evokes the high, poetic, tragic qualities of the theater of *supplice* again and again, it would be absurd to conclude from this that he is proposing this form of punishment—and the political structure supporting it (the Ancien Régime)—as positive alternatives to the present. Rather, Foucault uses the distance and difference between "high" and "low" forms of judicial theater to highlight and dramatize the negative effects of the low form when seen from the perspective of the high. He does this in order to assume a radical critical position on the problems of surveillance and punishment in general without proposing a specific practical alternative to them. For Foucault wants to avoid at all costs what he calls the reformist position, the naïve belief that prison conditions can be improved within the same general structure of punishment. This, for him, is the "trap" of all discourses on prisons in which "for a century and a half the prison had always been offered as its own remedy: the reactivation of the penitentiary techniques as the only means of overcoming their perpetual failure" (268).

Foucault attempts to situate his own critical perspective on surveillance and punishment in disciplinary society *between* high and low forms of the theaters of punishment—in a place that cannot be occupied as such by any group, class, party, or any other political or economic entity. His is not the perspective of any world view, ideology, or political program; the relations of power he analyzes cut through and situate all these other supposed "origins" or spaces of power. He attempts to situate his own critical perspective in such a way as to avoid all nostalgia for the past, as well as all forms of evolutionary, utopian, reformist optimism projected onto the future. In this particular instance, his goal is to delimit prison discourse and the institutions supporting it, and which it supports, without being delimited in its turn by another form of the prison or the "microtechniques" associated with it. Foucault's critical goal is to describe the exercise (and not possession) of power without exercising it himself—or, if this is impossible, without exercising it in the same way that other strategies and techniques of analysis do. His attempt to exercise "critical power" in order to expose and ultimately undermine the bases for the power-knowledge networks that regulate disciplinary society (without letting their mechanisms of regulation enter on stage) needs, therefore, the distance that an overtly violent and potentially disruptive form of judicial theater provides. His perspective is not so much situated in the tragic theater of *supplice* as in its distance from "modern" forms of judical theater and the incarceratory institutions associated with them.

There is, in fact, one other "public space" where Foucault claims the direct confrontation between criminal and sovereign took place, a space associated with the open theater of the public execution, but written, rather than theatrical, in nature. It is the "literary" space constituted by the different forms of gallows literature recounting the last words of the condemned. This popular literature constituted a sort of "battle ground around the crime, its punishment and its memory" (67), says Foucault, a form of discourse as action— insomuch as it was an "equivocal," two-sided literature that in painting the evilness of the condemned man, made him also into a great hero: "Black hero or reconciled criminal, defender of true right or an indomitable force, the criminal of the broadsheets, pamphlets, almanacs and adventure stories brought with him, beneath the apparent morality of the example not to be followed, a whole memory of struggles and confrontations" (67). In the same way that the theater of *supplice* itself becomes dangerous to the authorities, this literature is dangerous: in both, the play and conflict of power is not hidden, and thus a reversal of forces is always possible.

When these pamphlets are banned, argues Foucault, crime literature becomes "aesthetic" and loses its marginal, disruptive force:

> There is a whole aesthetic rewriting of crime, which is also the appropriation of criminality in acceptable forms. In appearance, it is the discovery of the beauty and greatness of crime; in fact, it is the affirmation that greatness too has a right to crime and that it even becomes the exclusive privilege of those who are really great. . . . The split [*partage*] was complete; the people was robbed of its own pride in its crimes; the great murders had become the quiet game of the well behaved [*les sages*]. (68–69)

The difference, then, is between two "aesthetics": the first a disruptive, popular aesthetics whose "beauty" is in the cruelty of the acts being recounted; the second is an aesthetics of the "fine arts," which makes the criminal a "great man," a "genius," thus elevating him above the public sphere and eliminating the threat he poses to it by keeping him at a safe distance from it.

Like the turning point or division that structures the narrative of *Madness and Civilization* and is located in Descartes's *decision* to exclude madness from philosophy, Foucault structures the narrative of *Discipline and Punish* in terms of this movement away from the "open struggle" of traditional crime and punishment and the literature recounting it. Crime literature becomes moralistic and one-sided as the people's place in the scenes of punishment is now eliminated; as they are removed to a safe, aestheticized distance, their capacity to resist is, at the very least, diminished if not destroyed. All future battles seem to have been won in advance by disciplinary society—because the distance appears to be much too great to cross and the forces policing it much too strong, hidden, and diversified to do effective battle with.

In order not to perpetuate this "aestheticization" of crime and crime literature, Foucault explicitly identifies with the perspective of the literature before the "death" of the tragic form of judicial theater, with the disruptive force and the possibility of resistance he claims such dramas and texts offered—insomuch as power is exercised openly in the space they delineate. In making the exercise of power visible again throught his analyses, one of his goals is to unmask the actors in the little theaters of power-knowledge of contemporary society and to make us see the different techniques and

practices of disciplinary society as weapons in a battle that does not necessarily have to be declared over before it begins. Foucault offers no master
plan or strategy for winning the wars of power-knowledge that are going on
everywhere—such wars, if they are certainly not lost in advance, are perhaps
at the same time unwinnable, perpetual. The point is to force the battle on
stage so that resistance is possible, so that techniques of transgression and
reversal can be developed and the status quo not accepted as inevitable. In
this way, the war may never be over—but it will never be quite the same
war either.

Now is the moment to return to the question with which we opened this
chapter: of what does the "beauty" of Rivière's frightening memoir consist,
if it is not the beauty being criticized in *Discipline and Punish* as an aestheticization and appropriation of criminality? In other words, how does Foucault distinguish his own critical approach from previous approaches to criminality and from other critical discourses vying for prominence on the
battleground of theory today? In his introduction to the Rivière volume,
Foucault begins to answer this question by attacking what can only be called
caricatures of other possible approaches to the documents being discussed.
His purpose is to dismiss the positions he feels are in contention with his
own as quickly as possible, to make them seem as absurd as possible—
especially his "bête noire," what he calls "the outdated academic methods
of textual analysis and all the concepts which derive from the monotonous
and scholarly prestige attributed to writing" (*I, Pierre Rivière*, xi, t.m.).

Foucault claims, in order to set up his own approach as *the* counter-ap-
proach to any interpretative strategy focused on writing, that by not treating
the dossier as either a *work* or a *text* his seminar was able to avoid all the
limitations he attributes to methodologies that depend on such concepts. He
even offers rather self-serving congratulations to his seminar for its decision
(similar in form to the "decisions" he analyzes in other works in terms of its
power of exclusion) "not to interpret" Rivière's discourse, "not to subject it
to any psychiatric or psychoanalytical commentary" (xiii).[12] Not to interpret
means here to let the documents stand on their own—but this too must, of
course, be considered a way of interpreting.

The *decision* to take the opposite perspective from the approaches being
denounced—to exclude from one's own interpretative strategy all psychoanalytical influences, for example, or even all concepts associated with a certain
notion of writing—is much more easily said than done. It could be shown
that the essays in the collection are all marked by the very theories they most
strenuously attempt to avoid. It is not as easy to lock up or exclude the
theoretician of writing or the psychoanalyst as Foucault seems to feel. They
might even be of some assistance in the critical battle Foucault wants to
wage.[13] It is never simply a question of deciding not to do something or not
to be influenced by something—for exclusions, divisions, and such decisions

never really accomplish what they claim to—as Foucault's own work, sometimes in spite of its declared aims, forcefully demonstrates.

More important than these polemical statements against psychoanalysis, theories of writing, and interpretation in general is the precise way Foucault situates his own critical strategy in terms of Rivière's memoir. Like the public executions and the gallows literature discussed above, the memoir and the documents associated with it constitute a battleground. They constitute, says Foucault, "a confrontation, a relation of power, a battle of discourse and through discourses. And to call it a battle is not enough; many combats took place at the same time and intersected one with the other. . . . I think the reason we decided to publish these documents was to draw a map, so to speak, of those combats, to reconstruct these confrontations and battles, to recognize the play of these discourses, as the arms, as the instruments of attack and defense in the relations of power and knowledge" (x–xi, t.m.). The problem is how to draw such a map without simplifying the struggle—for maps are unilinear, two-dimensional, flat, and the position of the mapmaker has a great influence on what areas of the territory are given prominence and which are slighted or even ignored. What is to ensure that this map will be different?

In fact, it is the beauty of the memoir that is called upon to guarantee that this mapping will be different than others, not just another interpretation of the territory under fire and the different combats taking place within it. And if the beauty of the memoir is to have these effects, its distance and difference from the discourses that attempt to explain and master it must be maintained at all costs. Even though, or rather, because it produces terror, it must be revered. For it is because of what Foucault calls a "kind of reverence and terror for a text which was to carry off four corpses with it" that he and his seminar let it reign supreme: "We did not want to superimpose our own texts on top of Rivière's memoir." Rather than try to subjugate the parricide it recounts, the seminar let itself be "subjugated by parricide" (xiii, t.m.). Claiming to have freed themselves of all subjective interests and theoretical-ideological influences, Foucault argues that the members of the seminar were thus able to respond to the beauty of the memoir as such and take on its perspective—rather than impose their own upon it. Beauty here is more than beauty then. It inspires at one and the same time reverence *and* terror, pleasure and pain, as it transgresses the limits of reason and the imagination. This theater of cruelty implies not an aesthetics of the beautiful, but a transgressive aesthetics of the sublime.

Being subjugated by parricide, by this extreme form of transgression— parricide having replaced regicide as the most horrible of all crimes, the one that recalls the past system of punishment and demands "an infinity of punishment" (*Discipline and Punish,* 113)—is to occupy a position that is at the limits, or beyond the limits, of the modern system of punishment and the discourses supporting and emerging from it. It has all of the characteristics of a *disinterested* perspective from which the struggles and battles of power-knowledge can supposedly be understood and described as they are, without distortion—a perspective from which the attempts of all the other discourses in the dossier to explain the memoir and the acts it recounts can be seen as futile attempts to control and diminish the violent, disruptive force of the memoir, to conceptualize its extra-conceptual beauty. As Foucault says, the memoir was used as "a zero benchmark (*point zéro*) to gauge the distance between the other discourses and the relations arising among them" (xiii). His goal is to develop a "non-interpretive" critical strategy that links up with, and even tries to protect, the disruptive force of the memoir, and, by doing so, guarantees its own critical power.[14]

But the strategy of non-interpretation is difficult to practice. As Foucault himself admits, he and his seminar "could hardly speak of it [the memoir] without involving it in one of the discourses (medical, legal, psychological, criminological) which they wished to speak of from its perspective" (xiii, t.m.).[15] Avoiding interpretation thus means that one lets the memoir have the first and determining word, to speak only in its terms. To do otherwise and interpret it—no matter what strategy of interpretation is used—is to make it subject to, and to subjugate oneself to, the relations of power-knowledge one is attempting to situate, analyze, and undermine. "If we had done so," says Foucault, "we would have brought it within this relation of forces whose reductive effect we wished to show, and we ourselves would have been its victim" (xii, t.m.). Better, in that case, not to speak at all; better not to interpret it, but stand silently in reverence and terror before it. How else can one avoid "the trap it lays for everyone" (xiii). To speak without speaking, to interpret without interpreting, is the contradictory and impossible task Foucault assigns himself in this instance; one could argue that this is the case whenever it is a question in his work of transgressive or disruptive discourses.

Without the transcendent perspective on the history of reason, the order of things, and the systems or theaters of power-knowledge provided by such texts, there would, however, be no space left within or at the limits of the discursive field for his own critical discourse; his analysis would be as reductive of their transgressive beauty, as *caught* in traditional philosophical-historical traps as those being opposed or denounced. And, yet, in terms of such a transcendent perspective, any discourse, no matter how critical, must be considered inadequate. The best strategy, Foucault seems to suggest, is to say (interpret) as little as possible and to let the transgressive beauty and disruptive power of these discourses act on their own.

In all such instances the limits of critical discourse are clearly and forcefully indicated. But, it seems to me, one could legitimately ask at what costs? When the "beauty" attributed to a hideous crime or a text recounting it places beauty above all investigation, when transcendence and "beauty" do not themselves

127

become explicit questions of power-knowledge, then the positive critical effects of revealing the limits of critical discourse are diminished. By identifying with transgressive texts, and, in some sense, claiming to be at one with their disruptive force (which Foucault claims has been distorted and reduced by every other form of interpretation), Foucault lightens his own load and frees himself of the more tedious, but still necessary, task of analyzing and challenging the limits of "beauty"—as well as the benefits critical discourse derives from this extra-discursive *force*. The transgressive "beauty" of such limit texts in Foucault's work certainly pushes critical discourse beyond its own limits. But when it is evoked to legitimate a particular critical position and denounce the shortcomings of all others, it is highly questionable. It seems evident by now that both tendencies can be found in Foucault's work, intertwined one with the other, difficult, if not impossible, to separate.

I would even say that the force of Foucault's critique would be more powerful, more disruptive, if it were less subjugated by these texts; if the disruptive beauty of texts such as Rivière's, Sade's, Artaud's, Bataille's, etc., were not "revered," but analyzed more critically; if those approaches he opposes were not ridiculed or dismissed, but were more carefully considered in terms of their relation to his own. Yet, it should also be clear by now that I am not suggesting here that Foucault's references to these texts be ignored or considered simply a regrettable excess of his early work. On the contrary, the problem of the critical function of a "transgressive" form of literature in his work is more complicated and contradictory than that. The disruptive "beauty" of these texts offers Foucault both a critical, paraesthetic perspective on the limitations of theory in general *and* a way out of the traps set by history, philosophy, literature, and politics—a means of delineating and escaping from the relations of power-knowledge claimed to be in play everywhere else. It constitutes, at least in part—in both early and late works—an aestheticist solution to serious philosophical, historical, and political problems—no matter how negative, transgressive, or cruel the aesthetics is claimed to be.

The cruel beauty of transgressive literature could be considered both a critical opening *and* the literary-aesthetic trap from which Foucault has not escaped, precisely insomuch as a certain literature is treated by him *as an escape.* I would argue that no discourse, no matter how disruptive it is claimed to be, can ever ensure in advance such an escape from history and the traps that history lays for all of us. Critical discourse loses the very power it claims for itself when it *identifies with* such disruptive discourses, when it claims for itself the privileges it grants to them. Here, as in other cases, however, the distinctions between paraesthetic and aestheticist, critical and "romantic" strategies cannot be considered as clearly delineated. To attempt, as some theorists have done, to cleanse Foucault's work of its aestheticist tendencies and make it more analytically or politically coherent would also be to diminish greatly its critical force—the very force it derives from art and literature.

In one of his last essays, Foucault eloquently defines what he sees as our most positive inheritence from the Enlightenment: a "philosophical ethos that could be described as a permanent critique of our historical era" ("What is Enlightenment?", in *The Foucault Reader,* edited by Paul Rabinow [New York: Pantheon, 1984], 42). He also says at the end of the essay: "I do not know whether it must be said today that the critical task still entails faith in Enlightenment; I continue to think that this task requires work on our limits, that is, a patient labor giving form to our impatience for liberty" (50). As we have seen, an important part of Foucault's own contributions to such a permanent critique, and one of the signs of his own impatience for liberty, has always been his interest in self-reflexive, transgressive forms of literature and art and in the critical perspectives they provide on all limits. Throughout his work, they are what makes it possible for "patient [critical] labor" to be undertaken and pursued.

I would even go so far as to claim that in those places where Foucault's work best embodies the philosophical ethos he describes in this essay, literary texts or paintings have set the stage or opened up the field of analysis and made it possible for Foucault to assume a critical perspective on the field. Even when his descriptions of these texts or paintings might be considered too reverential (perhaps even naïvely "romantic"), and, thus, cut short the patient critical labor necessary to exceed the limits of the field, his own impatience for liberty is strongly felt. His work could, in this sense, be considered to fluctuate between a negative—but nonetheless transcendent aestheticism—and a disruptive, critical paraesthetics, the one ultimately inseparable from the other. A certain radical, disruptive form of art and literature can thus legitimately be considered the locus of one of the most forceful and contradictory aspects of Foucault's work: of the repeated play between limit and excess that makes the best of his work so powerful.

C H A P T E R　　S I X
B O R D E R L I N E　A E S T H E T I C S

D　E　R　R　I　D　A

> Deconstruction must neither reframe nor dream of the pure and simple absence of the frame. These two apparently contradictory gestures, systematically inseparable, are the very functions of what is being deconstructed here.
>
> —Jacques Derrida, *La vérité en peinture*

1. Working the Frame

The difficulties faced by any critical theory of art in determining its relation to its "object" are, undoubtedly, no different in kind from those faced by theories of history, language, society, etc., in relation to their "objects." A great number of these difficulties are directly connected to the problem of how to avoid abstract theorization: that is, how to avoid predetermining the object being theorized and constituting it primarily as an object *of* theory. The various forms of empiricism could, in this sense, all be considered anti-theorisms (but not anti-theories, as many claim them to be); they argue against the theoretical predetermination of their object and attempt to develop strategies of analysis that allow the specificity of the object to affect and transform—if not determine—the theory being used to approach and give meaning to it. In times dominated by theoretical abstraction or even obfuscation, an increased concern with the empirical nature of "objects" could, at least up to a point, serve an important critical function. This may help explain why—no matter how often the limitations of empiricism have been indicated in the history of modern philosophy from at least Hegel on—philosophy has repeatedly returned to some form or other of empiricism. The call of the "object," the desire to be at one with it, and the frustrations

131

of dealing with ever-increasing theoretical complexities all continue to make empirical solutions tempting alternatives to theoretical investigation.

If the problem of the relation between theory and its "objects" is a general problem for any theory and not specific to theories of art or literature, the aesthetic field (assuming it is a field), cannot be taken at the outset to be intrinsically different, more complex, inherently more resistant to theorization and determination from the outside than any other field. Any theory that wants to assert such a status for art cannot simply assume this to be the case in general, but must, in each instance, carefully show under what conditions art resists attempts by theory to encompass it and how the form of this resistance is specific to art. To proceed otherwise would be to assign art a nature, that is, to accept the most classical determination of art by philosophy—even for the expressed purpose of saving art from, or raising it above, philosophy or theory. Today, at what could be called a time of crisis for art and theory—when each is questioning what it is and how it functions—it would seem very difficult (even though the effort is still being made) to put an end to this kind of questioning by determining arbitrarily and dogmatically what art is, or, what, under ideal conditions, it should be.

Without the possibility of such a predetermination coming from art or from theory, the question of the relation between the two becomes crucial; how to avoid or undo all philosophical and aesthetic determinations becomes one of the most important critical tasks, not just for theory, but for art as well. To meet the challenges of such a task, a double critical perspective is necessary on both traditional and nontraditional art and on traditional and nontraditional aesthetic theory. At the very least, the borders separating art and theory and determining what is specific to art should not be assumed and fixed once and for all. They should continually be questioned, mobilized, and reinscribed if art is to have a critical, transformative effect on theory. There may be no art without the borders that distinguish it from non-art. But there is no critical theory of art that does not, in some way, question the determination of these borders, the frames assigned or imposed on art by theory or "freely" projected and taken on by art itself.

Jacques Derrida's essays on art in *La vérité en peinture* (Paris: Flammarion, 1978) have, as their principal critical goal, the displacement of the established borders of art and theory. Art is questioned in terms of its borders and the effects on it of forces coming from "outside" its borders which interfere with its integrity, self-knowledge, and even with its own representation of self. These essays are not, really, as much *on art* as on the difficulties the major philosophies of art and art itself have in fixing the border between theory and art. Since Derrida considers the notion of a fixed border to be a sign of critical dogmatism, his questioning of art and the theory of art takes the form of a critical dialogue with the major philosophies of art—chiefly those of Kant, Hegel, and Heidegger—in order to determine, as he says, "if it is possible

132

and under what conditions to exceed, undo or displace the heritage of the great philosophies of art that still dominate this entire problematic" (*La vérité en peinture*, 14).

The problem of the limits of theoretical discourse (of philosophy) have, of course, been a central concern for Derrida from the very beginning. In his earlier work, he addresses what he calls the problem of the "closure of metaphysics," the process of totalization or systemization that philosophy has as its aim to accomplish, the image of self it produces and reflects back on itself in order to ensure its integrity and mastery. The break with philosophy, the movement outside and beyond its borders, Derrida has always argued, is only possible when the language of philosophy is not ignored or rejected, but assumed and undermined from within—when the problem of the relation between break and closure is articulated directly. For instance, in "Violence and Metaphysics," an essay on Emmanuel Lévinas, he argues: "And, if you want, by means of philosophical discourse from which it is impossible to extricate yourself completely, to attempt a breakthrough toward the beyond of philosophical discourse, you cannot possibly succeed *within language* . . . except by *formally* and *thematically* posing *the question of the relations between belonging and breaking out, the question of closure*" (*Writing and Difference*, 110, t.m., Derrida's emphasis). In like manner but applying Derrida's comments to aesthetic closure as well as philosophical closure, I would argue that a breakthrough beyond the limits of the philosophical discourse on art cannot be achieved unless the question of the relation between belonging to and breaking with the aesthetic is also raised as a problem for both theory and art.

An investigation of the problem of the specificity of art, then, must be considered an important part of a critical strategy that strives to achieve such a breakthrough. This means, at the very least, that criticism and theory have to take seriously the problem of the various kinds of frames used to distinguish art from its surroundings. At the same time, a certain disrespect for the frame is also necessary—for it is not at all clear, or necessarily the same in all instances, *how* the frame of a work of art sets the work off and distances it from its surroundings, and what kinds of relations the frame in fact does allow with these surroundings. In any case, the thesis that the frame prohibits all relations with the outside is one which inhibits the potential critical effects of the work of art and of critical approaches to art as much as does any theory that simply ignores the effects of the frame and treats art either as if it were not framed or as if the frame had no significant effects on its relations with the "outside."

Given the intensity of debates that continue to rage over the nature and status of art and literature, it would seem that much is at stake for both art and theory in this question. And yet, all too frequently the debates amount to little more than a clash of diametrically opposed positions on the impact of the frame or border of art—on whether, for example, aesthetic or historical-political concerns should determine a critical approach to art. The stark alternative offered by each of the opposed positions consists of a choice between being *for* or *against* the frame of art, between accepting or rejecting the concept of aesthetic specificity. It is as if one were being forced by both sides of the debate to choose between simplified versions of the Kantian and Hegelian traditions, between literary-aesthetic specificity and philosophical-historical truth, aestheticism and sociological-political determination. The categorical nature of the alternative itself imposes serious limitations—not only on the critical investigation of art and literature, but on the determination of the so-called outside fields as well. One of the most pressing problems facing contemporary theory seems, to me, to be how to overcome the limitations that this alternative imposes on art and theory.

Derrida's investigation of the relation of theory to art has, as one of its chief goals, to undermine the limitations of the most important philosophies of art by critically investigating the way they frame art. In describing his own approach to the question of art, Derrida argues that it is important that a critical approach to this question not let itself be framed by the theories it is investigating or by art itself—but it should not remain outside and at a distance from the frames of each, either. For Derrida, a theory of art can be considered critical only if it "works the frame, makes it work, lets it work, makes work for it" (*La vérité en peinture*, 16). To work the frame is to make work for theory and art, to attempt to force openings in each and to transform each and the relations each has with the other—without, however, determining either by the other. "Working the frame" is, thus, Derrida's strategy for breaking with the sterile alternative that both aestheticist and historical-philosophical systems have imposed on the question of art—a way of using the question of aesthetic specificity to develop alternative theoretical possibilities.

Derrida argues that, for Hegel and an entire history of philosophy, the empirical existence of works of art has provided a starting point for the philosophical investigation of the meaning and origin of art (*La vérité*, 24).[1] The purpose of the philosophy of art, in this context, is to raise the empirical nature of art to a higher level and endow it with historical and philosophical meaning: to negate and transcend the specifically aesthetic elements of art. The aesthetic "object" is, in this way, predetermined in terms of the historical-philosophical end it is made to serve.

But even if such an end were not imposed on art and if it were possible to approach art only on its own terms, with art as its own end, the questions that would then have to be asked of this "nondetermined concept" of art, argues Derrida, would in themselves predetermine what one means by art. And this holds true not just for traditional philosophical questions (such as what is the truth of art? its meaning? its origin?), but also for "modern" questions concerning the form of a work, its internal functioning, its performative effects. Each of these questions assumes, at the very least, an opposition or set of oppositions— truth/falsehood, meaning/form, internal/external, saying/doing, etc.—that limits and predetermines the definition of art and how it will be treated. Art could be considered to be predetermined, therefore—not only in those theories intent on making art serve some exterior end or purpose, but also in theories whose purpose is to have art serve only its own internal purposes.

The point is not just that art "suffers" when it is in the grasp of the major philosophies or theories of art, but that theory "suffers" as well. For, if it is true that all philosophies of art reduce or even ignore the formal complexity of art (as formalist aestheticians have often argued), in the same way, they seriously limit the possibilities of theory. "The philosophical," says Derrida, "encloses art in its circle but also lets its discourse on art be caught in a circle" (27). Even in assuming only what seems to be a minimal notion of art which presupposes nothing more than its existence, philosophies of art reproduce their own limits by assigning an inside and an outside to the work and thus to themselves: "Discourses on painting are perhaps destined to reproduce the limit that constitutes them no matter what they do or say: there is for them an inside and an outside of the work from the moment there is a work" (16). In accepting the art object as a work—that is, as unified, completed, integral—theory relegates itself to a specific place outside and determines its relation to art as that of an outside to an inside. The question Derrida pursues in his essays on art is how to break out of the enclosure determined by this inside/outside opposition—not in order to destroy all notions of aesthetic specificity, but to conceive of specificity in some other manner; not in order to diminish the status of theory, but to make it more critical and effective, less dogmatic. The transformation of art and the transformation of theory thus go hand in hand.

The first part of *La vérité en peinture,* "Parergon," consists of a close reading of important sections of Kant's *Critique of Judgement.* This is only one of many examples of a renewed concern with Kant in France in recent years; not only Derrida, but also Lyotard and Nancy,[2] to name only two, have devoted important studies to a reevaluation of Kant. This interest in Kant might seem to American theorists to have been long overdue and a sign that French critical thought has finally freed itself from what appeared, at times, as an almost obsessive concern with Hegel—even if it was most often in an attempt to refute him or move beyond him—and post-Hegelian phenomenology at the expense of Kant. This evaluation is perhaps true in part. But the recent "return" to Kant in France, especially the Kant of the *Third Critique,* and to such questions as aesthetic judgment and the sublime, has produced a very different "Kant" than the "Kant" with whom most American literary theorists are familiar—that is to say, the "Kant" of the New Criticism. If Kant's *Third*

Critique, for the New Critics, served as the cornerstone of an aesthetics or poetics that privileged the aesthetic or poetic object, that assigned it a formal integrity, an originality, and even, in some cases, a being—that considered the break between the aesthetic and the nonaesthetic to be essential—the recent "return" to Kant in France has tended, rather, to challenge the premises in Kant that support such a formalist or aestheticist reading and to emphasize instead the complicated ways the aesthetic and the non-aesthetic are inter-related in terms of their differences.

Derrida, for example, challenges the notion that Kant's *Third Critique* pro-vides an irrefutable defense of the frame of the aesthetic or poetic. He attempts to show the difficulty Kant has in dealing with this frame and placing it se-curely around art. In placing a frame around the aesthetic, as Derrida claims all philosophies of art do, Kant, at the same time, reveals its problematical status. Derrida's point, in fact, is to show how the frame itself—even as it delineates an inside and an outside for each art work—permits, and even encourages, a complicated movement or passage across it both from inside-out and outside-in. The integrity of the aesthetic is assured only when such movements across the frame are interrupted or prohibited; the New Critical reading of Kant was, for the most part, oriented towards emphasizing these interruptions and prohibitions. Derrida's reading, on the other hand, empha-sizes both the limiting effects of formalist prohibitions of this type and the consequences for art and the theory of art if the aesthetic cannot be effectively isolated in all instances from the non-aesthetic.

In following Kant step by step as he attempts to frame the aesthetic, Derrida reveals the contradictory status of what could be considered the inaugural gesture of modern aesthetics: the delineation of the work of art and the defi-nition of its specificity. And yet he argues that there is no such thing as a Kantian aesthetics per se and that any aesthetics derived from Kant would be just that—a derivation and a reduction of the Kantian project which is transcendental and not practical in nature:

> This critique of taste doesn't concern production; it has in mind nei-ther "formation" nor "culture," both of which it can quite easily do without. And as the *Critique* will show that one cannot assign con-ceptual rules to the beautiful, it will not be a question of constituting an aesthetics, no matter how general, but of analyzing the formal conditions of possibility of an aesthetic judgment in general, and thus of aesthetic objectivity in general. In terms of this transcendental aim, Kant demands that he be read in an uncompromising manner. (*La vérité*, 50)

The difficulties in generating a "practical" aesthetics from the Kantian critique of the conditions of possibility of aesthetic judgment in general are many and situated on various levels. Derrida is concerned, above all, with not reducing them in any way and making the formulation of a Kantian aesthetics too easy a task.[3]

Much of the commentary on the *Third Critique* insists on the revolutionary significance of Kant's notion of disinterestedness in aesthetic judgment in order to use this notion to speculate about the intrinsic nature of the art work. Derrida cautions that, insomuch as disinterestedness is a way of distinguishing between an inside and an outside of the work, it can be compared to other strategies having the same purpose. Like them, it presupposes an already existing frame:

> We have to know what we are talking about: what *intrinsically* concerns the value of beauty and what remains exterior to the immanent sense of beauty. This permanent request—to distinguish between the internal or proper sense and the circumstances of the object one is talking about—organizes all of the philosophical discourses on art, on the meaning of art and on meaning alone, from Plato to Hegel, Husserl, and Heidegger. It presupposes a discourse on the limit between the inside and outside of the art object, in this instance a discourse on the frame. (53)

For Derrida, then, the "originality" or specificity of Kant's approach to the aesthetic is not that he delineates an intrinsic aesthetic space and separates the aesthetic from the nonaesthetic. What is specific to Kant is *the way* he treats the frames that delineate aesthetic interiority and his strategies for deflecting questions that would seriously jeopardize the integrity of these frames.

In the *Third Critique*, the question of aesthetic judgment is virtually indistinguishable from that of reflective judgment—that is, from a form of judgment that functions in the absence of determined rules, and, in which (because the example precedes the law), one can never apply a predetermined rule to a particular case. On the contrary, the general law can only be postulated, in each instance, in terms of an example. To choose an example is already to take a position in terms of a law that is not yet determined. As a result, Derrida's choice of the *parergon* as the primary example on which his own reading of Kant focuses, can be seen as his way of taking a position on the difficulty of taking a position in Kant's work in general—but especially in terms of the frame of art. It is, first of all, an example that reveals how much Kant needs the notion of the frame in order to position his own discourse in relation to art. But Derrida also focuses on the example of the *parergon* in Kant in order to complicate the notion of the frame, to question it as an effective closure around art. In this way, he reveals its ambiguous

137

and contradictory function in Kant's work—how it, in fact, displaces or de-positions as much as it positions.

Kant's examples are crucial for an understanding of how the *Third Critique* positions itself. And Derrida's choice of examples from Kant's text are equally significant for understanding his own position on Kant. Derrida argues that in the examples of *parerga* given by Kant—the frames of paintings, the cloth-ing of statues, the columns around an edifice (*The Critique of Judgement*, translated by James Creed Meredith [Oxford: Oxford University Press, 1978], 68)—their exteriority to the work per se defines them less than does the necessity that links them to the internal structure of the work. In other words, no *ergon* without *parergon*: "What constitutes them as *parerga* is not simply their exteriority or surplus nature, it is the internal structural relation that attaches them to the interior lack of the *ergon*. And this lack would be con-stitutive of the very unity of the *ergon*. Without this lack, the *ergon* would have no need of a *parergon*" (*La vérité*, 69). The problem becomes, then, how to take a position in terms of an exteriority which is necessary to the interior integrity of the work—necessary because the interior lacks something in its interior and needs to be set off from an outside it cannot really do without. How is it possible to determine, in such a situation, what truly be-longs to the inside and what does not?

Derrida argues that Kant answers the question of what a frame is in terms that hardly support the notion of the closed interiority of the work: The frame is a "*parergon,* a combination [*un mixte*] of outside and inside: it is a com-bination that is not a mixture [*un mélange*] or a half-measure but rather an outside that is drawn inside the inside in order to constitute it inside" (74). The difficulties Kant has in resolving the problem of the intermixing of inside and outside especially interest Derrida; he devotes an important segment of his analysis to the effects of Kant's confrontation with these difficulties on his theory of aesthetic judgment. It could even be said that his position on Kant is to make it as difficult as possible for Kant to return from the *parergon* to the *ergon*, to make the closure, that a certain neo-Kantian aesthetics has always depended on, as difficult to defend as possible.

The question of form cannot be separated, argues Derrida, from that of the frame. Only formal judgments, judgments distinguished from those of content or matter, can be considered judgments of taste in the Kantian sense. Derrida claims that in Kant, it is a question of "formality as the space of aesthetics in general, of a 'formalism' that instead of representing a determined system is indistinguishable from the history of art and aesthetics itself. And the effect of formality is always linked to the possibility of a system of framing that is at the same time imposed and erased" (79). The *Third Critique* itself is caught in the same "parergonal logic" that it applies to art. Just as it frames itself by using the analytical concepts of the *First Critique*, it, at the same time, attempts to erase this frame by claiming that no concept determines the

138

judgment of the beautiful (89). The question thus becomes how to distinguish the good frame from the bad—or, at least, how to determine when to evoke the frame and when to ignore it or argue against it. And this is not just a question of the application of theory to art; it is also one internal to both theory and art. A too visible frame detracts from the work and destroys its integrity; a frame that is not visible enough produces a lack of differentiation between inside and outside, thereby having the same effect. Thus, working the frame and making the frame work constitute a critical approach to art that originates neither inside nor outside art, that is neither of theory or of art alone—for it consists in moving constantly from one to the other.

Is it possible, then, according to Derrida, to delineate a purely aesthetic space, and, if it is, does Kant succeed in doing so? The major thrust of Derrida's reading of the *Third Critique* is to answer the latter question in the negative and to suggest, through an analysis of Kant's "failure," that there are insurmountable difficulties in realizing the project of aesthetic purity or autonomy in general. This does not mean that the aesthetic becomes a subset or derivative of the philosophical or the discursive or that it does not push against and exceed the limitations theory imposes on it. It suggests, rather, that the aesthetic resists theoretical closure from within a space that is not entirely aesthetic in nature. In fact, for Derrida, even the attempt to grant the aesthetic the privileges of autonomy or integrity—and from this derive its "freedom" or universality—constitutes a way of limiting and framing it. The aesthetic for him is always a little less and a little more than what both its staunchest defenders and most vocal critics claim; it is occulted in the very act of locating and defining it, never completely contained by the frame placed around it and thus never completely "itself."

Derrida argues that Kant's approach to the aesthetic is not as undetermined as Kant claims, for a certain notion of man plays an important role in determining the frame of the aesthetic. Derrida finds the limiting effects of Kant's "humanism" almost everywhere in the *Third Critique*, especially in those places in Kant's text that have traditionally been considered to be the most formalist.[4] He argues, in other words, that Kant's formalism and humanism go hand and hand and that each implies the other. A certain notion of man will reappear in Kant in the very place from which he is excluded by the frame of art.

In the famous definition of the beautiful (under the category of relation) as a "finality without an end" (*Zweckmäßigkeit ohne Zweck*; purposiveness without purpose, say the standard translations of the *Third Critique*), the "internal" form of the object is held up as the only finality, a finality with no exterior purpose, self-sufficient and self-contained. As Derrida puts it, summarizing his analysis of this often quoted and analyzed, but still enigmatic phrase: "Finality, an oriented movement, is necessary, for without it there would be no beauty, but equally necessary is that the orientor (the end that

139

originates) be missing. Without finality, no beauty. But none either if an end were to determine this beauty" (99). Derrida concludes from this that, for Kant, finalized forms without ends are beautiful only insomuch as they immediately display their lack of attachment to an end, as the "pure cut" separating them from all other ends and purposes is evident in their frame.

We are thus led back to the frame—not to a material frame, but one made out of an absence of a very particular nature. "Thus it is the finality-without-end that is *said* to be beautiful. . . . Thus it is the *without* that counts for beauty: neither finality nor end, neither the purpose that is lacking nor the lack of purpose, but the border in the *without* of the pure cut, the *without* of the finality-*without*-end" (101). More fundamental than the finalized form without an end is the border that finalizes it and, at the same time, cuts it from its end—the border that keeps us from knowing its end and therefore from knowing it. The "without" out of which the frame is made is both the guarantee of the integrity of the inside and the point of passage from inside to out.

For Derrida, Kant's humanism weighs most heavily on his notion of the beautiful in terms of the finality of form and its non-relation to an end as its only end. Even so, man's place is not that easy to determine. Kant claims, paradoxically, both that: 1) the form of man cannot be the object of a judgment of pure taste, that is, considered beautiful in the sense of free beauty, for it "presupposes a concept of the end that defines what the thing has to be, and consequently a concept of its perfection" (*Critique of Judgement*, 73); and 2) the ideal of beauty is "only to be sought in the human figure" (79). Man is, thus, both present and absent at the same time: present because "he" occupies a privileged place in nature as the only ideal of beauty and yet absent as an anthropologically defined unity or end in the judgment of pure, free beauty.

This double, absent-present status is also evident, Derrida claims, in terms of man's place as the subject of aesthetic judgments:

> If the subject performing these judgments is not recognized as an anthropological unity, if the play of its functions (sensitivity, imagination, understanding, reason) is not bound by means of a finalized organization under the name of man occupying a privileged place in nature, none of this is intelligible, and certainly not this opposition between free and dependent beauty. If, on the contrary, a determined anthropology intervenes in this critique of aesthetic judgment, an entire theory of history, society, and culture decides the issue at what is formally the most critical moment. It weighs with all its content on the frame. (*La vérité*, 120)

All theories of history, society, culture, art, etc., may be excluded by Kant

140

from aesthetic judgment in the name of disinterestedness. But they reappear with the presence of man in nature and as the subject of aesthetic judgment—since for Kant man is the only being capable of determining his own ends. Present and absent, these anthropologically determined theories of society and culture weigh on the frame that excludes them and reappear inside in another form. Exclusion, here, is really a form of displacement; the excluded term does not disappear, but, rather, takes on a different form and place "inside" by being forced "outside."[5]

Derrida challenges an entire post-Kantian aesthetic tradition when he questions whether *The Critique of Judgement* in fact provides the means for determining the radical heterogeneity or specificity of the aesthetic. For he claims that aesthetic judgment in Kant cannot be totally cut off from what weighs on the frame delineating the aesthetic: "The *Third Critique* depends in an essential way . . . on a pragmatic anthropology and on what could be called in more than one sense of the term a reflective humanism. This anthropological resource, recognized in its juridical and formal instances, weighs massively by its content on this supposedly pure deduction of aesthetic judgment" (*La vérité*, 123). Although Derrida insists on the limiting effects of the weight of Kant's humanism on the aesthetic, this does not mean, however, that he is an anti-Kantian whose critical goal is to collapse the aesthetic into the philosophical, the moral, or the socio-historical. On the contrary, the issue of aesthetic specificity remains central to his investigation of Kant and the focal point of his attempt to rethink the relations between the exterior and the interior across and on each side of the frame. The aesthetic and the theoretical are, for him, too interconnected to be effectively separated by any frame or border drawn arbitrarily between them. And yet, as Derrida repeatedly points out, neither can do effectively without the notion of the frame either.

In order to break with the notion of the frame basic to the aesthetic, what would be needed is a form of judgment that functions without any borders whatsoever. In the *Third Critique*, one of the most important functions of the sublime—which lacks or exceeds the *parerga* characteristic of the beautiful—is to indicate the limitations of the aesthetic. As Derrida puts it, "If art takes form by limiting, indeed by framing, there can be a *parergon* of the beautiful, the *parergon* of a column or the *parergon* as column. But there cannot be, it seems, any *parergon* of the sublime. The colossal [the primary example Kant gives of the sublime] excludes the *parergon*, first of all because it is not a work, an *ergon,* and secondly because the infinite presents itself there, and the infinite does not let itself be bordered" (146). The unbounded or unlimited characteristics of the sublime seem, in this sense, to constitute a radical break with the aesthetic and the contradictory limitations of the frame.

But the sublime raises another series of questions for art and theory, ques-

141

tions that are still, at least indirectly, related to the problem of the frame. These questions have to do with how philosophy is to measure (up to) the immeasurable (in the form of the colossal or in some other form), or, in terms of the problem of presentation, how it is to present the unpresentable. Derrida's analysis of the Kantian sublime focuses on the various responses Kant gives to these questions, and, especially, on how the problem of the frame continues in a contradictory way to play a role in the presentation of the unpresentable:

> A concept can be too great, *almost too* great for presentation. *Colossal* (*kolossalisch*), therefore, qualifies presentation, the staging or making present, or rather making visible of something that is not a thing because it is a concept. And it is the presentation of this concept insomuch as it is not presentable; but not simply unpresentable: *almost unpresentable*. . . . How is it possible to conceive, in the presence of a presentation, the holding-oneself-erect-there (*Darstellen*) of an excess of size that remains only *almost* excessive, on the border of a delimiting trait barely crossed? . . . The *almost-too-much* forms the singular originality, with neither border nor simple overflow of border [*débordement*], of the colossal. (143)

For Derrida, the Kantian sublime is not the simple transcendence of all borders. Without borders the overflow itself cannot be measured, the *almost*-unpresentable cannot be presented. The sublime differs, for him, from the aesthetic in that the movement across the border or frame is an explicit element of its excessive nature and that the unpresentable is a basic component of the dynamics of its presentations.

The sublime, in this sense, is not placed by Kant in opposition to the beautiful, for as Derrida points out, "opposition can only arise between two objects that are determined, with their contours, borders, and finiteness" (145). The sublime is found only in an "'object without form,'" where the "'without-limits' 'represents' itself" (146). The sublime constitutes, therefore, more of a difference within the aesthetic. As Jean-Luc Nancy puts it, the sublime, whether it is called by its name or not, "is always a distance [*écart*] within the aesthetic or a distance from the aesthetic. . . . In the sublime, art itself is disturbed, given still another destiny; it has its destiny in some sense outside itself" ("L'offrande sublime," 76–77). The aesthetic, inasmuch as its frame can be argued to have a contradictory role—because it both separates the aesthetic from the nonaesthetic and opens the aesthetic up to what it is not—already contains the sublime "within it" in the form(lessness) of everything that cannot be contained or given form within its frame, starting with the frame itself.

The sublime, then, can in no way be considered a resolution of the paradoxes inherent in the placement/displacement of the frame of art. Rather, it constitutes in some sense the paradox of the aesthetic itself: the paradox of the pleasure of displeasure and the presentation of the unpresentable. The sublime pushes art and the theory of art outside the specifically aesthetic realm so that the questions raised by art can be linked in a nondetermined way to historical, political, and ethical questions—questions which are themselves displaced and transformed by being formulated in terms of the sublime. The sublime, thus, is not so much defined by an absence of frames as by the constant passage from one side of the frame to the other. Or, as Derrida puts it in terms of the colossal, "The size of the colossal is neither culture nor nature but at the same time the one and the other. It is perhaps, between the presentable and the unpresentable, the passage from one to the other as much as the irreducibility of one to the other: size, border, the boundaries of the cut, what passes and happens, without passing, from one to the other" (164–65). In such a situation, the focus on just one side of the frame of art, whether on aesthetic specificity "inside" or the historical-political "outside," would constitute a serious reduction of both art and those extra- or paraesthetic forces pressing against its frame and continually modifying and displacing art, as well as being modified and displaced by it.

Through the Kantian sublime, Derrida raises the problem of the frame of art from the "outside," inasmuch as the sublime has to do with the presentation of the infinite, the absolute, the unbounded. In this case, Derrida shows how the unbounded itself needs to be set off in terms of a frame it exceeds; without the frame, the immeasurable could not be measured in any way and the unpresentable would not be a problem for presentation but its negation. To insist on the contradictory role of the frame in terms of the sublime is to confront art and the various theories of art with their limitations. But it also makes the sublime a question of and for art. The sublime, considered in this light, constitutes a radical way of working the frame of art and opening the aesthetic up to the paraesthetic elements constituting, and at the same time, deconstituting its specificity.

Derrida's reading of Kant, then, demonstrates why theory can neither accept nor ignore the frame of art. Kant's own difficulties with the problem of the frame delineating the aesthetic become, in Derrida's interpretation, exemplary of what he calls "parergonal logic"—where the interiority of art and its exteriority are seen to be interconnected in fundamental, paradoxical, and undeniable ways. The question of the specificity of the aesthetic (which in its modern form, at least, is derived from Kant), is recast by Derrida so that it no longer can be seen as a simple defense of art, but, rather, as a way of relating to the "extra-aesthetic" from the critical distance—no matter how slight—instituted by the frame of art. At the same time, however, the aesthetic is itself revealed to contain within the area delineated by the frame paraesthetic elements which it cannot do without. Thus, the entire question of the aesthetic is itself recast in terms of paraesthetic issues and forces that are as much intrinsic to art as external to its specificity.

Derrida's critical investigation of the aesthetic and the sublime in Kant does not provide the foundation for a practical aesthetics. Rather, it reveals the limitations of both "the practical" and "the theoretical" when it comes to the question of art. The term that perhaps best characterizes Derrida's approach to art (not just in his essay on Kant, but in all of the essays of *La vérité en peinture*), the term that is fundamental to what could be called his borderline aesthetics—an aesthetics that is situated on both sides of the aesthetic—is a term that appears frequently in his essays: *passage*. For Derrida's goal is to push against the limitations of theory and produce a form of critical discourse mobile enough to pass from art to theory and back again without terminating in either one. His work on art "mobilizes" both theory and art by rethinking each in terms of the frames that both separate them and link them together, that both block and permit passage or movement between them. In terms of Derrida's essays on art, it is possible to argue that the question of the specificity of art (that is, the question of its frame), can be considered a critical rather than aestheticist question when it leads to a critical investigation and recasting of the fields and discourses bordering the aesthetic: when the question of aesthetic specificity is made a means of passage "outside" rather than a form of blockage "inside."[6]

2. Framing the Work

If the specificity of art remains a pressing but unresolved question after and (as we have seen from Derrida's reading), because of Kant, the case of literature is equally if not more complex. In any case, what distinguishes the literary from the nonliterary, that is, what constitutes the frame of literature, certainly continues to be a much debated issue in contemporary theory. Many of these debates are centered on the question of self-reflexivity and whether (as certain formalist theories claim) the specificity of literature can be equated with the self-reflexive procedures by means of which a literary text reflects (on) how it functions and what makes it "literary." The advantage of such an equation is that it resolves all questions concerning the frame of literature—because the true frame of literature is considered to be the border that literature constructs "on its own" to ensure that the extra-literary "outside" is kept outside. How can the frame of literature be ignored or challenged, the formalist asks, when specific texts explicitly highlight the formal and rhetorical devices that constitute their formal integrity and thus their "literariness?"

Through various rhetorical and formal devices, poems, novels, and plays can create an effect of framing. In contemporary theory, these devices have often been emphasized in order to argue that the literary text has a different nature and function from all other kinds of texts. Whether it is in terms of the self-referential characteristics of poetic language, the self-conscious nature of a narrator or narrative function, or the self-reflexivity of a play within a play, the construction of the frame used to distinguish the literary from the nonliterary has, more and more frequently, come to be seen as an important and even primary function of the literary text itself. One could legitimately wonder, however, if this emphasis on the frame that literature projects for itself is due to the fact that the problem of literary specificity has been resolved (as many formalists imply when they define literature in terms of self-reflexivity), or whether, on the contrary, it indicates a deep insecurity and uncertainty—that of both literature and literary criticism and theory—concerning the literariness of literature.

Faced with texts that explicitly stage their own closure, theory has sometimes responded by accepting as-is the frame that literature delineates around itself. By not questioning this frame, theory is not necessarily motivated primarily by a desire to respect the integrity of literature, however. For theory is, in fact, able to deal (and dispense) with literature more easily when literature is enclosed by a frame it determines by itself rather than one theory imposes on it. In other words, when theory can point to the frame literature projects around itself, it does not have to invoke and, then legitimate, its own authority to frame literature. It simply acknowledges literature's authority to frame itself and determine what it is—most often in order, ultimately, to have authority over that authority.[7]

It is even possible to argue that formalist approaches which emphasize the specificity of literature as being a product of self-reflexivity are not necessarily any more "faithful" to literature than any other approach. They are simply more dependent on the frame projected by literature and are "faithful" or subservient to the devices and commentary within individual texts that delineate an inside and outside of the text. Formalist theories thus tend to ignore the paradoxical status of the frame—even one projected by the literary text itself—and refuse to make the frame work except as a barrier between literature and its contexts. Passage from inside-out and outside-in is prohibited—if for no other reason than that it interrupts and complicates the process of self-reflection and, thus, the mastery the specific literary text has over itself.

Perhaps the most complex and interesting examples from Derrida's work of his analysis of the impact of the problem of the frame in the relation of theory to literature are to be found in his readings of psychoanalytical texts. And, for reasons that will soon become clear, the question of self-reflexivity is central to his discussion of these texts. Derrida shows how psychoanalysis, like all other forms of theory, imposes a frame around literature—but only after it has, in some sense, acknowledged the priority of literature and let itself, at least in part, be led outside itself, beyond its boundaries, by certain

145

literary texts. Derrida will focus on the place of literature in psychoanalysis in order to force open the frame that psychoanalysis ultimately encloses literature (and itself) within; but he will do this by using critical weapons supplied by psychoanalysis itself. Thus, in his work, it is not a question of choosing literature over psychoanalysis or psychoanalysis over literature, but of making the one work on and transform the other, across the frames separating them from and linking them to each other.

It is, of course, well known that in numerous places in his work, Freud evokes "the poets" as his predecessors and the supreme authorities on truths that psychoanalysis is just belatedly discovering (and sometimes not yet able to prove scientifically)—truths that the poets, however, "always knew." Throughout his work, a certain literature—that is, myth, drama, poetry, or fiction—serves as the model for psychoanalysis itself: it already contains the truths psychoanalysis is trying to discover and even, at times, dramatically figures the process of analysis needed to uncover these truths. Freud, in this way, inscribes psychoanalysis and certain of its truths within the frame of literature and relies on literature's authority (and assumed universality) to support psychoanalysis.

But there are other instances when the analyst (theorist), who comes after the poet just as the adult comes after the child,[8] appears to have an advantage over him: the advantage of analysis over intuition. In these instances, Freud obviously puts the poet or artist in his place, usually only after having declared the great respect he has for his "art." Psychoanalysis, by explaining the sense of the "play" of the artist in terms of the child and determining in this way the ultimate context of all "play," imposes a frame on literature that is, at least in part, a frame literature has created for itself through its "play." The framed entity (psychoanalysis) frames the framing entity (literature) and is framed in turn by it. The authority of psychoanalysis demands that literature have authority over it so that it can then have authority over that authority. Within the field of psychoanalysis itself, this results in a fierce and endless struggle between psychoanalytical theory and literature for territory and domination.[9]

Throughout his work, Freud characteristically follows the lead of poets and tries to achieve "scientifically" what they have intuitively grasped through their imagination. Quotations from literature repeatedly fill in the spaces that science and his own experience leave blank. At the beginnings and ends of chapters, at crucial moments of his argument and narrative, whenever science, history, logic, reason, and experience all come up short, the authority of literature and the authority of myth (the literature of the collectivity) are called upon to support the speculations of the analyst. Freud does not bring literature into his discussion to resolve the problems that the various modes of theorizing are unable to resolve. Rather, he brings in literature to make it possible to continue to speculate, to offer hypotheses, to suppose things to be a certain way, when—because of inconclusive or contradictory evidence—one cannot *know* or *prove* they are that way. In other words, "the poets" make it possible to take positions (perhaps in an "athetic" way)[10]— no matter how tenuous or uncertain they may be, no matter how often the positions have to be changed—on questions that no philosophical, scientific, or political theory has succeeded in answering conclusively.

In general, the function of "poetry" is to be already at the origin and end of the difficult journey on which Freud takes his readers and for which he apologizes "for not having been a more skillful guide and for not having spared them empty stretches of road and toublesome *détours*." "There is no doubt," Freud also admits, "that it could have been done better" (*Civilization and its Discontents, S.E.,* v. 21, 134). Without the aid of poets, however, the road would have even been more troublesome and the journey truly endless with no "sigh of relief" possible when the end is finally in sight: "And we may well heave a sigh of relief at the thought that it is nevertheless vouchsafed to a few to salvage without effort from the whirlpool of their own feelings the deepest truths, towards which the rest of us have to find our way through tormenting uncertainty and with restless groping" (*S.E.,* v. 21, 133). In this context, literature and the truths revealed in it serve as the "destination" of psychoanalysis. Effortlessly, from the depths of their own feelings, poets express the truths psychoanalysts can only hope, with great uncertainty and torment, to stumble onto and make their own.

This is undoubtedly a difficult position for any "science" to be in. Even if uncertainty and restless groping might be considered one way to approach the truth, a more direct path with fewer detours, a path that was more psychoanalytical in form and content—assuming that something like a psychoanalytical specificity without relation to the poetic or the literary could be determined—would have provided a better defense of psychoanalysis.[11] The problem is that it simply was not available for the study of the "objects," drives, and principles psychoanalysis proposes to determine, isolate, and study. The ungrounded hypotheses, speculations, suppositions, detours, and misdirections characteristic of this text, and perhaps of the psychoanalytical journey in general, are all necessary and inevitable—given the elusive and deceptive, or, as Samuel Weber characterizes it, the dislocated and dislocating, the disfigured and disfiguring nature of its principle object, the unconscious.[12]

As if to keep dislocation and disfiguration within potentially manageable, "scientific" limits, Freud assigns them a location in literature, a location where they seem to be framed (by the "art" of the poet) and manageable, where the truths and objects they locate and figure through dislocation and defiguration are still kept intact. In such instances, critical investigation in Freud stops here—in literature, within a frame that encloses the truths of psychoanalysis and that psychoanalysis recognizes in order, in its turn, to be better able to enclose. Because Freud repeatedly pulls back from critically investigating the frame provided by literature—that is, the specific characteristics of the "art" of the poets which provides the context for the truth of psychoanalysis—it remains one of the principal limitations of all applications of psychoanalysis to literature and all "returns to Freud" in which literature and/or lanaguage play(s) an important role.

The most important of these "returns to Freud" is undoubtedly that of Jacques Lacan. In his analysis of Poe's "The Purloined Letter," which is part of his general rectification and return to the letter of the Freudian text and "its truth," Lacan finds it "convenient" to leave Freud's text and take a detour through a "fiction" in order, all the better, to return to Freud. He even gives "'The Purloined Letter' the privilege of opening" his *Ecrits* (Paris: Seuil, 1966) "despite its diachrony" (9)—that is, despite the fact that, chronologically, his seminar on Poe's text would have to be placed somewhere in the middle of the collection. He is, in this sense, in approximately the same position as Freud in relation to literary texts and poets or writers of fiction. But coming after Freud, he seems to have an advantage over him. For Poe's fiction is treated by Lacan as an illustration of a truth that he now can call "Freudian." Thus Lacan, in a sense, completes the journey from psychoanalysis through literature back to psychoanalysis, closing the frame around literature and usurping the critical power and "truth" psychoanalysis projects onto literature. In spite of Barbara Johnson's ingenious efforts (in a text that has much to say about frames[13]) to argue the contrary, it seems impossible to deny this aspect of Lacan's text: its identification of Poe's text with "Freudian truth" and its attempt to situate itself within the frame provided by this truth. Through a masterful reading of Poe's text and the problem of rivalry and mastery contained within it, Lacan's project is clearly to return this text to Freud and psychoanalysis, to make its truth a Lacanian-Freudian truth.

It is precisely the authority and frame of Lacanian psychoanalysis that Derrida questions in "Le facteur de la vérité."[14] In the process of doing so, it might at first seem that Derrida simply reverses the framing and the framed entities and the hierarchy between them—that is, that he privileges Poe's text, and perhaps even literature in general, in terms of their power to resist and exceed the frame psychoanalysis, or any other theory, would impose on them. Derrida does use a certain literature to undermine the frame and authority of psychoanalysis—especially Lacanian psychoanalysis—but this reversal is only a moment of a more complicated critical strategy, and not an end in itself. The trump cards Derrida uses in this struggle may be cards that are often associated with literature. But they are not necessarily only literature's to use, or even specifically literary in nature. The question that needs to be asked is not just what happens to psychoanalysis in this struggle of powers (Derrida and Lacan, literature and psychoanalysis), but, also, what happens to literature? Does it come out of the struggle with no wounds? does

148

its frame remain intact? Is literature really the frame within which Derrida situates his critique of Lacan and the end towards which his critique is oriented?

Derrida begins his essay by focusing on the claims of psychoanalysis to universality, claims made evident in the manner in which psychoanalysis projects and thus finds itself, that is, finds confirmation of itself, everywhere. According to Derrida, it does this without seriously investigating the effects on it of the very contexts in which it finds itself; these are the effects he proposes to analyze:

> Where then? Where does psychoanalysis, already, always, find itself? That in which it is found, if it is found, let us call it text. Not only for the purpose of recalling that the theoretical and practical inscription of psychoanalysis (in the text as "language," "writing," "culture," "mythology," "history of religion, of philosophy, literature, science, medicine," etc., in the text as an "historical," "economic," "political" realm, a field of "drives," etc., in the heterogeneous and conflictual fabric of difference, defined elsewhere as *general text*—and without boundaries) must have effects that have to be taken into account. But also for the purpose of defining the space of a particular question. ("The Purveyor of Truth," 31–32, t.m.)

No context, literature included, Derrida insists, can be considered the original, or dominant, or most extensive field, the field of all fields. The "general text without boundaries" far exceeds and precedes the division into fields, thus making all boundaries—those each field assigns itself or has assigned to it— appear relative and secondary. Given the characteristics of the "general text," the framing of any field by another—whether, for example, literature by psychoanalysis or psychoanalysis by literature—can never be considered conclusive.

Derrida finds evidence in Lacan's reading of Poe (and in psychoanalysis in general) of a repeated neutralization not only of the literary, but also of the historical, philosophical, and political[15] contexts of psychoanalysis itself. In order to dramatize the effects of such neutralization, he focuses on Lacan's use of Poe's text and Freud's use of similar literary texts. Literature is here being used, he says, not only to stage psychoanalytical truth for the benefit of psychoanalysis, but also to stage the process of analysis used by the psychoanalyst (or any other theoretician bent on discovering the truth of the text) to decipher the truth. In such a situation, the literary text is clearly one step ahead of the psychoanalyst-theorist, lying in wait of the theorist as if to entrap him:

> What happens in the psychoanalytical deciphering of a text when the

149

deciphered (text) already explains itself? When it reveals a great deal more than the deciphering text (a debt acknowledged more than once by Freud)? And above all, when it inscribes in itself *in addition* the scene of deciphering? When it deploys more force in its staging and derives [diverts] the analytical process down to the last word, for example, the truth? . . . But the truth, is it an example? ("The Purveyor of Truth," 32, t.m.)

What happens is that such literary texts—but are they simply and exclusively literary?—are taken as authorities; they have on their side the powers of self-reflexivity, and, some would even say, self-deconstruction or auto-(psycho)analysis. Nothing can be done to them that they either have not already done to themselves or that they have not anticipated will be done to them. No truth can be found in them that they have not already explicitly staged, whose discovery they have not already thematized and dramatized—perhaps only all the better to undermine or deconstruct it.

The self-reflexive text thus lays a trap for everyone and everything, for all theoretical discourses that attempt to penetrate, decipher, enclose, and master it. Because the self-reflexive staging process is displayed and presented as being primary, everything else is dependent on it. Thus, psychoanalysis can only find here what the text—seemingly in full control of itself, its frame, and its staging powers—lets it find. And it can only find what it finds in the way the text allows it to find it. The frame of the literary text, in these instances, seems inviolable and its authority unquestionable, its self-reflexivity, total and pure. A restrictive self-reflexivity of this type could even be considered as the chief characteristic of the most prevalent form of contemporary literary–formalist dogmatism: when the powers of the literary text are such that they constitute the text as self-constituting and all-encompassing (as concerns any theory of the text), then literature has become the frame of all frames and theory has been relegated to the subsurvient role of reflecting and repeating literature's truths from outside its frame.

Lacan (and Freud before him), by choosing self-reflexive texts to serve as examples of psychoanalytical truth—that is, by choosing to locate psychoanalysis within the frame these texts construct—reveal that these texts possess a critical advantage and power over psychoanalysis. But is Derrida claiming more than this in his critique of Lacan? Is he not making, in his turn, claims about the ultimate authority and inclusiveness of a certain form of literature that is capable of such staging, and about the authority of all literature when it is defined as the self-reflexive staging of itself? Is he even claiming that the sense and truth of literature is to be found in the staging process itself—which would then be taken as a process or technique of framing that is prior to, and that encompasses, all others? This could be argued only if self-reflexivity constituted for Derrida an effective means of framing,

150

of keeping the outside and inside clearly distinguished and separated from each other. Self-reflexivity in his analysis, however, has decidedly different, nondogmatic effects as concerns both psychoanalysis and literature.

When a literary text situates within itself the analytical scene of deciphering, when it highlights the process of the production or discovery of meaning, truth, or even form, Derrida argues that it is, in fact, situating the production, investigation, and discovery of the truth—not just within itself, but also within a long and complicated historical-intertextual process that no historical moment and no single text dominates or frames. This situation can be considered no more typical of literature than of history or philosophy or anything else, because it is a fundamental possibility of the text in general: "This overrun does not express the mastery of an author, or even less, the meaning of fiction. It would rather be the regular effect of an energetic framework. Truth would play a part in it: extracted by the philosopher or analyst from within a more powerful functioning" ("The Purveyor of Truth," 33, t.m.). Literary theory— when it attempts to make literature into the master term of such a process, when it equates the process with literature and finds itself and its truth in it—performs the same reduction that, Derrida claims, the analyst performs when he searches for the truth of psychoanalysis in literature. It extracts, from within a complicated intertextual and intercontextual network, one of the forces inscribed there and it resolves the conflict of forces and contexts making up this network in the name of one of the forces and contexts: literature. Again, it is not a question of choosing between literature and truth, fiction and psychoanalysis, text and theory; it is, rather, a question of accounting for the "overrun" of one into the other.

In discussing Freud's analysis of dreams of nudity in *The Interpretation of Dreams,* Derrida shows how the mode of analysis used by Freud—the penetration of the veils or disguises of various fictions in order to discover the truth in its unveiled state, the reduction of texts to their "naked truth, but also to truth as nakedness" (34)—has already been thematized and performed by the fictions on themselves. In this case, the text Freud refers to is "The Emperor's New Clothes:"

> If we take into account the more than metaphorical equation of veil, text, and fabric, Andersen's text has the text as its theme, more precisely, the determination of the text as a veil within the space of truth, the reduction of the text to a movement of *aletheia.* It stages Freud's text when he explains to us that the text, e.g. that of the fairy tale, is an *Einkleidung* of the nakedness of the dream of nakedness. What Freud states about secondary revision (Freud's explaining text) is already staged and represented in advance in the explained text (Andersen's fairy tale). This text *also* described the analytical scene, the position of the analyst, the forms of his discourse, the metaphorico-

151

conceptual structures of what he is looking for and what he finds. One text is located [finds itself] in the other. Is there no difference between the two texts? Yes, of course, there are many, many differences. But their co-implication is undoubtedly more complex than one would think. (37–38, t.m.)

The argument that there is a fundamental co-implication of the theoretical and fictional texts, that each frames and is framed by the other, is a comment not only on truth (whether psychoanalytical, philosophical, historical, etc.), but also on fiction. It implies that fiction is never a simple antidote for the truth, that it does not exist in and by itself as its own truth simply because it admits or stages its own fictiveness, because it appears to frame itself and all interpretations of it within itself.

The overlapping of the two realms, the overrun of fiction and truth indicates for Derrida that the frame of fiction, even one put into place through a process of self-reflexivity, is open. This does not mean, however, that it should be ignored. By ignoring and neutralizing the effects of the general narrator in "The Purloined Letter," Derrida argues, Lacan reduces seriously the complexity of Poe's fiction:

> We are faced with a problem of framing, of bordering or delimiting which demands an absolutely precise analysis if the effects of fiction are to become evident. . . . There is an invisible but structurally irreducible frame around the narration . . . and such complication suffices to point out everything that is misunderstood about the structure of the text once the frame is ignored. . . . Missing here is an elaboration of the problem of the frame, the signature, and the *parergon.* This lack makes it possible for the scene of the signifier to be reconstructed as a signified, . . . writing as the written, the text as discourse. (52–53, t.m.)

Lacan's reduction of the process of narration and his failure to elaborate or even recognize the complex process of framing in Poe's text limits the scope of his reading and its theoretical implications. But if this were all that was at stake in Derrida's critique, analysts might rightfully question if this had any significant bearing on psychoanalysis itself. Derrida's argument is, however, that the reduction of the narrative frame has direct effects on Lacan's theoretical position within psychoanalysis and cannot be separated from it.

In Derrida's reading, Lacan's reduction of the process of narration corresponds to a triangularization of the analytical scene extracted from Poe's fiction. This triangularization (or Oedipalization) constitutes, for Derrida, an indication of the dogmatic characteristics of Lacanian psychoanalysis in general—and not just in terms of its relation to literature: "Not taking this complication into account is no fault of 'formalist' literary criticism, but rather the operation of a psychoanalyst-semanticist. . . . In framing in such a violent fashion, in cutting the narrated figure itself off from a fourth side in order to see only triangles in the text, a certain complication, which is indicated in the scene of writing and perhaps Oedipal in nature, is avoided" (54, t.m.). In this instance, the reduction of the narrative frame and the rigidity of a theoretical position are interdependent.

As Barbara Johnson correctly points out, however, Derrida's principal criticism of Lacan is not just that he doesn't respect the frame of Poe's fiction and imposes, instead, a rigid triangular-Oedipal frame around it. More importantly, he criticizes Lacan for not taking into account the "textual drifting" that no frame can enclose: "Lacan has eliminated not the frame but the unframability of the literary text" ("The Frame of Reference," 481). Or, as Derrida puts it, "Our purpose is not to prove that 'The Purloined Letter' functions within a frame . . . but to prove that the structure of the effects of framing is such that no totalization of the border is even possible. Frames are always framed: therefore, framed by a piece of their content. Pieces without a whole, 'divisions' without totality" ("The Purveyor of Truth," 99, t.m.). The place of theory (not just psychoanalysis but any theory) in relation to such a situation cannot be fixed. The "paradoxes of parergonal logic," as Derrida calls them, prevent the theorist or critic from occupying a secure position on either side of the frame—which is what he sees Lacan doing in his text: attempting to dominate Poe's text from a metalinguistic position outside the frame, Lacan has, following indications the text itself gives, imposed on it.

For Derrida, Poe's fiction as fiction is not only situated just outside the frame imposed on it by psychoanalysis, but also outside the frame it imposes on itself: "The rest, the remnant, would be 'the Purloined Letter,' the text that bears this title, and whose place . . . is not where one was expecting to find it, in the enclosed content of the 'real drama' or in the hidden and sealed interior of Poe's story, but in and as the open letter, the very open letter, which fiction is" (64). Thus, by having a frame imposed on it—even one that it seems to project itself—a fiction does not ensure its integrity, but is displaced outside its own frame by the framing process itself.

The paradoxes of parergonal logic, paradoxes Derrida reveals at the basis of Lacan's attempt to frame Poe's text, have unsettling implications—not just for literature and literary theory, but even for theories not specifically "literary" in form or intent.[16] For, no determined logic or theoretical system can be relied on with any certainty to deal effectively with the question of the frame—even though a critical investigation of logic and theory might very well be the only way to approach such a question without predetermining the answers one gives it. Not only theory, then, needs the constant and rigorous investigation and displacement of its frame in order to remain alive and critical, but literature does as well.

153

In Derrida's work, the critical investigation of the question of the specificity and integrity of art or literature leads to the displacement of the frame separating the "inside" of art and literature from the "outside," as well as to the displacement of the theories dependent on such frames. It could be argued that Derrida's pursuit of the *question* of aesthetic or literary specificity *as a question* holds a significant place in his overall critical strategy and in the displacement and "mobilization" of theory—not because art and literature have a specificity that can be used "against" theory, but because their specificity is a fundamental issue for art and literature and the theories that strive to account for them: precisely because art and literature cannot be enclosed in any frame and reduced to what is specific to them, and because theory cannot, therefore, be kept "outside."

CHAPTER SEVEN
THE AESTHETIC AND THE POLITICAL

L Y O T A R D

With the sublime, Kant advances very far into the parathetical in such a way that the solution to the aesthetic antinomy appears more difficult in the sublime than in the beautiful.

The *Begebenheit* that marks what has been labeled postmodernity to designate our era . . . is the feeling of a fission of this enormous, deliberative political core. . . . [The *Begebenheit*] which we have to consider, as philosophers and moral political thinkers, and which is in no way homologous to the enthusiasm of 1789 (because it is not aroused by the Idea of an end but by the Idea of several ends or even by the Ideas of heterogeneous ends), this *Begebenheit* of our era, then, would induce a new kind of sublime, even more paradoxical than that of enthusiasm.
—Jean-François Lyotard, *L'enthousiasme*

1. The Rules of the Game

If, for Hegel, art is "a thing of the past,"[1] Lyotard's notions of postmodern and avant-garde art make art for him always a "thing" of the future. Hegel and an entire philosophical tradition claim to *know* what art is and by knowing what it is to put it behind philosophy or under its domain. It is precisely this *knowledge* that is in question in any approach to art that could be considered paraesthetic. Lyotard insists that knowledge must be suspended as concerns art—for what art is depends on the experiments *to be* performed and the forms *to be* invented, rather than in what has already been formed or performed. The importance of the avant-garde for Lyotard is that it continually

155

puts into question the art we already know (or think we know) by producing forms and constructs that force us to ask whether they can be considered to be taken as art and whether, therefore, we really do know what art is and whether we ever shall know. The avant-garde, for Lyotard, always gives to the question "Do we know what art is?" the response "Not yet."

In "Answering the Question: What is Postmodernism?" Lyotard character-izes the postmodern artist and writer as "working without rules in order to formulate the rules of what *will have been done*. . . . *Post modern* would have to be understood according to the paradox of the future (*post*) anterior (*modo*)."[2] The future anterior in which Lyotard situates postmodern art in-dicates that, for him, one of the primary functions of art is to keep the knowl-edge we have of it from ever being actual—either a present knowledge or one anticipated in a future that will some day constitute the present. When art is known or knowable, it no longer is art, but has become a category of knowledge. Lyotard's entire critical project rests, to a very large extent, on keeping knowledge and the aesthetic as distinct categories that can be linked to each other only across the irreducible gap which separates them. For Lyotard, as long as art remains in some sense "postmodern," it will never be completely "of the past."[3]

Not knowing what art is means not knowing its rules. And yet, throughout his work, Lyotard has insisted on the importance of rules—for without rules there is no art. For him, what separates the "game of art" from the "game of knowledge" is, primarily, the different set of rules governing each. This con-tradiction between the knowledge of the rules necessary to distinguish art and knowledge and the assertion that a knowledge of art (and thus of its rules) constitutes a destruction of art is, in fact, one of the most difficult and perplexing aspects of Lyotard's approach to art. His own experimentation in his most recent work with different critical strategies reflects the complexity of the problem of how to establish and maintain the distinctions among the various categories, genres, and language games (and thus defend the spec-ificity of art and other fields), without, in the same process, defining the specific nature or the rules governing art and making art simply another object *of* knowledge.

It is certainly easier to proclaim that art cannot be known than to develop strategies for dealing with art, strategies that do not assume or imply such knowledge. In fact, knowledge of some sort is undoubtedly always implied by any strategy—no matter how critical it is of the limitations of knowledge. The difference between a traditional theory or philosophy of art and an ex-perimental critical method like Lyotard's (which frequently changes strate-gies) is that the latter, like experimental art, is never satisfied with the knowl-edge that it cannot help but project; it is obliged to look constantly for alternative approaches to art, for different ways of categorizing art, and new rules for playing a constantly changing game. If a critical strategy is to maintain the indeterminacy of art, it cannot itself be determined by exterior forces and theories; it must attempt to ensure its *own* indeterminacy—at least up to a point.

In an attempt to achieve and maintain an indeterminacy of critical strategy, Lyotard has experimented in recent years with various terms as possible starting points for critical discourse and as weapons in its attack against theoretical dogmatism. As in *Discours, figure,* he seeks to develop a critical discourse that is "free" of metaphysical implications, that is not determined by ideology, and, thus, that is as *critical* as art is claimed to be. But rather than argue that discourse approximates art when its regulation of negation and meaning is disrupted by figural language and discontinuous spatialization (as he did in the first half of *Discours, figure*), Lyotard now attempts to reduce discourse as much as possible—to the point where it is not yet fixed or determined by anything other than the way it functions on its own and determines the relations of its various parts. This self-regulation of its own internal relations is what he calls the pragmatics of discourse. In a certain sense, his aim is to empty critical discourse of all "exterior" content and determination and have it approximate the separation or distance from knowledge he considers all true (that is, experimental) art to establish; only in this way can discourse be considered self-determining and critical. For Lyotard, critical discourse, like art, has, ultimately, less to do with knowledge per se than with the limitations of knowledge and the categories, genres, and language games that can be distinguished from those of knowledge.

This desire to free critical discourse from exterior determination may help explain the narratological strategies of *Instructions païennes* (Paris: Galilée, 1977), *The Postmodern Condition,* and *Au juste* (Paris: Christian Bourgois, 1979—translated by Wlad Godzich as *Just Gaming* [Minneapolis: University of Minnesota Press, 1985]). In these texts, Lyotard focuses on the plurality, heterogeneity, and self-regulating characteristics of what he calls "little narratives"—predominately the narratives of social exchange and daily life—as a way of combating all totalized philosophical systems (which he refers to as grand or metanarratives). In the same texts, he also invokes a Wittgensteinien notion of language games for approximately the same reasons: it provides the means for distinguishing among the various rules that make the "games" of science, art, politics, etc. possible and for maintaining the heterogeneity of the discursive universe. His insistence on the positive critical value of Kant's tripartite division of the faculties in *Just Gaming* and *Le différend* (Paris: Minuit, 1983) has the same critical ends in view. By separating the faculty of judgment from those of understanding and will, Lyotard argues that Kant frees judgment from determination by either of the other two faculties and analyzes the conditions of self-determination in general. Heterogeneity among the faculties is, thus, guaranteed when no one faculty determines the other two.

157

In much the same vein, in *Le différend* Lyotard postulates a notion of the phrase which, he claims, has neither a philosophical nor a linguistic definition and is thus a neutral, self-presupposing entity, as empty of content and philosophical-ideological implications as possible. The phrase is for him what I would call "pre-categorical": it determines all of the categories in which it can be placed, but is not determined by any one of them in particular. In each of these works, then, Lyotard seems to be in search of an absolutely minimal term—one that is not a concept and not even really a fixed entity, but, rather, a fundamental given that is not a category or genre itself but a mere difference between categories and genres. And it is certainly not inconsequential that the term of differentiation is constantly changing from work to work, that no one term is able to embody by itself the minimalism being sought.

In the *Postmodern Condition,* Lyotard opposes the heterogeneity of "little narratives" to the dogmatism of "grand narratives," whose reign he unequivocally proclaims is over. No longer, asserts Lyotard, are the grand philosophical narratives considered as effective means of legitimating science, thought, and political action. Broadly speaking, the grand or metanarratives have, for him, the speculative or emancipatory form of systematic, totalizing philosophy and political theory and are called on to support science from the "outside," by legitimating its origins and ends. He considers the crisis in legitimation provoked by this disbelief in metanarratives basic to what he calls the postmodern condition: "Simplifying to the extreme, I define *postmodern* as incredulity toward metanarratives" (xxiv). A disbelief in metanarrative forces science to legitimate itself on its own terms (in terms of performativity) and also provokes an explosion of non-totalizable "little narratives"—the smaller and more diversified, in Lyotard's view, the better— whose conflictual multiplicity and heterogeneity resist all forms of totalization. Narrative, at least as long as it remains "little," is taken by Lyotard to be a kind of open, highly mobile form that, in each instance, determines on its own how the various elements it contains or refers to will be interrelated. The little narrative is, in this sense, a kind of "zero degree" of differentiating discourse—the form discourse takes to express diversity and unresolved conflict and, thus, resist homogenization.

There can be no general theory of little narratives because, Lyotard argues, they do not depend on any social, historical, or philosophical metanarrative for legitimation. They are constituted primarily in terms of their own pragmatics, that is, the complicated and mobile set of relations that exist among "narrator and what is narrated, narrator and listener (reader), and listener and the story being talked about by the narrator" (*Instructions païennes,* 16). Pragmatics focuses on the relations established within the narratives and ignores or underplays their "content" or context, except insomuch as it is an effect of the specific narrative relating it. In a manner similar to speech act theory, narrative pragmatics shifts the emphasis from the truth value of the narrative—that is, whether it represents accurately the truth of its referent— to its force of telling, its "dramatic" or performative effects.[4]

Because of the performative character of narrative for Lyotard—that is, because in the postmodern age there is no general context or universal mas- ter-narrative from which little narratives can draw their authority—each little narrative must be taken as the source of its own legitimacy. Lyotard considers the right to narration—what he calls "a force of narrating practically invin- cible in everyone" (*Instructions païennes,* 17)—to be the basic, "inalienable" right of alterity: that is, not the right of the individual subject to be and express him/herself, but rather the right of the other to be other, of the alien to differ from the norm. The invincibility of this force is used by him to challenge all systems and theories that would try to contain, repress, or even theorize the force of the other—that is, assign it a specific place within a metanarrative.

He has argued, for example, that the loss of credibility of the Marxist me- tanarrative is largely due to the unjust effects it has produced in every in- stance in which it has been executed completely (*Instructions,* 11)—the most evident of these injustices being the way it denies even the "heroes" of the Marxist narrative (that is, the workers who are also its addressees) the right to narration (23). Being denied narration is not just a metaphor for injustice for Lyotard, it is already a form of injustice itself.

The totalitarian state is, for him, one in which all narrative functions are fixed and assigned in advance and where all deviations from the master- narrative are immediately repressed:

> As a citizen of one of these regimes, you are taken at the same time
> for the co-author of its narrative, for the privileged listener, and for
> the perfect executor of the episodes that are assigned you. Your place
> is thus fixed in the three instances of the master-narrative and in all
> the details of your life. Your imagination as a narrator, listener or
> actor is completely blocked. . . . A mistake in execution, an error of
> listening, a lapsus of narration, and you are locked up. . . . You are
> forbidden narration. Such is devastation. (31–32)

The imposition of a master-narrative perpetuates injustice because it con- stitutes a denial of the imagination, a denial of the right to respond, to invent, to deviate from the norm—in other words, the right to little narratives that are rooted in difference rather than in the identity established by the grand narrative. In a certain sense, the totalitarian state is a radical extension and perverse application of the governing principles of all metanarratives: the assignment of all narrators, listeners, and actors to a fixed place and function; the universalization of a particular plot; the unification and totalization of a basically diversified and heterogeneous field. The master-narrative does not respect the differences and heterogeneity established by the individual pragmatics of little narratives and, thus, is unjust *in its very form.*

An insistence on pragmatics opens up a space of difference and heterogeneity within the narrative universe. But narrative does not consist only of the rules and formal relations established in each instance among narrative elements. In fact, here and elsewhere, Lyotard insists on the differences among the rules distinguishing various games—but he rarely, if ever, describes in any detail what the rules are. The rules of the game of narrative distinguish it *in principle* from other games. But there is obviously more to narrative than knowledge of its rules (or knowing that there are rules): there is even what could be called an "art" of narrative that no rules can explain. Lyotard uses the term "the faculty of narratives" (20), a "faculty" characterized by a "narrative imagination" (24). It is as if he were adding a fourth faculty to the three defined by Kant, with narrative being considered a form of imagination which also acts as a force of resistance within the social-political realm. Unauthorized narratives represent, for Lyotard, the possibility (and necessity) of alternative social configurations. They are a kind of "shadow of civil society made of distended circuits and improvised circulations" (33). Subversive in their pragmatics (and not necessarily in *what* they recount), these unofficial narratives do not provide an alternate picture of society, a view of what society should be (a way of determining the social that Lyotard always condemns). They *act* as open and flexible sets of relations not governed by any truth or rules other than their own. The "art of narrative" is, thus, fundamentally aesthetic and social at one and the same time.

Narrative imagination could be defined as the capacity to respond to any narrative with a counter-narrative, to occupy a different place than that assigned by any master-narrative, to improvise and deviate from the assigned plot. The faculty of narratives constitutes for Lyotard something like a faculty of the political in a critical sense—little narratives testifying to a political force of resistance, transformation, deviation. Lyotard makes them carry an incredibly heavy burden—the burden of political resistance and justice— totally disproportionate to their size. The smaller the narrative entity, it would appear, the more critical weight it can carry; the bigger the narrative, the more the weight of its content and its own structure contain, if not prohibit, diversity and critical alternatives.

On the one hand, the "little narrative" is, for Lyotard, a self-governing, self-generating, open, discursive form. Because it is determined solely by its own pragmatics, it represents the critical mode of the political. On the other, narrative is for him—at least in those texts that use a critical strategy indebted to narrative pragmatics—the principal critical mode of literature, inasmuch as the conflictual heterogeneity it is rooted in is as far removed from the supposed uniformity of knowledge as possible. "The narrative form, unlike the developed forms of the discourse of knowledge," claims Lyotard, "lends

160

itself to a great variety of language games. . . . The areas of competence whose criteria the narrative supplies or applies are thus tightly woven together in the web it forms" (*The Postmodern Condition,* 20). Behind this view of narrative as an *art* of combination lies a general view of literature as a heterogeneous mixture, a conflict of discourses and language games that no one set of rules can account for and no theory resolve. Lyotard's discussion of narrative—which is primarily directed at understanding the conditions of postmodern knowledge and raising the problems of legitimacy and social justice in a critical way—frequently drifts outside the scientific and social fields to where it confronts the problem of literature and art. This constant movement from pragmatics into aesthetics (or paraesthetics) constitutes an important component of his critical strategy—his way of connecting sociopolitical and philosophical issues to questions of art and literature without predetermining the responses to be given them.

Opposed to knowledge of the truth, literature is, for Lyotard, related to dialectics in the Aristotelian rather than Hegelian sense of the term:

> [Aristotle] opposed learned didactics to the art of discussion, where opinions confront one another, that is to say, where little narratives of common people enter into competition with each other. A literary work can give rise only to this dialectic. Only conceptual madmen can make of it material to be taught, that is theorized. . . . There is no literary theory because of a lack of literature that is teachable. (*Instructions,* 41)

Literary theory is an enterprise of "conceptual madmen" because it attempts to theorize, that is, explain and situate within a totalized master-narrative, what cannot be theorized in this way—what is, for Lyotard, clearly and categorically not a category of the theoretical.

Accusations, like those against conceptual madness, are certainly meant to be categorical and taken as a condemnation of any attempt to theorize (to "know") literature—that is, to forge a link between or to combine in any way two games (the theoretical and the literary), games Lyotard posits as being played by totally different rules. Samuel Weber considers such statements in *The Postmodern Condition* and *Just Gaming* to be the work of a "great prescriber" who insists that the purity and singularity of each game be respected in order to avoid the injustice inherent in the domination of one game by another. But, as Weber argues, the great prescriber cannot make such statements without promoting the "domination of the prescriptive" game over all others ("Afterword: Literature—Just Making It," in *Just Gaming,* 104). As Weber also points out, this is a way of *proscribing* "while obscuring the necessity for proscription," a way of making sure that "no game plays games with any other" (104–105). Do not play the game of knowledge with literature,

161

the "great prescriber-proscriber" seems to be saying, or you will be considered "mad" or, even worse, unjust.

This uncompromising position concerning language games constitutes what I would call Lyotard's pragmatic, categorical, or categorizing side—a side which, though certainly not a madness per se, could be considered just as restrictive as the conceptual madness it attempts to combat (at least it would be as restrictive if it were ever to be taken unproblematically, as a generalized prescription). But how can we take it literally, in Lyotard's own terms, when to do so is to promote the domination of the prescriptive game in an effort to do away with domination? And even if this were not the case, is it really possible to play all games by their rules? By what rules is the game of literature to be played, for example, if there is no theory of literature to make them known? How can we even be sure that there are rules if knowledge and theory are excluded from the game as forms of madness?[5]

The proscription not to confuse the various games, and especially, the game of literature and the game of justice with the game of knowledge, leads to an impasse. A strict interpretation of the rules of the game of game-playing makes it impossible to move beyond the isolated singularity of each game and play more complicated games whose rules overlap with each other or where an "ambivalence" exists in the rules themselves of any of the games (Weber, 113). The entire notion of language games (a notion which is based on the possibility of making clear distinctions among the various games), seems, if followed literally, to allow for no slippage between games and to exclude, as well, the possibility of games that do not fit into one category alone. As we have seen, Lyotard strenuously argues against such slippage throughout *The Postmodern Condition* and *Just Gaming* in order to preserve the heterogeneity of the discursive universe. The practice of producing and circulating discrete "little narratives" constructed in terms of their own rules—which are not authorized by the dominant master-narratives—is an important sign of the possibility of justice in the political realm, a justice of the heterogeneous.[6] At the same time, however, and without explicitly discussing the problems this raises for the "great prescriber," Lyotard makes the "art" of combining heterogeneous games the chief characteristic of literature in its "untheorizable," critical form.

Literature is not the only game that resists theorization, even if it is the most obvious one. Politics is also considered a game played outside the rules governing knowledge: "There is no political theory," Lyotard claims in *Instructions païennes,* "because politics is not didactic material" (41). The gaps, tensions, and conflicts that arise when one attempts to theorize what resists theorization are, in fact, important critical weapons against both abstract, dogmatic theorization, and, I would add, against equally abstract, dogmatic categorization. The fact that, for Lyotard, both literature and politics are situated outside the domain of theory and the way each could be said to "resist theory" should not, however, be considered proof that theory should be abandoned. On the contrary, they point, rather, to the need for a critical theory able to account for this resistance.

Literature and politics, precisely because they are not, for Lyotard, games of knowledge per se, indicate that the knowledge of games and of the distinctions among them is no guarantee that one will "play" them well or justly. It seems to me, however, impossible to conclude from this insufficiency that knowledge must be *excluded* from these forms of game-playing—as Lyotard at times argues. When one is "just gaming" or playing the game of the just, one is playing many games at once; no game of prescription or proscription can really determine that any game is just what it is prescribed to be. Is it really "just" or judicious to claim that one has to be mad to think that theory, even if it does not dominate all games, has an important role to play in (the) just playing (of) them? Is a notion of a language game or a pragmatics of narrative really sufficient to describe art or politics if neither really plays by a particular set of rules? Without the possibility of combining and transforming the rules, or inventing new rules, art and politics cannot be considered experimental or critical. On the contrary, they end up being determined by a formalist aesthetics, in the first case, or a fixed set of prescriptions or laws, in the second.

In Lyotard's work, the uncompromising, absolute proscription—made in the name of a notion of justice rooted in heterogeneity—not to mix up the various games is counterbalanced by the fact that he considers literature in general and narrative in particular to be *arts* of combination. This, in fact, constitutes their critical advantage for him over other games. He even asserts that the strategy of approaching discourse in terms of language games implies a notion of what he calls general literature:

> This implies that the task is one of multiplying and refining language games. I mean that, ultimately, what does this thesis lead to? To a literature, in the best sense of the term, as an enterprise of experimentation on language games, to a general literature if one can put it this way. (*Just Gaming,* 49)

All forms of combination, therefore, are not equal. Some destroy the singularity and heterogeneity of the various games, while others maintain it. What Lyotard undoubtedly considers mad in the project to make literature an object of theory is the belief that theory can ever regulate and totalize the radical and conflictual heterogeneity that, he argues, literature constitutes.

I would argue that in spite of what the proscription (not to combine or confuse the rules of separate games) seems to indicate, Lyotard's ultimate critical project is, itself, concerned with the impossible theorizing of the untheorizable, with linking and combining elements, games, faculties, etc. that are fundamentally (that is, categorically) incommensurable—without destroying their incommensurability. Such an "art" of linkage falls outside the domain of narrative pragmatics and the rules of language games per se. But its necessity is certainly felt in the fundamental heterogeneity each attests to, but leaves to the extra-pragmatic, not completely rule-governed powers of art and politics to deal with.

2. Phrasing the Political

Like little narratives and language games, Lyotard argues that the notion of phrases he proposes in *Le différend* has the critical advantage of being "immediately presupposed (to doubt that one is phrasing is in any case to phrase, to be silent is to phrase)" (*Le différend*, 9). This is to say that any definition or description of a phrase must necessarily be given in a phrase. And to claim that something exists before or outside of the universe of phrases, "your phrase presents it. It presents it as being there before any phrase" (50). To deny the existence of phrases is also to phrase denial: "There is no phrase is a phrase" (101). Phrases do not constitute one genre or category of discourse, however, as is the case of narrative. They cut across the various categories and genres: thus their advantage over narrative. They also do not imply a subject-player who exists outside or prior to the universe of language games in order to play them (as Wittgenstein's notion does). Rather, they situate all "players," all addressees, all referents, within the universe they present. The phrase is, for Lyotard, what little narratives and language games were also supposed to be: a minimal, self-presupposing, "purely analytical" entity.

The phrase could be considered the smallest of discursive units, too small to fit into any one category or genre, too diversified to be contained by any linguistic definition. To define what a phrase is would be to situate it in terms of one of its *régimes*—to reason, know, describe, tell, question, show, command, etc. (10)—at the expense of its place in others. Thus, Lyotard's strategy is to avoid defining what the phrase is: "There is no definition of a phrase because every attempt of this sort leads to the concept of a well-formed totality. One must say rather that definition is a family of phrases, and its demand for the 'well-formed' corresponds to the universe it presents and varies according to whether the definition is logical, grammatical, linguistic or analytical."[7] There is, thus, no need for a "great prescriber or proscriber" when it comes to phrases—for heterogeneity and singularity seem guaranteed without him.

Lyotard's focus on the phrase brings to the fore the problem of linkage. That the relations between phrases is a central problem in *Le différend* indicates the shift in emphasis from *The Postmodern Condition* and *Just Gaming* (where the force of the prescription to distinguish among language games obscured, somewhat, the fundamental importance of the problem of linkage among games and categories). Given a phrase, and it is given, for Lyotard, that a phrase is always given, that no phrase is the first or the last phrase— "for a phrase to be the last phrase, another phrase is necessary to declare this, and thus it is not the last one" (27)—the most fundamental question is how to respond to, or link up with, the given phrase. The possibilities are, at least in principle, infinite.

Lyotard's strategy in *Le différend* remains, if not formalist, then, at least, to a great extent, logical or analytical—that is, rule-bound—in its concern for the differentiation of categories and the possible rules of linkage. Critical philosophy is still, for Lyotard, first and foremost the art of making distinctions. He relies on those philosophers (mainly Aristotle, Kant, and Wittgenstein) who draw distinctions among territories, genres of discourse, families of phrases, faculties, etc., and who by doing so set the stage for the postmodern context in which he situates his own work. "The free examination of phrases leads to the (critical) dissociation of their *régimes* (the separation of the faculties in Kant, the disentanglement of language games in Wittgenstein). They prepare the way for the dispersion (diaspora, writes Kant) that . . . forms our own context" (12). What seems to matter, above all, is that distinctions are established, whatever their nature might be.

Lyotard could perhaps be criticized, therefore, for initially accepting such distinctions and categories at face value and for not questioning the philosophical assumptions that, in each case, support even the "freest" examination of phrases and produce distinctions on one level or in one area rather than in another—in other words, that decide before the fact where differences lie and what their nature is.[8] But it could also be argued that his use of such categories is always strategic, and that by shifting from one set of categories and distinctions to another he is in fact pluralizing the concept of language behind each of them and refusing to accept one version of language over another as definitive or determining. Language consists of an unresolvable plurality and conflict of languages for Lyotard; the phrase is, above all, no matter its conceptual limitations, an indication of this heterogeneity. The most critical level of language is, thus, for him not "a deeper ground of language" (as it is, for example, for Heidegger), but the surface of language. In other words, Lyotard's strategy consists in the infinite deferral of the question of the ultimate ground of language by assuming not what language is, but only, regardless how language is defined, that there are phrases.

Lyotard is interested primarily in the effects of distinguishing or categorizing. The more fundamental the category and the greater the dispersion it produces the more critical he would consider it to be. But after the dispersion produced by the categories has been affirmed and the problem of linkage raised, he challenges and parts company with the presuppositions underlying the various sets of categories and their metaphysical and teleological implications. He criticizes, for example, "the debt to anthropomorphism which encumbers the heritage" of Kant and Wittgenstein (12). But this does not stop him from using, for his own purposes, the categories and distinctions which are also a part of that heritage. More precisely, in the case of Kant, he opposes the teleology that directs the tripartite division of the faculties towards a unqiue end, but he insists on the critical significance of that same division when it is oriented in his own work towards a plurality of ends.

Lyotard's strategy, then, is not to challenge formalist or analytical categories on the level of the distinctions they make, but, rather, to challenge them only when the distinctions are unified or subsumed into a unique system or in terms of a general end. He intervenes critically in the systems of all of the philosophers whose categories he uses precisely at the moment in their work when dispersion is synthesized; his intervention, in each case, constitutes an attempt to maintain dispersion at all costs against the particular end imposed by the system. His philosophy of phrases could, in this sense, be considered a "patchwork" of various philosophies whose categories it uses but whose ends it disputes. Like his notions of little narratives and a general literature, his philosophy of phrases is an art of combination that refuses to respect only one set of rules or play only one game at a time.

How to respond to a phrase, how to link one phrase with another, is always matter for dispute—for there are no general rules determining how links are to be made. The only necessity, argues Lyotard, is linkage itself: "That there not be a phrase is impossible. It is rather: *And a phrase* is necessary. It is necessary to link [Il faut enchâiner]. This is not an obligation, un *Sollen*, but a necessity, a *Müssen.* To link is necessary, how to link is not" (103). The choice, then, of one response, one linkage, over all the other possibilities, does not resolve the question of linkage, but reopens it; not only must another phrase follow every phrase, but there remains the problem of all the un-phrased phrases that underlie what is actually phrased. On the most fundamental level and in terms of the slightest of relations, then, there is dispute, "dissensus," a *différend*. If "it is impossible for there not to be a phrase," it is also impossible for there to be an end to dispute, given the nature of linkage. The principle of disputation, of *dissensus,* is located on too basic a level ever to be completely overcome; to overcome it would be to give the last phrase and terminate linkage—both of which are, by definition, impossible.

The phrase and the problem of linkage that Lyotard associates with it, constitute not just formal problems, however. On a very basic level, he claims, they are also political issues: "The linkage of one phrase with another is problematic, and this problem is politics" (11). If linkage is political, it is not in the usual sense of politics on the grand scale—the politics of parties, groups, classes, ideological conflicts, economic interests, etc.—but on the smallest of scales. Without denying the impact of politics on the grand scale, Lyotard's philosophy of phrases recasts such a politics in order to undermine

those political philosophies which claim that politics constitutes the totality—the most general category under which all other categories can be subsumed or the most fundamental category from which all others can be
derived.

Lyotard's philosophy of phrases has another political purpose: to diversify
the question of what is political by considering even the least significant link
of one phrase with another to be political—that is, to attest to the multiplicity
underlying any linkage and the possibility of alternative links to any phrase:

> If politics were a genre and if this genre had the pretention of at-
> tributing to itself a supreme status, then it would be quite easy to
> show its vanity. But politics is the threat of the *différend*. It is not a
> genre but the multiplicity of genres, the diversity of ends, and above
> all the question of linkage. . . . Everything is political if politics is the
> possibility of the *différend* on the occasion of the slightest linkage.
> But politics is not everything if what is believed by this is that it is
> the genre that contains all genres. It is not *a* genre. (200–201)

This simultaneous extension and minimalization of the political—which radicalizes critical strategies that are already evident in *Instructions païennes,
The Postmodern Condition,* and *Just Gaming*—displaces politics from its sovereign position either above or below all other domains and makes the political the problem of relations, both among the various domains and within
each of them. The critical force of such a recasting or rephrasing, of course,
depends (at least in part) on how convincing are the links made between this
minimal level of the phrase and the historical-political on a larger scale, on
how effectively a philosophy of phrases reveals, not only the limitations, but
also the particular stakes of the historical-political in general.

As might be expected, given Lyotard's other work, art and literature have
an important role to play in rephrasing the political in this way. The aesthetic
and the political both have as their stakes the discovery of their stakes. They
have as their only rule the search for their rules, which, Lyotard insists, cannot
be thought to preexist their experimentation with rules but can only be discovered by means of it. Art (at least avant-garde, postmodern art) serves as
a kind of model for Lyotard's investigation of the political, because art is
considered by him to question continually its own foundations and stakes
and experiment with new strategies and forms without knowing in advance
exactly where they will lead:

> When Cézanne takes up his brush, the stakes of painting are ques-
> tioned; when Schönberg is before his piano, so are the stakes of music;
> when Joyce takes hold of his pen, those of literature. Not simply new
> strategies for "winning" are tried out, but the nature of "success" is

questioned. . . . Painting will be considered good (will have realized
its end, will have approached it) if it obliges its addressee to ask
himself what it consists of. (201)

If Lyotard considers art to have experimentation as its defining characteristic,
it is not experimentation for its own sake, but, rather, experimentation with
a particular (though undeterminable) orientation: that is, a form of experimentation whose aim is to question the very foundations of art.[9] In this sense,
art is considered to be a "genre" without a specific end, a genre whose end
is always in question and *to be* determined, never already determined. For
Lyotard, the political "genre" is also of the same undetermined nature. This
means that neither art nor politics is really a genre at all. Their boundaries
can never be conclusively delineated or fixed, the categories used to distinguish them from other genres can never be considered totally appropriate.

The aesthetic and the political are, thus, areas explicitly constituted and
dominated by unresolved *différends*—where the absence of a general rule
produces a continual questioning of, and experimentation with, rules and
forms, with no ultimate resolution possible. Lyotard describes the term *différend* in the following way:

Different from a litigation, a *différend* would be a case of conflict
between (at least) two parties that could not be resolved equitably
for lack of a rule of judgment applicable to the two modes of argumentation. That one is legitimate does not imply that the other is
not. If the same rule of judgment is applied to each in order to resolve
their *différend* as if it were a litigation, then one inflicts an injustice
[*un tort*] on one of them. . . . An injustice results from the fact that
the rules of the genre of discourse according to which one judges
are not those of the genre(s) of discourse being judged. . . . The title
of this book suggests . . . that a universal rule of judgment among
heterogeneous genres is in general lacking. (9)

What makes the problem of the *différend* especially central to the aesthetic
and the political—and we can now add the philosophical to this list, at least,
when it is critical rather than dogmatic or didactic—is that the heterogeneity
described as existing among different genres is found within each of them.
Each is a psuedo- or heterogeneous genre—what I would call parageneric—
in the sense that heterogeneity is basic to each. Any generic rule, no matter
how it is conceived, is insufficient for regulating their conflictual diversity;
when one is nonetheless applied, it inflicts an "injustice" on all the elements
of the field that cannot be fairly judged in terms of that rule.

Art, philosophy, and politics are linked, then, in their particular search—
and each search is particular, for were each identical to the others, then the

168

heterogeneity that distinguishes each pseudo-genre would be destroyed—to express *différends* while leaving them unresolved:

> The *différend* is the unstable state and instance of language in which something which ought to be able to be phrased cannot yet be phrased. This state requires silence, which is a negative phrase, but it also calls for phrases that are in principle still possible. . . . Much searching is necessary to find new rules for the formation and linkage of phrases capable of expressing the *différend* . . . if you do not want this *différend* to be immediately smothered within a litigation. . . . The stakes of a certain literature, philosophy, and perhaps politics, are to bear witness to *différends* by finding idioms for them. (29–30)

In this sense, the *différend* is, for Lyotard, the principle of differentiation and conflict on its most fundamental level, the minimal level of all minimalization and, thus, the one with the widest possible extension. Lyotard links literature, critical philosophy, and politics in the task of maintaining and finding ways to phrase *différends*, that is, the task of keeping the critical task unresolved. This is why consensus of any sort, whether "freely arrived at" or imposed, could be considered the principal obstacle to Lyotard's politics and aesthetics of *différends*.[10]

3. Auschwitz and the "Signs of History"

It is no exaggeration to say that, in spite of the emphasis he gives to rules and categories, Lyotard has never really liked playing by the rules. Rules, for him, are ultimately made to be broken, categories to be transgressed and combined with other categories—no matter how vehemently he argues at times that they must be respected. With the notion of the *différend*, he builds into the very recognition of and respect for rules and categories the problem of the conflict and dissension basic to them—in the sense that any application of a rule or delineation of a category rules out other rules and categories and, thus, provokes at least implicit dissent. In fact, in his recent work, the problem of justice is intimately connected to what now must be called the necessity of dissent and a sensitivity to what is ruled out when any rule is followed. Justice is less a function of respecting the singularity of each language game—as it was in *Just Gaming*—than in respecting and finding an idiom for what is ruled out in playing a game only by *its* rules.

Within each genre, there are elements that explicitly demand treatment in terms of a logic or rules different from those of the genre. Within the historical genre, for example, there are names of places where historical events occurred that signify much more than what occurred there, that signify in a way that no logic of the event could account for. The limit case of these names

169

is "Auschwitz," which, for Lyotard, following Adorno, testifies once and for all to the limitations of rational history. "Everything that is real is rational, everything that is rational is real: 'Auschwitz' refutes the speculative doctrine. At least this crime that is real . . . is not rational" (257). Or, as Adorno asserts in *Negative Dialectics* (translated by E.B. Ashton [New York: Continuum, 1983]): "After Auschwitz there is no word tinged from on high, not even a theological one, that has any rights unless it underwent a transformation" (367). In other words, for Adorno and Lyotard, "after Auschwitz," all discourse is delegitimized, all philosophical and historical claims to rationality are suspect. Auschwitz, a name that has a particular and horrible historical signification and determination, puts the entire historical genre into question.

To argue this, Lyotard claims that Adorno makes Auschwitz a model rather than an example, the illustration of an idea:

> The idea of a model corresponds to the reversal of the destiny of the dialectic: the model is the name of a kind of para-experience in which the dialectic meets a non-negatable negative and remains in the impossibility of redoubling it into a "result." A para-experience in which the wound to the spirit does not heal. . . . The model "Auschwitz" designates an "experience" of language which stops speculative discourse. The latter cannot go on "after Auschwitz." Here is a name "in" which speculative thought does not occur. It is thus not a name in the Hegelian sense, a figure of memory that assures the permanency of the referent and of its meanings when the spirit has destroyed its signs. It is a name without a speculative "name," which cannot be raised up into a concept. (*Le différend*, 133)

For Lyotard, the horrendous crime that the name Auschwitz evokes presents the problem of linkage in its most difficult and radical form. For if "it is necessary to link" one phrase with another, how is it possible to do so in terms of this impossible "para-experience of language?"

In terms of this extreme "model" or "para-experience," the rules no longer regulate, the categories and genres no longer separate and distinguish. For if there is a logical, analytical necessity to link one phrase with the next, this necessity has here become so problematical that it is experienced as an impossibility; it takes on the characteristics of a duty. We *must* (and no longer, it is necessary to) link phrases with this impossible name, precisely because it is impossible to do so. A logic of phrases has become an ethical obligation. Another logic is needed, suggests Lyotard, a logic that does not have a speculative result: "Because it has no speculative name does not mean that it is not necessary to speak of it. The question that 'Auschwitz' raises is that of the genre of discourse that will link up with 'Auschwitz.' If this genre is not speculative, what can it be? . . . Is it possible that another kind of phrase,

regulated by another logic, could occur 'after' the anonymity 'Auschwitz'"
(134–35)? If there are no general rules for linkage, here, discourse confronts
most directly the abyss underlying all linkage, the lack of solid ground or
necessity for one particular linkage rather than another. There is certainly
no need to add, especially in terms of Auschwitz, however, that it can never
be a question of "anything goes." The speculative genre, for example, no
longer works; in its inability to conceptualize Auschwitz and generate a "result" from this "experience," a general problem of knowledge is also raised:
Is Auschwitz only what can be *known* of it?

This is the most fundamental of all historical questions, because "knowledge" is, of course, not irrelevant to the question of the death camps—as
Claude Lanzmann's remarkable film *Shoah* so movingly demonstrates. (The
film also demonstrates that emotions are not irrelevant to knowledge either.)
The importance of knowing as much as possible about the camps is especially
evident at a time when the existence of death camps and the implementation
of the final solution is still being denied by a small group of revisionist historians—whatever their bad faith and reactionary political motivations might
be in doing so. As Pierre Vidal-Naquet argues in his "Un Eichmann de papier,"—and it is outrageous that such responses on this basic level still have
to be argued—the existence of the death camps has been abundantly proved
and verified by accepted historical procedures.[11] Lyotard wonders if a response such as Vidal-Naquet's (argued in the logic of the historian and no
matter how necessary) is adequate, if something more isn't at stake in the
various silences associated with "Auschwitz": the silence imposed on the
millions of victims who were exterminated, the silence which is also the
response of many survivors of the camps to the horror they lived through,
and a certain silence imposed on the historian by the enormity of the crime
and the incapacity of reason and logic to deal with it adequately, to have
exclusive domain over it. This is not the "silence of forgetting," insists Lyotard, but rather "a feeling"(91). It is through an interpretation of the role of
feeling in history that Lyotard attempts to challenge the limitations of the
historical field, to push history beyond itself, and to testify to the irresolv-
ability of *différends*.

Lyotard interprets the silence imposed by Auschwitz to be a "sign" in the
Kantian sense, a sign that something that should be phrased cannot be
phrased in the idioms of history:

> The silence that the crime of Auschwitz imposes on the historian is
> for everyday people a sign. Signs . . . are not referents to which ver-
> ifiable significations are attached under the cognitive *régime*. They
> indicate that something that should be able to be phrased cannot be
> in the accepted idioms. . . . The silence surrounding the phrase:
> *Auschwitz was the camp of annihilation* is not a state of soul; it is

171

the sign that something that is not phrased and that is not determined remains to be phrased. This sign brings about a linkage of phrases. The indetermination of meanings left unformulated, the annihilation of the means to determine them, the shadow of negation emptying reality out to the point of dissipating it, in one word, the injustice done to victims that condemns them to silence—it is this and not a state of soul that calls out to unknown phrases to link up with the name of Auschwitz. (91)

In one sense, this silence and the injustice it indicates are merely signs of the multiplicity of meanings not yet uncovered by the historian. In another and more radical sense, they indicate that historical means are necessary but not sufficient for the task of linkage. The feeling that there is something at stake in history besides knowledge opens the historical field up to linkages it would in itself exclude or at least devalue, to phrases that do not conform to the rules of historical verification.

Something will always remain to be phrased, and the historian cannot, Lyotard argues—and this is especially evident as concerns Auschwitz—remain indifferent to the silence that is a sign of all the phrases not phrased and never to be phrased. Lyotard insists that this silence should not be considered a wrong that can be rectified through litigation, no matter the nature of the court claiming authority in such matters—but a *différend* arising out of the enormity of the injustice perpetuated. The historian's obligation here is to listen to this silence and respond to it:

It is necessary that the historian break with the monopoly granted to the cognitive order of phrases over history and risk lending an ear to what is not presentable in the rules of knowledge. Every reality carries within it this demand insomuch as it carries within it the possibilities of unknown meanings. Auschwitz is the most real of all realities in this respect. Its name marks the limit where historical knowledge sees its competency challenged. It does not follow that one enters then into the realm of nonsense. The alternative is not: either the signification established by science or absurdity. (92)

By means of such an argument against the monopoly granted to knowledge in history, the historical field is blown wide open—but with the risk of chaos, confusion, superstition, prejudice, mysticism, irrationality: everything philosophy and history since the Enlightenment have combated. But, above all, there is the risk of limiting the pertinence of the tools that an historian such as Vidal-Naquet uses to refute a Faurisson—limiting to such an extent that the latter's denial of the existence of the extermination camps would have as much right to claim validity as any other thesis. Such is not the case,

Lyotard would argue, 1) because research, documentation, and verifiable historical argumentation still determine the historical field almost in its entirety, and 2) because what is not determinable in all its aspects by knowledge is still regulated by the question of justice. Auschwitz is the irrefutable sign, for Lyotard, that no matter how limited the rules and logic of historical validification might be, what cannot be determined by the rules or logic of knowledge or reason per se can in no way be considered to be outside the realm of critical judgment and the problem of justice. If feeling cannot be evaluated in terms of cognitive criteria, it, too, must still stand the test of judgment: the question of justice cannot be avoided.

For Lyotard, critical judgment does not have the logical or generic limitations of knowledge. It cannot be situated in one field, genre, or *régime* alone, but cuts through and makes links among them all. In other words, it is always necessary to judge. Where there are no fixed criteria—and there are no fixed criteria for either the just or the beautiful—one must judge, case by case, without criteria. The "signs of history" are, thus, matter for judgment. This means that the responses of the historian or critical philosopher to the silences of Auschwitz, to the unpresentable as it is *felt* and not *known*, may not all be determined by the rules of historical linkage. But they all must, nevertheless, still be judged to be just or unjust in terms of *différends* that can never be litigated. The question of justice thus supplements that of knowledge; the problem of the signs of history and the role of sentiment in history explicitly raises the question of the ethical-political. A philosophy of phrases may initially constitute something like an analytic of the historical-political, but, in Lyotard's hands, it leads ultimately to a critique of the analytical and conceptual and to what could be called a demand for a historical-political receptiveness—not only to the facts, but also to the signs of history.

4. A Critique of Political Judgment

It is not surprising that when the problem of critical judgment becomes the chief focus of Lyotard's work, Kant begins to hold an increasingly important place in it. In *Instructions païennes,* Lyotard already admits to being a "Kantian"—but, he claims, only in terms of the Kant of the *Third Critique*: "not the Kant of the concept or the moral law but the Kant of the imagination, when he cures himself of the illness of knowledge and rules" (36). In *Le différend,* Lyotard clearly identifies with the Kant he characterizes as a "critical watchman" who maintains at all costs the distinction among the cognitive, ethical, and aesthestic realms and resists the temptation to derive the latter from the former. Such derivation is the principal symptom of the "illness of knowledge," and in the ethical-political realm, Lyotard argues, it has often been fatal.

It is the Kant who distinguishes among the faculties, then, (not just the

Kant of the *Third Critique,* it turns out, but also of the *Second Critique*), who provides Lyotard with a basis for his recasting of the historical-political apart from the cognitive faculty. Lyotard is especially interested in Kant's argument in the *Critique of Practical Reason* (translated by Lewis White Beck [Indianapolis: Bobbs-Merrill, 1956]) that the moral law is "certain" but neither deducible nor confirmed by reason or experience: "The objective reality of the moral law can be proved through no deduction, through no exertion of the theoretical, speculative, or empirically supported reason; and even if one were willing to renounce its apodictic certainty, it could not be confirmed by any experience and thus proved a posteriori. Nevertheless it is firmly established in itself" (48). Showing how the moral law—obligation in Lyotard's sense—can be "firmly established in itself," but not demonstrable as such, will constitute an important part of Lyotard's reading of Kant. Lyotard's Kant is the Kant for whom "the law remains nondeduced," and "at the same time as dependence on the law is presented as a feeling, independence in relation to the order of knowledge is presented as a mysterious presupposition" (*Le différend,* 179). As Lyotard reads him, independence from the cognitive faculty and the central role given to a "feeling" for the law characterize the ethical-political for Kant. The inevitable "conflict between the faculties" such independence provokes is what makes him a philosopher of *différends* as well.

Kant is, first of all for Lyotard, the critical philosopher who, along with Lévinas, offers the best means of exposing the "transcendental illusion" of revolutionary politics—of perhaps all politics in the narrow sense—which is to "confuse what is presentable as an object for a cognitive phrase with what is presentable as an object for a speculative and/or ethical phrase, that is, schemas and examples with *analoga*" (233). In the ethical-political realm, no example can be given of the law, no direct presentation can be made of what constitutes justice. But this does not mean that one is totally "abandoned" by the law and placed in an ethical abyss, left with only subjective whim or the uncontrollable flux of libidinal drives that act in the absence of knowable laws (as, for example, Lyotard had argued in *Economie libidinale*). One is, rather, left with feelings, signs, and *analoga*, and in Lévinas's terms, "hostage" to an obligation that cannot be defined in terms of a knowable law or moral code.[12] What cannot be presented directly is evoked indirectly, presented in terms of its unpresentability, as unpresentable except by means of analogies.

Kant makes "being hostage" to the unpresentable bearable, so to speak, by regulating its non-determined, "subjective," characteristics in terms of an Idea. An Idea, in Kant's sense, is different from a concept in that it does not correspond to any object and thus cannot be proved to exist; yet, it nevertheless can be (in fact, must be) presumed as a regulating principle. It has an "as-if" rather than an actual existence; thus, analogy could be said to be its principal mode of indirect "presentation." Because Ideas regulate but do not determine, links to Ideas always remain problematical—as do the possible links among the various faculties that Ideas encourage because they imply a certain form of universality.

Linkage among the various faculties is accomplished largely by means of analogy. But the strategy of analogy Lyotard derives from Kant is one in which a similarity of procedure in dealing with different fields in no way cancels out or even diminishes the radical differences among them. One proceeds "as if" there were similarities in order all the better to highlight both the similarities *and* the differences: "The analogy that results from the *als ob* is an illusion when differences are forgotten and the *différend* smothered. It is on the contrary critical if the modes of formation and validation of phrases are distinguished from each other and if the *différend* . . . is thus fully exposed" (181). Kant will, thus, provide Lyotard with a critical strategy by which links can be made across the "abyss" separating the various faculties, but one which resists homogenization and totalization of the faculties in terms of a knowable ideal or concept.

Argument by means of analogy is the most fragile and risky form of argumentation, for there is a very fine line between "good" and "bad" analogy. Analogy is, in fact, less argument than suggestion; it uses more paralogical than logical procedures. Given that there cannot be any predetermined rules to distinguish one form of analogy from the other, each analogy must be judged in each instance to decide if, on the one hand, it maintains the differences between the terms while linking them, or, on the other, it collapses them into each other. Each analogy, if critical, will result in the introduction into each field of a perspective that is, at least in part, that of the other field. In this way, each field remains open, always to be determined: if analogy is basic to a field, the field can never be thought to exist or to function only by and in itself. It can never present itself in its own terms or be presented as it is. The Kant of critical judgment is, for Lyotard, therefore, the Kant of critical analogies, of an "as if" which never becomes a simple "as."[13]

The first, and one could say, most far-reaching analogy Lyotard uncovers in Kant is between Kant's notion of critique in general and the historical-political realm in particular:

> The one and the other have to judge without having any rule of judgment, which is different from the juridical-political (which has in principle the rule of law). In other words, just as a critique in Kant's sense, cannot give rise to any doctrine (but to criticism), there must not be any doctrine of the historical-political. This relation is perhaps more than an affinity; it is an analogy: a critique (still in the Kantian sense) is perhaps the political in the universe of philosophical phrases, and the political perhaps a critique (in the Kantian sense) in the universe of socio-historical phrases. ("Introduction à une étude

du politique selon Kant"—in *Rejouer le politique [Paris: Galilée, 1981], 91).*[14]

If one follows this analogy—and with an analogy it is never completely certain how far to follow it before going too far and equating the two terms—Lyotard is not arguing that all philosophy is political or all politics philosophical; rather, he is saying that they have in common a certain relation to a notion of critique which highlights rather than diminishes the important differences existing between them. Analogy in this sense thus works to keep each domain from becoming doctrinaire or dogmatic and from being determined by itself entirely on its own terms.

The specific relation of the critical and the political—which has to do with the fact that they both demand a form of judgment that functions in the absence of any specific doctrine or rules—is not explicitly developed at length by Kant in any particular work, but, rather, evoked in various texts on history and politics written near the end of his life. As Lyotard notes, Kant never wrote a "Fourth Critique," and Lyotard finds this lack of a specifically political critique to be a sign of the radical heterogeneity of the political: "The Critique of political reason was never written. It is legitimate, within particular limits that remain to be determined, to see in the dispersion of the historical-political texts of Kant a sign of the particular heterogeneity of the political 'object'" (*Le différend*, 189). But Kant did write *The Critique of Judgement,* and Lyotard will focus on this *Critique* in order to investigate the political outside its determination by the cognitive—that is, in terms of an analogy with the aesthetic.

The "quasi-faculty or 'as-if' faculty" of judgment, as Lyotard calls it, is, in Kant, the faculty of links or "passages" (*Übergänge*) between faculties. It is given "an enormous privilege in its capacity to unify at the same time as it suffers from an enormous lack in its capacity to know the object that is proper to it: in other words, it has no determined object" (190). Judgment in the *Third Critique* is, at least initially, not specifically aesthetic (or teleological) and not even specific to this critique; the lack of a particular object to which judgment is to be applied keeps it from being inscribed in one territory alone. It permits it, however, to "delimit the territories and domains which establish the authority of each genre. . . . And it is able to do this only thanks to the commerce or war that it maintains among the genres" (191). Judgment, thus, is not the property of one faculty or territory alone but constitutes a kind of parafaculty of territorializing in general.

The problem remains as to why Kant moves from judgment in general to aesthetic judgment in particular. In his "Preface to the First Edition" (1790) of *The Critique of Judgement,* Kant gives the following "explanation" for beginning with aesthetic judgment—and, it could be added, for conceiving (to a large extent) all judgment in terms of it. It has to do with the difficulties involved in discovering the particular principle belonging to this faculty:

> For this principle is one which must not be derived from *a priori* concepts, seeing that these are the property of understanding, and judgement is only directed to their application. It has, therefore, itself to furnish a concept, and one from which, properly, we get no cognition of a thing, but which it can itself employ as a rule only—but not as an objective rule to which it can adapt its judgement, because, for that, another faculty of judgement would again be required to enable us to decide whether the case was one for the application of the rule or not. It is chiefly in those estimates that are called aesthetic, and which relate to the beautiful and the sublime, whether of nature or of art, that one meets with the above difficulty about a principle (be it subjective or objective). And yet the critical search for a principle of judgement in their case is the most important item in a Critique of this faculty. (5)

Aesthetic judgment is thus for Kant a form of judgment for which the difficulties in discovering a principle are the most serious, and, yet, in which the search for a principle is "the most important item." The aesthetic is chosen as the context in which to investigate critically the problem of (reflective) judgment in general, therefore—not because it provides a ready-made model for judgment or because it is an area in which problems of judgment have been resolved. On the contrary, it is the area where the antinomies (the *différends*) basic to judgment are the most extreme because its concept cannot be derived from the a priori principles of understanding. Judgment as concerns the aesthetic, therefore, is primary and fundamental. For these reasons it serves as a kind of model for all other instances in which knowledge is not determining, a model for judgment which must operate in the absence of models.

A crucial analogy between the aesthetic and the political has to do, therefore, with the indeterminate status of their respective "objects"; one of the most important tasks Lyotard gives to critical judgment in each field is to undermine all existing determinations of the aesthetic or political reality of the object—that is, in his terms, to "derealize" their object:

> The importance of the philosophy of the beautiful and the sublime in the first part of the *Third Critique* rests in the derealization of the object of aesthetic feelings and at the same time in the absence, strictly speaking, of any faculty of aesthetic knowledge. It is the same, but in an even more radical way, for the historical-political object, which has no reality as such, and for a faculty of political knowledge,

177

which must remain nonexistent. ("Introduction à une étude du politique selon Kant," 112–13)

In the aesthetic and political realms, critical judgment cannot be derived from
what can be seen and known. It is one thing to perceive, calculate, measure,
and determine the characteristics of an art object, Lyotard argues (following
Kant), and it is another to judge it to be beautiful: "The aesthetic object is
not an object of experience, and there is no intuition of it, at least not of its
aesthetic qualities. Its form is perceivable, but the beauty of its form is not"
(*Le différend*, 192). In the same way, one could say that it is one thing to
perceive, gather together, evaluate, and understand phenomena from the historical-political realm; it is another to judge that an action is just or unjust
in terms of ends that are not determined but that remain open to debate.

In this context, the "signs of history" could be considered, through analogy,
to be what is "aesthetic," that is, critical within the political. Signs in this
sense refer in Kant to Ideas, not concepts, to what cannot be determined as
a cognitive object. One of the reasons Ideas (such as progress toward the
better, the human community, freedom, etc.) cannot be presented directly
as objects of knowledge is that they have as their referent a future which
they, in some sense, anticipate but in no way determine. Any yet, it is not
enough to dream of such things. If progress, community, justice are not pure
foolishness or idle fantasies—and there is always a chance they are—they
must be demonstrated as having some sort of existence. They must be indicated indirectly even if they can't be present directly. An historical event
must be found, argues Lyotard, "that would only indicate (*hinweisen*) and
not prove (*beweisen*) that humanity is capable of being the cause (*Ursache*)
and the author (*Urheber*) of its progress. . . . This *Begebenheit* must itself
not be the cause of progress, but only its indication, . . . a sign that recalls,
shows, anticipates" (236). The "signs of history," therefore, are analogous to
the judgment of the beautiful: both demand or anticipate disinterested, universal agreement. From a particular case or example, a judgment is made
with universal implications—but without the knowledge of the form of that
universality. Analogy could here perhaps be considered to be on the most
tenuous of grounds, for the universal that regulates the links between the
aesthetic and the political must remain, by definition, unpresentable.

The signs of history, then, like aesthetic judgment in general, imply a certain
form of universality. The French Revolution is the principal example Kant
uses of an historical event that provoked feelings which could be taken as a
sign of disinterested universality. Kant is less interested in the Revolution as
an historical event than he is in the responses of those spectators to the event
who are profoundly moved by it, yet can be judged to be disinterested. Like
the aesthetic spectator who must go through the critical process of freeing
himself of all interest in the object he is contemplating and of emptying the

aesthetic object of all utility before he can judge it to be beautiful, the spectator to history must also be free of all personal interest—if his "sympathy for the players on one side against those on the other" is to be taken as "universal" and "disinterested" (Kant, "An Old Question Raised Again: Is the Human Race Constantly Progressing?"—in *On History*, Lewis White Beck, editor [Indianapolis: Bobbs-Merrill, 1963], 143). The historical truth of one version of the Revolution as compared to another is not the issue here, but, rather, how certain feelings about the event under very particular conditions can be considered by Kant to be indications of progress—something the event itself cannot be demonstrated to be as long as the specific form and sense of progress must remain indeterminate rather than determined. In Lyotard's term, progress, as such, cannot be presented as a concept, but can only be "felt" and evoked through "signs"—if the historical-political is to be treated in a critical rather than doctrinaire or dogmatic way.

The "proof" of the disinterestedness of the spectators to the Revolution is that their participation in the event is "wishful" and "borders closely on enthusiasm, the very expression of which is fraught with danger" (*On History*, 144). A partiality that "could become very disadvantageous for them if discovered" (143) is the proof of impartiality and universality; it "not only permits people to hope for progress towards the better, but is already itself progress" (144)—which the Revolution in and of itself (as it manifests the conflict of partisan interests and degenerates into the violence of the Terror) is not. The political risks run by the spectators indicate that their enthusiasm cannot be "grafted onto self-interest," but that it moves toward "what is ideal and, indeed, to what is purely moral" (145).

It could be argued that the Kantian "critical watchman" moves too quickly here and is not enough on his guard against the possibility that enthusiasm in spectators—even if it entails risks—could still be self-interested: the sign of a desire to have the revolution spread to their own country in order to improve their own condition. For Kant, this is not the case. He puts the spectators to the Revolution in his own place, in the place of someone who fears and condemns revolution as much as he participates in the enthusiasm it provokes. Taken within a very narrow framework, Kant could here be considered to be proposing an aestheticism of history: a notion of an approach to historical events that demands "subjects of history" who are emotionally active (enthusiastic or sorrowful, in the case of negative signs), but, nonetheless, passive when it comes to any form of action or participation—purely aesthetic spectators reduced always to contemplatation from a distance. The danger would be that in the name of the signs of history and the "feeling" that things are progressing toward the better (toward a universality that can never be presented as such), that history in its everyday sense would be left to the partisan, self-serving groups and forces who follow their interests—no matter where they might lead. In such a situation, the gap between the signs of history and history proper, between aesthetic-historical spectators and participants, would continue to increase; the enthusiasm of the former would look more and more like naïve idealism, a way of fleeing history for the safety of aesthetic sentiments and pure contemplation.

Such a reading of Kant is, of course, not without its textual support in Kant; it could also be linked to certain aestheticist tendencies of the neo-Kantian tradition. Compared with Lyotard's, it is a fairly narrow reading in terms of the critical force of Kant's work, not only in relation to the historical-political, but to the aesthetic as well. It inflates the latter to the point where it becomes its own end and the end of everything else. Lyotard is quick to point out that such is not the case, because Kant never allows one realm to be collapsed into the other. Lyotard argues that the risks run by the enthusiastic response of spectators to the Revolution indicate, not the political value, but the "aesthetic value of their feeling. What must be said of their enthusiasm is that it is an aesthetic analogue of a pure republican fervor" (*Le différend*, 241). As an analogue, it does not replace "republican fervor" with an aesthetic sentiment, action with contemplation. It links them together while maintaining, and even emphasizing, their differences: "As for a politics of the sublime, there is none. If there were, it could only be the Terror. But in politics, there is an aesthetics of the sublime" (*Le postmoderne expliqué aux enfants* [Paris: Galilée, 1986], 112–13).

Sublime enthusiasm indicates that there is something more in the historical-political realm than the politics of interested parties. But, at the same time, because there is no politics of the sublime (or the beautiful) except in the form of terror, republican fervor and political action in general indicate that contemplation can never be an end in itself. The distance (retreat)[15] from the historical-political (which makes manifest the interested and partisan nature of the political) may be considered disinterested—but only in terms of what it cannot express, and not in terms of what it does express. The aesthetic or sublime analogue is, thus, a sign of the limitations of the historical-political, a distance within it. But the latter could equally be taken as an indication of the limitations of the aesthetic and its illusory nature when it is taken to be a replacement, rather than an analogue, for the political.

What makes this enthusiasm a sublime feeling is the extreme tension, or the tension of extremes, it contains within it. As Lyotard puts it, Kant argues that humanity must be considered to be "in progress" because it was able to "feel, even in the crime committed by the Jacobins, the 'presence' of the unpresentable Idea of freedom" (112). The enthusiasm is not a feeling directly linked in any causal way to the drama being observed from afar. It is linked to no definite object, but emerges out of and manifests the gap between the baseness of the crime of regicide and the nobility of the Idea of freedom that such a crime, nonetheless, also suggests. The Idea of freedom is, thus, evoked in circumstances that in themselves seem as far removed from that Idea as

180

possible. Sublime enthusiasm is, in this context, constituted by horror and joy at one and the same time. Its distance from the Idea is also a sign of its proximity to it.

What Kant values in the "objects" at the source of this enthusiasm is not their form, but, rather, as in the case of all other disruptive historical events, their formlessness. Lyotard claims that they are, for Kant, "the unformed and the without-figure of historical human nature" (240)—at least they remain unformed for the enthusiastic spectators. The diverse participants in the Revolution have undoubtedly fallen prey to "the political illusion" that a form of the republic can be taken for the Idea of the republic; they fight for a particular form against all those who oppose the republic, but also against all those who defend a different form. In the formed, there can be no universality— for it is always a local, regional phenomenon, confined to its context. If the universality that is evoked in aesthetic judgment is not a consensus but a *sensus communis* (a universality that is anticipated in its undetermined form but never present in any determined form), the universality anticipated by the sublime is even less determined, because no determined object evokes it. With the sublime both the object and the "public" remain unformed.[16]

The sublime feeling, as we have seen, is simultaneously a feeling of both pleasure and displeasure, or, as Lyotard puts it, "different from taste, the regulation of the sublime is good when it is bad. The sublime implies the finality of a non-finality and the pleasure of a displeasure" (*Le différend,* 238). The enthusiasm of the spectators of the Revolution is sublime, therefore, precisely because it is not determined by, and does not present, any concept or specific example of freedom—the Revolution itself cannot be used as such an example. Yet, in this inadequacy, the greatness of the Idea is felt even more strongly and with more intense pleasure, because of the pain that accompanies it:

> Enthusiasm is a modality of sublime feeling. The imagination tries to furnish a direct, sensual presentation of an Idea of reason (for the totality is an object of an Idea, for example, the totality of practical, rational beings), but it does not succeed and thus experiences its impotence. But it discovers at the same time its destination, which is to realize its agreement with Ideas of reason through an appropriate presentation. It results from this blocked relation that instead of experiencing a feeling for the object, one experiences when confronted with this object a feeling "for the Idea of humanity in us as subjects." (238)

"The Idea of humanity" is felt all the more intensely because its presentation is experienced as a radical impossibility.

The notion that the ethical-political community—here the Idea of the re-

181

public—cannot be presented as an object achieves its most extreme and therefore most powerful manifestation in the sublime.[17] Given this limitation of and in presentation, Lyotard concludes that the task of a critical politics is, nevertheless, to present the unpresentable, to present the fact that the unpresentable exists and that it concerns the future of the human community: "'Our' destination . . . is to have to furnish a presentation for the unpresentable, and thus when it is a question of Ideas, to exceed everything that can be presented" (238–39). The Kantian sublime indicates, for Lyotard, that the spectator to the Revolution or the critical "reader" of other signs of history can never be secure in his contemplation—not only because his feelings are torn between pleasure and displeasure, but also because the signs he reads demand more than contemplation from him. They demand that he surpass the presentable in search of the unpresentable, that he acknowledge that whatever is presented as an example of true community, freedom, humanity, etc. must be judged to be inadequate in terms of Ideas that can never be realized, as such, but which can (and must) only be sensed indirectly and serve as regulating alternatives to what is presentable.

The sublime sentiment in the historical-political is, thus, a case of analogy at its most extreme point, the point where the differences separating the faculties are most intensely felt at the same time as the links between them are precariously postulated. It is analogy at the point of simultaneously breaking apart and fusing together, the least certain and the most powerful of such cases. Lyotard argues that "the sublime sentiment constitutes an 'as-if presentation' of the Idea of civil and even cosmopolitan society, and thus of the Idea of morality, there where it cannot, however, be presented: in experience" (244). Because all presentations of the Idea can only as "as-if" presentations, analogy lies at the very heart of a critical approach to the historical-political in Kant. It is the principal critical weapon Lyotard uses against the derivation of the political or its reduction to what already exists or even to what can be presented in experience—and this includes, of course, aesthetic as well as historical-political "experience." As Lyotard puts it, "we have in it the most inconsistent 'passage' imaginable, the impasse as 'passage'" (239). Thus the only critical path to the Idea is one that makes of its inability to present directly the Idea a way of indicating it indirectly by analogy.

For Lyotard, the primary political question would seem to be how to conceive of the gap between historical reality and the Ideas of progress and freedom, and in a way that is not the simple negation of reality or the withdrawal into aestheticism or idealism. There are, of course, no simple answers to such a question. But it must be clear by now that the aesthetic—especially when it has the paraesthetic form of the sublime—is a kind of critical safeguard against the dogmatism of the theoretical in general. The sublime serves to push philosophy and politics into a reflexive, critical mode, to defer indefinitely the imposition of an end on the historical-political process. By emphasizing the gap between Idea and concept, the notion of the sublime in the historical-political highlights the tension between the desire to surpass "what is presentable" for something beyond presentation, as well as the critical awareness that no concept of the social is adequate to the Idea of freedom and none, therefore, can be considered to embody it.[18]

Lyotard's own critical position is rooted in the tensions and irresolvable contradictions (or *différends*) he considers basic to history and politics and which he makes the stakes of his entire critical project. This may help explain why his own critical strategy consists of two widely divergent and even conflictual tendencies. On the one hand (whether in terms of narrative pragmatics, language games, or a philosophy of phrases), there is a decidedly cold, analytical-pragmatic side to his strategy—what I have characterized as his search for an impossible minimal element, or "zero degree" of critical discourse, that would be without presuppositions. On the other hand, one finds throughout his work an insistence on the role of libidinal drives, desire, sensation, and feeling as undeniable elements, not only of the aesthetic, but of the historical-political as well. In his strategy, the analytical and the affective seem to be locked in a struggle he makes no attempt to resolve, one which he, in fact, continually exacerbates, moving from one extreme to the other to increase the tension between them.

What could be called the "coup analytique" is continually countered in his work by the "coup du sentiment," both of which are contained or, rather, do battle in the term *différend* itself. For the *différend* is, at one and the same time, a kind of limit case of both the analytical and the affective. It is an analytical category in the sense that it depends on the existence of rules that regulate how links between phrases are made and is rooted in the plurality of existing and possible rules that makes linkage a fundamental problem. But *différends* also provoke feelings of injustice and stimulate a sensitivity to what, in a given situation, has not been phrased. At the same time, a focus on *différends* motivates the search for idioms that testify in some way to the silences of the not yet phrased and the unphrasable, which constitute the stakes of a critical philosophy, politics, and art. Lyotard's goal is to make the presentation of the fact—that the unpresentable exists—as much the concern of a critical politics as of a critical or para- aesthetics. The aesthetic supplements the historical-political and the theoretical in general in his work as a means of pushing the theoretical beyond itself in pursuit of what it cannot capture or present, that is, conceptualize.

Lyotard's critical position, then, pursues the implications, not of what Hegel called the "end of art," but, rather, of what could be called the end of metatheory—if by metatheory is meant philosophy in its systematic, totalized (metanarrative) form. But the conflictual pluralism that such a crisis in theory and legitimation produces is itself regulated by the problem of justice and the obligation to judge, to differentiate, to take a stand in terms of conflicting "opinions," critical strategies, and theories. Critical judgment lacks criteria, but it does not, however, because of this lack, take place in the void.[19] Judgment, for Lyotard (as for Kant), cannot occur without some connection to an Idea (in the Kantian sense)—just as it cannot be considered critical unless the Idea to which it is linked remains unpresentable. If Lyotard eventually parts company with Kant, it is because "in contradistinction to what Kant thought, this Idea is not, for us today, an Idea of totality" (*Just Gaming*, 88). The Lyotardian notion of the Idea, then, is itself a conflictual heterogeneity whose unity is not given, but problematical. The notion of the sublime allows him to make this irresolvable tension between the presentable and the unpresentable not only a necessary product of the "postmodern disbelief" in all forms of metatheory, but, also, the stakes of his approach to both the political and the aesthetic.

The distance instituted by the aesthetic in the political—which is equally the distance within the aesthetic itself, a distance I have called the paraesthetic—is the space in which both the limitations of theory, as well as the possiblities of exceeding these limitations, are revealed. The paraesthetic distance within and outside the theoretical thus marks not so much the end of all theory—even if such an end might be proclaimed in order to distinguish art from knowledge—but, rather, the possibility of critical forms of theory for which the question of art, as well as the problems of the political and "the just," are persistently pursued but never resolved.

C H A P T E R   E I G H T
THE UNDETERMINED ENDS OF THEORY AND ART

> With art, one is never finished.
> —Philippe Lacoue-Labarthe, *La Poésie comme expérience*

In the course of this book I have argued that a critical concern with the question of art and literature leads Foucault, Lyotard, and Derrida in different ways to confront all theories of "the end of art" and, implicitly, to challenge all theories of the "end of theory" as well. In their work, one is never finished with art, and one is never finished with theory either. At least, one is not finished with theory if it is continually pushed beyond and outside itself through a confrontation with art and literature, a confrontation that does not leave intact any of the terms or the fields they are supposed to determine. At the same time, these readings of Foucault, Lyotard, and Derrida point to the uncertain future of both art and theory and the undetermined nature of their relations. The paraesthetic strategies I consider as basic to their work are, in fact, directed at the question of the future of art and theory beyond their declared, predetermined ends.

In *L'entretien infini* (Paris: Gallimard, 1969), Maurice Blanchot approaches the question of art in Nietzsche in a similar vein. He argues that Nietzsche's famous phrase, "We have art ['Wir haben die Kunst'—not really 'we possess art,' as the English translation says]—lest we perish of the truth" (*The Will to Power*, 435, t.m.), taken on its own, appears to make art *the alternative* to philosophical-religious truth and the privileged means for undermining its restrictive and even lethal influence. The phrase suggests that Nietzsche believes that the "illusory," formal (Apollonian) characteristics of art constitute an impenetrable defense against the totalizing, dogmatic, and moralizing ef-

185

fects of the truth. Phrases like this—and there are not shortage of them in Nietzsche—encourage and sustain those readings of Nietzsche which consider his work to constitute a radical (aestheticist) defense of art against metaphysics—as if the only way to combat the limitations of philosophy were to posit art as a realm of pure illusion untouched by truth.

Blanchot obviously feels that such readings of Nietzsche are too narrow in their approach to the question of art. Reading Nietzsche's texts in a way that strives to be faithful to what he feels is their most radical thrust, Blanchot cautions that, despite appearances, the purely aesthetic (Apollonian) aspects of art do not really constitute a bulwark against the truth; form and illusion cannot be kept separate from force and movement, Apollo from Dionysus. As Blanchot argues, "Apollo, who had for some time already been dispersed in Dionysus, could no longer keep us from perishing if we ever were to confront the truth" (248). Blanchot wonders—against the prevalent aestheticist readings of Nietzsche—in what sense, after Nietzsche, we can still be considered "to have art": "But do we have art? And do we have the truth even if it is to perish from it" (248)? At the very least, the precautions Blanchot takes before approaching the question of art and its relation to the truth would be a way of resisting any attempt to generalize the aesthetic or to aestheticize the truth—as, in fact, has frequently been done in Nietzsche's name. I have found it necessary to take similar precautions while dealing with the question of art in Foucault, Lyotard, and Derrida, in order not to transform their critical approaches to art into mystifications of art.

My readings of Foucault, Lyotard, and Derrida have demonstrated that Blanchot's questions are important ones; art and literature lose their critical force if their place is taken for granted, if they are posited as alternatives to the truth. If, what I have called, their paraesthetic approaches to art and literature can all be linked in important ways to Nietzsche, it is only in terms of the distance from the aesthetic or the uncertainty concerning the nature and status of art and literature indicated by Blanchot's questions. The fact that all three emphasize the difficulty of answering if and in what sense we can be considered, still, "to have art" constitutes an important component of the critical force of their work.

My decision to approach the work of Foucault, Lyotard, and Derrida in terms of the question of art was influenced in part by Blanchot's reading of Nietzsche and my conviction that these three philosophers all fit in some way into a discontinuous series of critical thinkers—running, for example, from Nietzsche through Heidegger, Merleau-Ponty, and Blanchot, and interconnecting, in terms of specific issues, with Benjamin and Adorno[1]—who all make the pursuit of some form of the question of art and literature central to their critical investigation of philosophy, history, and politics. In the preceding chapters, I have argued that a crucial component of the work of Foucault, Lyotard, and Derrida is not their *theory* of art as such, but, rather, how their determination to keep art and literature unfinished, undecidable, or un-determined—as "unwork" rather than work—serves to confront both theory and art with their limitations and to transform and displace each in terms of the other. This indeterminancy or undecidability of art must, in each instance, however, be argued anew and meticulously analyzed, rather than simply de-clared. It is only through such analysis that the question of art has critical effects on and within theory.

The most important links among these three critical philosophers consist, then, not in what they *say* about art and literature, but, rather, in what they *do* with art and literature and what they make art and literature do for them. They are perhaps closest to each other when they confront the limitations of their own strategies and theory in general and search for ways to push art and theory beyond these limitations. The links among the three philosophers remain tenuous, however, and can legitimately be made only in terms of the varied, and sometimes even opposed, critical strategies characteristic of the work of each and the different critical effects that each strategy produces.

Even though I have not made the differences among these three philoso-phers an explicit topic of my analyses, I am not suggesting that they should in any way be ignored or underplayed. Foucault's polemical response to Der-rida's analysis of *Madness and Civilization* ("Cogito and the History of Mad-ness" in *Writing and Difference*) and his persistent attack on Derrida's notions of writing and textuality are evidence enough that important differences sep-arate them.[2] Lyotard's *Discours, figure* contains numerous critical references to Derrida and *Economie libidinale* includes "deconstruction" among the list of theories being attacked. Even when Lyotard and Derrida explicitly agree on a number of crucial philosophical and political issues—as they did, for example, at the Cerisy Colloquium devoted to Derrida's work in 1980—dif-ferences of strategy and style continue to separate them.[3] My main point in analyzing the work of these three philosophers in terms of the question of art is to show how the relentless pursuit of this question leads, in each case (but in a different way), to the breaching of theoretical and aesthetic closure and the displacement of theory. Beneath, or to the side of, the polemics, differences, and critiques separating them from each other can be found a concern for the question of art in its undetermined sense, a concern which serves as a starting point for three very diverse critical projects.

Paraesthetics, then, does not in any sense define a critical school or a methodology of reading—whether such a methodology were to be derived from or applied to either literature and art or philosophy—but points to a complex of questions which lead in turn to other questions. This is one of the senses in which one is never finished with art. "To have art" in this way implies that art and the theory of art are never given in themselves, but must be constantly reworked. In terms of paraesthetic approaches to art, there cannot be any *result* or *end*—either given in advance or simply anticipated—assigned to the investigation of art and its interactions with theory.

At a time when one senses a growing desire to "return" to history and politics and, in this way, to finish with theory, it is crucial that certain of the most important theoretical advances and modes of critical analysis of the last twenty years not be swept aside in the haste to get back to (what are declared to be) more empirical, concrete, and, thus, more easily determined issues or problems. One of my principal goals in this book has been to show that a concern for art or literature "on its own terms" does not constitute, in itself, a denial of history or a repression of socio-political issues—if the "terms" specific to art or literature are, at the same time, considered in terms of their paraliterary or paraesthetic implications. On the contrary, the pursuit of the questions of art and literature in the work of Foucault, Lyotard, and Derrida is an important critical tool in their respective reworkings of philosophy, history, and politics. If these questions were eliminated from their work, their investigation and displacement of the limitations of theory would lose much of its critical force.

The paraesthetic strategies of the three philosophers treated in this work constitute various ways of theorizing in the absence of any generally accepted philosophically or historically determined metatheory. In focusing on the question of whether we can be said to "have art," paraesthetics, at the same time, focuses on how and with what consequences we can claim "to have theory" and the philosophical, historical, political, and even aesthetic "truths" it determines. Paraesthetic critical strategies posit no end to art and no end to theory, because their ends are intricately intertwined and, thus, constantly in question within and outside each. The task of paraesthetic theory is not to resolve all questions concerning the relations of theory with art and literature, but, rather, to rethink these relations and, through the transformation and displacement of art and literature, to recast the philosophical, historical, and political "fields"—"fields" with which art and literature are inextricably linked.

N O T E S

1. Beyond Theorisms and Aestheticisms

1. This kind of reaction against recent theory is not just an American phenomenon. In a recent article entitled "La police de la pensée," Jean-François Lyotard and Jacob Rogozinski attack this tendency in a series of recent French publications: namely, in Jacques Bouveresse, *Le philosophe chez les autophages* (Paris: Minuit, 1985); Tzvetan Todorov, *Critique de la critique* (Paris: Seuil, 1985); and Luc Ferry and Alain Renault, *La pensée 68* (Paris: Gallimard, 1985). Lyotard and Rogozinski claim that what links these various texts, besides a refusal to analyze the texts they attack (those of Lacan, Foucault, Derrida, Barthes, and Blanchot), is "a common goal, the same will to *react* against the most radical advances of modernity and to return to the dogmas and values that reigned in previous days in the university and in right-minded cliques" (*L'Autre Journal*, no. 10 [December 1985], 30). Jean-Luc Nancy in *L'Oubli de la philosophie* (Paris: Galilée, 1986) in a similar fashion decries those who "on all sides proclaim that our era has forgotten true philosophy, its authentic duties, and the rectitude of its reflections. In truth, it is most often this call to order that testifies on the contrary to a forgetting of what philosophy is, of what it has become, and of what it is suitable to do with it or in its name. It seemed to me desirable and in short urgent to show what in such a stance is really being forgotten" (9).

2. Allan Megill in *Prophets of Extremity: Nietzsche, Heidegger, Foucault, Derrida* (Berkeley: University of California Press, 1985) considers Nietzsche to be an "agenda setter . . . to have set the order of intellectual priorities for those who follow. . . . The vision that he presented in his writings set the agenda not only for the three other thinkers whom I shall be considering in this book but for the whole of modernist and postmodernist art and throught" (1). My claims for Nietzsche are much more modest; suffice it to say here that, rather than being an "agenda setter," I consider Nietzsche's work to be one of the places—though not the only one—where art is used as a critical weapon against abstract theorizing and where the problems such a strategy entails are clearly visible. Megill's study is helpful in that it focuses on an important and too-often neglected problem in the history of modern thought: the role of a certain notion of aesthetics in four critical philosophers. My differences with Megill have to do with his characterization of all these thinkers as "aestheticists." He does claim that, for him, aestheticism does not denote "an enclosure within a self-contained realm of aesthetic objects and sensations," but rather "an attempt to expand the aesthetic to embrace the whole of reality" (2). This overinflation of the aesthetic, which is, I would argue, more in his interpretation than in the work of the three "post-Nietzschean" thinkers he treats, leads him repeatedly to undercut the most forceful aspects of his own analysis and make statements such as the following: "The truck that is coming down the road is fundamentally different from the interpretation 'Here comes a truck.' To believe otherwise—and the aestheticist does believe otherwise, or for heuristic or revolutionary purposes, claims that this is his belief—is to risk becoming trapped in an implausible and highly artificial form of historical idealism" (63). In my mind, this is precisely why none of the thinkers he treats should really be considered an aestheticist and why I shall stress what is critical, rather than aestheticist, in their use of art and literature.

3. Friedrich Nietzsche, *On the Genealogy of Morals*, translated by Walter Kaufmann and R. J.

189

Hollingdale (New York: Vintage, 1967), 76. The reference here is to legal orders but could be extended to any principle that is posited as sovereign and universal, including art.

4. Fink considers this, however, to be just one of four phases of Nietzsche's development, the phrase of the "metaphysics of the artist," which gives to *The Birth of Tragedy* its "romantic character" (17).

5. Martin Heidegger, *Nietzsche*, v. I, translated by David Farrell Krell (New York: Harper and Row, 1979), 67, 72—Heidegger's emphasis.

6. Fink takes exception to Heidegger's reading at this point and argues that a non-metaphysical origin for his thinking is to be found in his notion of "play" [*Spiel*]: "With his doctrine of will to power Nietzsche accomplishes, according to Heidegger, the metaphysics of modern times, which thinks substance as force and as identity. . . . However, the question remains *open* as to whether Nietzsche in the fundamental intention of his way of *thinking the world* did not already leave behind the ontological problem-level of metaphysics. A non-metaphysical origin of a cosmological philosophy can be found in his idea of 'play'" (*Nietzsches Philosophie*, 187).

7. Nietzsche's phrase, which Heidegger quotes, is the following: "Very early in my life I took the question of the relation of *art* to *truth* seriously: and even now I stand in holy dread in the face of this discordance" (142).

8. The problems having to do with Nietzsche's *Nachlass* are by now well known, and it is important to insist (as Kaufmann does in his introduction to the translation of *The Will to Power*) that "these notes were not intended for publication in this form, and the arrangement and the numbering are not Nietzsche's" (xv–xvi). See also Maurice Blanchot's discussion of the problems these notes pose in the section of *L'Entretien infini* (Paris: Gallimard, 1969) entitled "Nietzsche aujourd'hui" (201–215), and, especially, his presentation in a long footnote of Heidegger's critique of the editions of the notes existing in 1936–39 and his claim that the only legitimate order for the notes is a chronological one. There now exists of course a German edition of Nietzsche's complete works which includes the "Nachgesassene Fragmente" in chronological order: *Nietzsche Werke*, edited by Giorgio Colli and Mazzino Montinari (Berlin: Walter de Gruyter, 1972).

9. See Philippe Lacoue-Labarthe's two essays, "L'oblitération" and "Le détour," in *Le sujet de la philosophie* (Paris: Flammarion, 1979). In another essay from the same collection, "Nietzsche apocryphe," Lacoue-Labarthe claims that Heidegger *deliberately refuses* to take into account the "literary" side of Nietzsche's work, its "form" or "style," and that this cannot be considered an oversight or a failure" (81). It is, however, most definitely a limitation.

10. Friedrich Nietzsche, *The Birth of Tragedy*, translated by Walter Kaufmann (New York: Vintage, 1967), 83–84.

11. In "Genesis and Genealogy (Nietzsche)" from *Allegories of Reading* (New Haven: Yale University Press, 1979), de Man argues against the dominance of the diachronic structure of *The Birth of Tragedy* and claims that "it can be shown, however, that whenever an art form is being discussed, the three modes represented by Dionysos, Apollo, and Socrates are always simultaneously present and that it is impossible to mention one of them without at least implying the others" (85).

12. In *Nietzsche and Philosophy*, translated by Hugh Tomlinson (London: Athlone Press, 1983), Gilles Deleuze claims that tragedy is murdered not once but three difference times; "by Socrates' dialectic, . . . by Christianity, . . . and a third time under the combined blows of the modern dialectic and Wagner himself [in person]" (10–11).

13. Nietzsche is here following the German Romantics (especially Friedrich Schlegel) in their derivation of the novel from the model of the Socratic dialogues. M.M. Bakhtin makes the same observation: "the Socratic dialogues, which may be called—to rephrase Friedrich Schlegel—'the novels of their time'" (*The Dialogic Imagination*, translated by Caryl Emerson and Michael Holquist [Austin: University of Texas Press, 1981], 22).

14. Lacoue-Labarthe, for example, claims that Nietzsche's work has played an important role in focusing attention on the problem of the text: "Nietzsche is also among all the 'philosophers'

(Kierkegaard included) the one who has distinguished himself the most . . . by his contradictory and multiple, enigmatic and, let us say, unsettling practice of writing. This is true to such an extent that without him the 'question' of the text would never have emerged, at least not in the precise figure it has today" (*Le Sujet de la philosophie*, 80).

15. See, of course, de Man's well-known discussion of rhetorical questions (apropos of Archie Bunker's bowling shoes) in "Semiology and Rhetoric," the opening chapter of *Allegories of Reading*. De Man defines the *rhetorical* side of the rhetorical question in the following terms, ultimately equating rhetorical, figural potentiality with literature: "The grammatical model of the question becomes rhetorical not when we have, on the one hand, a literal meaning and on the other hand a figural meaning, but when it is impossible to decide by grammatical or other linguistic devices which of the two meanings (that can be entirely incompatible) prevails. Rhetoric radically suspends logic and opens up vertiginous possibilities of referential aberration. . . . I would not hesitate to equate the rhetorical, figural potentiality of language with literature itself" (10). It should again be stressed that even though de Man claims that rhetoric produces a situation of radical undecidability when it comes to meanings, he sees no need to hesitate when it comes to equating rhetoric with literature.

16. See Rodolphe Gasché's essays on "literay deconstruction" and the work of de Man that touch on de Man's use of literature: "Deconstruction as Criticism," *Glyph* v.6 (1979) and "'Setzung' and 'Übersetzung': Notes on Paul de Man," *Diacritics*, v. 11, no. 4 (Winter 1981). See also Suzanne Gearhart's reading of de Man in which she states her differences with Gasché: "Philosophy *Before* Literature: Deconstruction, Historicity, and the Work of Paul de Man, *Diacritics*, v. 13, no. 4 (Winter 1983). Gearhart, near the end of her essay, argues: "De Man's work constitutes a radical theory of literature, one that rejects all traditional forms of totalization, whether formal, aesthetic, hermeneutic, or historical. But in spite of de Man's resistance to all attempts to close off literature and treat it as a discrete object, his work persistently reassures us that literature, literary language, and the text are there all along, deconstituting themselves in a process that only confirms their priority and their privilege" (80).

17. Jacques Derrida, in the Wellek Library Lectures given at the University of California, Irvine in April, 1984, and which were devoted to de Man, makes the following comments on de Man's claims concerning the "reliability" of this perspective: "And aporicity evokes, rather than prohibits, more precisely, promises *through* its prohibition, an other thinking, an other text, the future of another promise. All at once the impasse (*the dead-end*) becomes the most 'trustworthy,' 'reliable' place or moment for reopening a question which is finally equal to or on the same level as that which remains difficult to think. . . . This 'reliability' will no doubt be precarious and menaced by what renders all 'promises' necessary and mad, but it will not promise itself any the less because of this" (*Mémoires: For Paul de Man* [New York: Columbia University Press, 1986], 133–34). A few pages later, Derrida goes on to make surprisingly sweeping claims about the implications of this phrase: "The formulation remains very prudent. . . . It is nonetheless a question of a strong recasting of what deconstruction can and could be, in its strategy and even in its politics" (136).

18. De Man's references to Lacoue-Labarthe are not completely positive, however: he disagrees that *The Birth of Tragedy* is Nietzsche's only genuine "Book" (*Allegories*, 83) and, more importantly, claims that Lacoue-Labarthe in this essay fails to "question its logocentric ontology" (89). In general, he feels that Lacoue-Labarthe's reading is "still preparatory and tentative at best" (104). What de Man here calls Lacoue-Labarthe's tentativeness I shall argue is, in fact, his reluctance to invest as much in rhetoric or in literature-as-rhetoric as de Man. It is not due to an oversight or "blindness" on Lacoue-Labarthe's part, or to the preparatory nature of his reading— I wonder whose reading would be considered in this case to be more than preparatory?—but due, rather, to a slight but significant difference in critical strategy.

19. Heidegger—Derrida after him will also make this an important component of his own critical strategy—criticizes the proclamations of simple alternatives to philosophy for their ahis-

torical characteristics and for being naïvely caught in the very tradition they claim to escape: "Whoever believes that philosophical thought can dispense with its history by means of a simple proclamation will, without his knowing it, be dispensed with by history; he will be struck a blow from which he can never recover, one that will blind him utterly. He will think he is being original when he is merely rehashing what has been transmitted and mixing together traditional interpretations into something ostensibly new. The greater a revolution is to be, the more profoundly it must plunge into its history" (*Nietzsche*, v. I, 203).

20. See Lacoue-Labarthe's recent texts on Nietzsche—namely, "Histoire et *mimèsis*" and "L'antagonisme"—in his *L'Imitation des modernes* (Paris: Galilée, 1986).

21. The key Derridean text on rhetoric is, of course, "White Mythology"—in *Margins of Philosophy*, translated by Alan Bass (Chicago: University of Chicago Press, 1982), which originally appeared in the same issue of *Poétique* (no. 5 [1971]) as "Le Détour."

2. Aesthetic Antagonisms

1. An obvious exception is Theodor W. Adorno's work on aesthetics, especially in *Aesthetic Theory*, translated by C. Lenhardt (London: Routledge and Kegan Paul, 1984). Adorno criticizes the determination of art by extra-aesthetic categories but also wonders if art, in what I would call its paraesthetic aspects, doesn't itself encourage such a determination: "Take a look at the widespread inclination . . . to perceive art in terms of extra-aesthetic or pre-aesthetic criteria. The tendency is, on the one hand, a mark of atrocious backwardness or of the regressive consciousness of many people. On the other hand, there is no denying that the tendency is promoted by something in art itself. If art is perceived strictly in aesthetic terms, then it cannot be properly perceived in aesthetic terms" (9). Adorno also asserts that "in actual fact, art today is virtually impossible unless it is engaged in experimentation, among other things" (55).

2. Edited by Roger McKeon (New York: Semiotext(e), 1984).

3. Lyotard's use of this term is not the same as Derrida's and is derived more from the deconstructive movement in art than from philosophy. For Lyotard, it is, in a certain sense, the radical alternative to all philosophy, even critical philosophy. Rodolphe Gasché in "Deconstruction as Criticism," in *Glyph*, no. 6 (1979), argues, however, that the two critical strategies are essentially the same: "*Discours, figure* is a monument of deconstruction similar to *Of Grammatology*. . . . Lyotard first reprivileges the hitherto secondary and necessarily inferior term of the dyad, that is to say, the figure. This first step is achieved by *reversing* the hierarchy of the given dyad. The second step consists of *reinscribing* the newly privileged term" (183–84). I think that Gasché moves a bit too quickly here when he equates these two critical strategies on such an abstract level—for it should be stressed that when Lyotard uses the term deconstruction he is not referring primarily to a philosophical strategy that is indebted to Heidegger (as Gasché himself argues the true philosophical sense of deconstruction is), but to certain aesthetic strategies of a particular form of art. I also wonder if either of the texts Gasché mentions can really be considered "a monument of deconstruction," if one of the chief purposes of deconstruction is to undermine all such monuments.

4. Adorno argues, in a similar fashion, that "from now on, no art will be conceivable without the moment of anti-art. This means no less than that art has to go beyond its own concept in order to remain faithful to itself" (*Aesthetic Theory*, 43).

5. Peter Dews in "The Letter and the Line: Discourse and its Other in Lyotard—in *Diacritics*, v. 14, no. 3 (Fall 1984)—particularly emphasizes Lyotard's insistence on the opposition between discourse and figure in this text, but does so at the expense of the mutual transformation of both figure and discourse which the overall movement of the book attempts to bring about. He is pushed into this position because his main polemical purpose in this essay is to oppose Lyotard to Derrida: "In direct opposition to the then-triumphant philosophies of the text . . . Lyotard here

takes up the defense of the perceived world against the imperialism of language" (40). It is certainly true that there are significant differences between Lyotard's critique of the "imperialism of language" in general and of that of structuralism in particular and Derrida's critique of all linguistic definitions of language and, in particular, of structuralism in its various manifestations. But to equate Derrida's notion of the text with that of language is a serious distortion of the entire issue of the visual and spatial characteristics of the trace and the process of *espacement* crucial to this notion. It would be more accurate to say that Derrida and Lyotard are equally intent on undermining the "imperialism of language," but that they use different strategies to do it. To oppose them the way Dews does is to simplify and seriously distort the position of each.

6. Rodolphe Gasché, in "Deconstruction as Criticism," analyzes the relation of Lyotard's notion of deconstruction to Merleau-Ponty's concept of surreflexion in the following terms: "This interrogation of the gaze of consciousness at itself, a gaze which is different from every possible object-relation and which gives access to the new mode of transcendental existence as an absolute present existence, takes in *The Visible and the Invisible* the form of a critique of reflexivity in general and of all philosophy of reflection. This critique interrogates the very possibility of reflection" (185).

7. Lyotard breaks with Merleau-Ponty over the issue of whether gesture can be considered to be constitutive of discourse. Lyotard characterizes Merleau-Ponty's attempt to posit gesture as the act lying outside and before speech which makes speech possible as "the last effort of transcendental reflexion." This effort fails, Lyotard claims, because the "system is always-already there, and therefore the gesture of speech supposed to create signification can never be captured in its constitutive function. . . . What can be shown in order to reach that order sought by Merleau-Ponty is how the beyond-the-Logos inhabits language, how it invades language to transgress in it the invariances, which are the keys to signification, and to arouse in language that lateral sense which surreality is" (*Discours, figure*, 56).

8. One of the later chapters on Freud emphasizes this characteristic of figure and discourse to be intermixed in phantasies. Its title is "Fiscours, digure, l'utopie du fantasme."

9. See Chapter 4 for Derrida's analysis of Mallarmé's place in this same "crisis."

10. All references to Freud will be to *The Standard Edition of the Complete Psychological Works* (London: Hogarth, 1953–74). Here the reference is to Volume V, 507.

11. Lyotard argues that the image-figure "deconstructs the contour of the silhouette; it is the transgression of the revealing trace" (277). It thus belongs to the realm of the visible as a visible transgression or distortion of the rules and conventions of the visible. The form-figure is located on another level of visibility and even more destructive of form. It "supports the visible as its nerve system without being seen, but it can itself be made visible. . . . The unconscious form-figure . . . would be an anti-good form, a 'bad form.' . . . It is an energetics indifferent to the unity of the whole, . . . the elimination a fortiori of every recognizable figure. It seems as if we have passed over into Bacchic delirium, descended underground where plastic 'invariants' . . . are brought to a boiling point, where energy circulates at an incredible speed from one point to another of the pictorial space, prohibiting the eye from locating itself anywhere" (277–78).

12. There can therefore be no "artistic" example given of the matrix-figure because it underlies visibility but is not visible itself—it must always be reconstructed from traces. See Jean Laplanche and J.-B. Pontalis, "Fantasme originaire, fantasme des origines, origine du fantasme," *Les temps modernes*, no. 215 (April 1964), for an analysis of the status of such phantasies in Freud that influenced Lyotard's thinking here.

13. This situation is strikingly similar, though argued within a very different context, to the heterogeneity characteristic of the *différend* in the work of the same name. Again see Chapter 7 for a discussion of this term.

14. For example, Lyotard treats Marx, and his most biting attacks are aimed at traditional Marxism, both as an old man whose beard should be "stroked without scorn or devotion" (*Economie*, 117) and as a young girl, whose romantic naïveté has to be exposed for what it is, the two

together in a "strange bisexual arrangement" (118). He considers semiotics to be a "nihilism," a "religious science par excellence," and the notion of polysemia to constitute a "little break-through of right thinking people, a little disorder of *frondeurs*, sugar-coated deconstruction" (64). The problem of the closure of representation is a "sarcastic find," this "sad news, this kakagospel [*kakangile*] that is only the converse of the gospel, this pathetic announcement . . . this bitter message" (12). He does not criticize mimetic theory as "an error, perversion, illusion or ideology," but rather dismisses it in an off-hand way: "If you get off on mimesis, gentlemen, then what objection can we have to that" (296)? And, finally, he says that the Heideggerian discourse on the retreat of being, "for profound reasons bores the hell out of me, just like religion" (306).

15. In the Wellek Library Lectures Lyotard gave at the University of California, Irvine in May, 1986, he refered to *Economie libidinale* as his "evil book, the book of evilness that everyone writing and thinking is tempted to do." But he also went on to "defend" it in the following terms: "The book did perform the ruin of the hegemony of conceptual reception. Compared with the mortal sin of consuming structures, *Economie libidinale* could be considered an honorable sac-rificial offering for that sin. In general, its rare readers disliked the book, which passed for a piece of shamelessness, immodesty, and provocation. Although it actually was all that, the ques-tion remained and has remained since whether 'being' is shameful, modest or well-mannered." These lectures, entitled *Peregrinations: Law, Form, Event*, will be published by Columbia Uni-versity Press.

16. See especially his "Pierce Souyri: le marxisme qui n'a pas fini," in *Esprit*, v. 61, no. 1 (January 1982).

17. In terms of a similar problem, see Lyotard's reading of Fredric Jameson's *The Political Unconscious*, entitled "The Unconscious, History, and Phrases: Notes on *The Political Uncon-scious*," translated by Michael Clark in the *New Orleans Review*, v. 11, no. 1 (Spring 1984). He praises that aspect of Jameson's work that critically evaluates Marxist criticism, for 'far from directing him to a master-method, a position that subsumes all methods, it leads him to reopen and to leave open questions that orthodox Marxism(s) present(s) as resolved. The Jamesonian interpretation of Marxist interpretation appears remarkable to me not for its totalizing or capi-talizing dogmatism but rather for its uneasiness: the critical task is not only endless; it might even be without fixed criteria" (73).

3. Self-Reflexivity and Critical Theory

1. See various essays by Jean Ricardou in *Problèmes du nouveau roman* (Paris: Seuil, 1967), *Pour une théorie du nouveau roman* (Paris: Seuil, 1971), and *Nouveaux problèmes du roman* (Paris: Seuil, 1978) and especially a work by Lucien Dällenbach entitled *Let Récit spéculaire* (Paris: Seuil, 1977).

2. Michel Foucault, *The Order of Things* (New York: Vintage, 1973), translator not given. For reasons that, to me, are unclear, in general. Foucault has not been well served by his translators, and this work is one of the most poorly translated of all. Perhaps this is why no credit is given to the translator. One exception is Richard Howard's fine translation of *Histoire de la folie—Madness and Civilization* (New York: Vintage, 1973)—but this is unfortunately only a part of the complete French text. The entire work obviously needs to be translated, and many of his other works translated again.

3. In this instance, as in *Madness and Civilization: A History of Insanity in the Age of Reason*, translated by Richard Howard (New York: Vintage, 1973), where Foucault constantly refers to the "tragic experience of madness" of certain paintings and texts, the notion of "experience" appears terribly insufficient. In *The Archaeology of Knowledge*, translated by M. A. Sheridan Smith (New York: Harper and Row, 1972), Foucault criticizes his own use of this term in *Madness and Civilization*. But his comments could apply to *The Order of Things* as well: "Generally speak-

ing, *Madness and Civilization* accorded far too great a place, and a very enigmatic one too, to what was termed an 'experience' [the English translation of *The Archaeology* mistakenly renders this as 'experiment'], revealing by this how close this text still was to admitting an anonymous and general subject of history" (t.m., 16). It would even be possible to argue in Foucault's own terms that the "raw being of order" and the "being of madness" point to the limitations of experience and cannot be experienced as such. Foucault's enigmatic notion of "experience," is really, therefore, a non-experience, or what I would call a paraexperience.

4. This is the aspect of the book on which I focused in an essay entitled "The Subject of Archaeology or the Sovereignty of the Episteme," in *Modern Language Notes*, v. 93, no. 4 (May 1978). In this essay I emphasized how each episteme, arising out of and located in a very precisely determined absence, functions as a unified "subject," whose unity, integrity, and presence are guaranteed by the closure constituted by its context. The present chapter looks more at the other side of the book: those elements that challenge, exceed, and undermine the sovereignty of the episteme and thus the notion of a closed epistemological field.

5. Joel Snyder in *"Las Meninas* and the Mirror of the Prince," in *Critical Inquiry*, v. 11, no. 4 (June 1985), attacks previous readings of the painting for "placing the source of our fascination with the painting in a single structural element, one which is, in an important sense, invisible— its perspective. This seems doubly curious to me: it locates the power of Velázquez's undeniable masterwork within its invisible structural elements and consequently reduces the various persons and objects depicted (as well as the manner of representation) to a secondary and almost in- cidental importance" (543). He is especially severe with what he calls Foucault's "theological" analysis, which he claims makes "the point of projection . . . the first principle, the *sine qua non* of the painting's perspective" (545). Snyder makes no attempt, however, to consider Foucault's reading within the context of *The Order of Things* and as part of an analysis of representation in the Classical age, nor to follow Foucault's argument when he describes the displacement of the point of projection by the painting and thus complicates the problem of perspective in general. His claim that Foucault, along with Searle, have not gotten "the facts about the painting straight" and that this "results in the invalidation of their arguments" (547) is undermined by the way he fails to get the facts straight about Foucault's analysis. When he claims that Foucault argues that "we must place ourselves" at the point of projection "in order to make sense of the picture" (550), it is clear that he has misunderstood how the displacement of perspective in Foucault's reading gives the viewer no privileged position to occupy, that the painting's projection of a point of projection is just one moment of a complicated process of exchange of positions and perspectives among viewer, painter, and model. If "there is something confused and confusing about saying" this, it is more Snyder's than Foucault's confusion.

6. This could be compared with Merleau-Ponty's notion of surreflexion in the way it highlights the impossibility of seeing oneself seeing, of the "seeing" and the "seeing-oneself-seeing" ever perfectly coinciding. Merleau-Ponty gives the example of the gap between hands when one hand is touching another while the second is touching something else.

7. Foucault's analysis shows how slippage or oscillation is characteristic of all of the functions of representation represented in the painting: neither the painter nor the spectator nor the model stabilizes what, for Foucault, is an infinitely "unstable play of metamorphoses," where "subject and object, the spectator and the model, infinitely reverse their roles," and where the place fixed by the look of the painter "never ceases changing content, form, face, identity" (5, t.m.).

8. Foucault is here, once again, close to Merleau-Ponty's analysis of the gap between "the eye and the mind," perception and language. As we have seen in Chapter 2, Jean-François Lyotard, in *Discours, figure*, also argues for the fundamental incompatability of language and painting in order to indicate the limitations of language when it is considered to be a closed formal or signifying system. Foucault's short text on René Magritte, *Ceci n'est pas une pipe* (Paris: Fata Morgana, 1973), focuses on how Magritte plays with what Foucault calls the "oldest oppositions of our alphabetical civilization: those between showing and telling, figuring and saying, repro-

ducing and articulating, imitating and signifying, looking and reading" (22). Magritte's purpose, claims Foucault, is "to prevert them and threaten in this way all the traditional relations of language and image" (23). In what Foucault calls the "absence of space, the effacement of the 'common space' between the signs of writing and the lines of images . . . the pipe has slipped away once and for all. . . . Nowhere is there any pipe" (34–35). Foucault's analysis is aimed at analyzing the representational effects of this radical absence Magritte inscribes at the heart of representation.

9. In Foucault's analysis of *Las Meninas*, it is the "visitor," depicted at the back of the scene among all the other portraits, paintings, and the mirror reflecting the vague image of the king and queen, who is an indication of the epistemological space not yet formed. "He is there in flesh and blood; he has appeared from the outside, on the threshold of the area represented— he is indubitable—not a probable reflection but an irruption. . . . The ambiguous visitor is coming in and going out at the same time. . . . a real man" (11).

10. I would translate "désoeuvrement" as "unworkness," but it is obviously not an easy term to translate; recent translations of Blanchot differ in their attempts to capture in English its complexity. Lydia Davis, in her translation of various essays collected under the title *The Gaze of Orpheus* (Barrytown: Station Hill Press, 1981), translates it as "worklessness." Ann Smock, in her translation of *L'Espace littéraire—The Space of Literature* (Lincoln: University of Nebraska Press, 1982), explains why she uses different words in different contexts to translate it: "I have most often translated *désoeuvrement* as "inertia," thereby emphasizing the paradox whereby the artist's relation to the work, the demand which he feels is made of him that there *be* a work, overwhelms him, not with creative powers, but on the contrary, with their exhaustion. . . . It *inspires* in him a kind of numbness or stupefaction. . . . The work excludes him, sets him *outside* it. . . . *Le désoeuvrement* is the absence of the work, l'absence de l'oeuvre. I come closest to expressing this when I translate *désoeuvrement* as 'lack of work'" (13).

11. The English translation is included as an appendix to *The Archaeology of Knowledge*.

12. See Edward W. Said's *Beginnings: Intention and Method* (Baltimore: Johns Hopkins University Press, 1975) for a discussion of the complexity of this issue in literature and theory— especially Chapter 5, "*Abecedarium Culturae*: Absence, Writing, Statement, Discourse, Archeology, Structuralism," as concerns Foucault. Said is more sympathetic to Foucault's critical project in this work than he is in his more recent work and tries to make it "serve a paticularly humanizing purpose" by claiming that since "the library" and "the archive"—he doesn't say the episteme, however—are "manmade," they can be subordinated to a "human motive" (313). In this way "the crisis of discontinuity," that Said claims is represented by Foucault and the structuralists, is countered for him by "an intentional process, a logic of writing, and of making texts, which *took place*" (343). Said's "beginnings" are thus far different from Foucault's and, moreover, they serve to cut short the critical process Foucault strives to push to the limit by originating it in "man" and "history" in an extremely conventional sense.

13. In *The Archaeology of Knowledge*, Foucault situates his own position in a similar fashion: "Hence the cautious, stumbling manner of this text: at every turn, it distances itself, takes its measures from wherever it can, gropes towards its limits, stumbles against what it does not mean, and digs out empty spaces to define its own path. . . . It is an attempt to define a particular site by the exteriority of its surroundings . . . to try to define this blank space from which I speak, and which is slowly taking shape in a discourse that I still feel to be so precarious and unsure" (17, t.m.).

14. This is the thesis of Hubert L. Dreyfus and Paul Rabinow's book on Foucault, *Michel Foucault: Beyond Structuralism and Hermeneutics* (Chicago: University of Chicago Press, 1982). Because they overemphasize one aspect of Foucault's later work—in a desire to convince us that Foucault did, in fact, move beyond both the structuralist and hermeneutical influences of his early work—they judge too severely and ultimately dismiss the aspects of Foucault's work that interest me here. Since the thesis of at least one of the authors, Dreyfus, is that Heidegger's

influence on Foucault was crucial, it seems strange that almost no mention is made of the latter's pursuit of the problem of the origin of language in his texts on literature, where, through Blanchot's work, the Heideggerian resonances are most evident. The notion that it is, rather, the most recent work of Foucault that links up best with Heidegger (largely, the early Heidegger) and not the earlier work of Foucault with the later Heidegger, as it seems to me is clearly the case, is an inventive approach to Foucault (and Heidegger), but one that does not, I fear, stand up to scrutiny.

15. See especially his "Monstrosities in Criticism," in *Diacritics* (Fall 1971), where he states: "Now, I have never at any moment pretended to be a structuralist" (58). In his "Foreword to the English Edition" of *The Order of Things* he is even more forceful and biting: "In France, certain half-witted 'commentators' persist in labelling me a 'structuralist'. I have been unable to get it into their tiny minds that I have used none of the methods, concepts or key terms that characterize structural analysis" (xiv). One can only wonder why associating his work with structuralism— even if admittedly inaccurate insomuch as he never based his work on the structuralist model for language—provoked Foucault's wrath against "half-wits" to such an extent, when he himself admits immediately afterwards that "there may well be certain similarities between the works of the structuralists and my own work."

16. In a chapter entitled "The Methodological Failure of Archaeology," which is perhaps the strongest chapter in the book, Dreyfus and Rabinow come down especially hard on this work: "In taking the view that meaning is, in effect, epiphenomenological, the archaeologist stands outside all discursive formations. Or, to be more exact, the archaeologist, like Husserl's transcendental phenomenologist, must perform an 'ego split' in order to look on as a detached spectator at the very phenomena in which, as an empirical interested ego (or in Foucault's case speaker), one can't help being involved" (87). This leads to what they consider to be the ahistorical implications of archaeology: "The archaeologist who claims to have emerged in history only to have stepped outside it, and thus to have totally and definitively understood it, tells a seamless story. His own discourse poses no problem for the archaeologist, who like the phenomenologist and unlike the hermeneuticist, does not even raise the problem of his historical language. . . . The language of the archaeologist . . . seems to have no history but is put forward as a transparent technical terminology, invented precisely to be adequate to the phenomenon. . . . as if archaeological discourse had to find its legitimation in an account of the productivity of discourse that flourished before history and will flourish again at its end" (97).

17. *Raymond Roussel* (Paris: Gallimard, 1963), recently translated by Charles Ruas as *Death and the Labyrinth: The World of Raymond Roussel* (New York: Doubleday, 1986). All references are to the French edition and are my own translations.

18. See, for example, Jean Ricardou's essay on Roussel entitled "L'activité roussellienne" in *Pour une théorie du nouveau roman* (Paris: Seuil, 1971). Ricardou's purpose is to show that Roussel's writing constitutes a "pure productive activity" (97), the credit for which should in each case be given to language itself (95). For Ricardou, self-reflexivity is the sign of the radical autonomy of language and literature.

19. Foucault's *Raymond Roussel* could be compared to another study with a similar intent: Jean Laplanche's *Hölderlin et la question du père* (Paris: Presses Universitaires de France, 1961). Laplanche's study is much more biographical than Foucault's and heavily indebted to a Lacanian perspective. Foucault reviewed the book favorably in an essay originally published in *Critique*, no. 178 (1962) and translated as "The Father's 'No'" in *Language, Counter-Memory, Practice*. What interests Foucault in Laplanche's study is his treatment of absence: the way he analyzes everything that "directs his [Hölderlin's] language to the fundamental gap in the signifier, that transforms his lyricism into delirium, his work into the absence of a work" (84). "The dissolution of a work in madness, this void to which poetic speech is drawn as to its self-destruction" (85) will be the dominant theme of all of Foucault's own work on "mad poets." And language retains a "sovereign position" here insomuch as "it comes to us from elsewhere, from a place of which

no one can speak, but it can be transformed into a work only if, in ascending to its proper discourse, it directs its speech towards this absence" (86).

20. Another example is to be found in Foucault's essay on Bataille entitled "Preface to Transgression": "Perhaps one day [transgression] will seem as decisive for our culture, as much a part of its soil, as the experience of contradiction was at an earlier time for dialectical thought. But in spite of so many scattered signs, the language in which transgression will find its space and the illumination of its being lies almost entirely in the future." Bataille's work indicates that future for Foucault, but not in what it is or says but only in what it destroys: "It is surely possible, however, to find in Bataille its calcinated roots, its promising ashes" (in *Language, Counter-Memory, Practice*, 33). In another essay from the same collection, Foucault envisions a future in terms of the work of Gilles Deleuze: "Perhaps one day, this century will be known as Deleuzian" ("Theatrum Philosophicum," 165).

21. Allan Megill, in his *Prophets of Extremity: Nietzsche, Heidegger, Foucault, Derrida* (Berkeley: University of California Press, 1985), addresses this question at some length—in fact it is the principal question he pursues in terms of all of the figures he treats in this work. He argues that "Foucault's project *is*, essentially, an aesthetic one" (216) and, as such, relates it to the work of the later Heidegger and especially Nietzsche. Megill finds the "aesthetic underpinnings" of Foucault's notion of discourse as evident in his later work as in his earlier work (231). The work of Nietzsche and Foucault, Megill claims, can only be understood in an aesthetic context where we "engage in the willing suspension of disbelief." Both "generalize this aesthetic context to cover the whole of the social and political world" (42). As I have indicated in an earlier note, much of what Megill says is pertinent to my own argument, and his book focuses attention on the positive critical functions served by the aesthetic in the various figures he treats. The problem with his book is the narrow way he defines the aesthetic—he opposes it to the "real"—and the fundamental contradiction in his approach: repeatedly, after analyzing at great length the positive critical benefits of an "aesthetic approach" to philosophical and historical problems, he abruptly changes perspectives and dismisses this approach. For example, after praising Foucault's critique of the limits of the rational, he goes on to say that "if Foucault's readers know that his allegedly historical writing is fictional, then that writing cannot by any rational standards have the desired effect on their politics" (42). And if "there is much that one can learn" from the generalization of the aesthetic, "at the same time, it can be seen as provisionally dangerous and, because it ultimately comes up against its contradiction, finally self-defeating" (42). Megill seems to want to have it both ways; his attacks on the various strategies that he had previously praised have to leave any reader of his book puzzled. I would argue it is his own refusal to see the aesthetic except as the opposite of the real that creates these problems in his work and leads him to contradict and undermine the strongest aspects of his own argument.

22. Many of the most important differences between Foucault and Derrida have to do with what each means by writing and the place each gives it in his overall critical strategy. When Foucault criticizes theories that grant "a primordial status to writing" for being theological and aesthetic, as he does in "What is an Author?" (in *Language, Counter-Memory, Practice*, 120), he clearly has Derrida in mind—even if his version of Derrida's notion is a carciature of what Derrida actually says about writing. See Chapter 4 for an analysis of the place of writing in Derrida's critical strategy and of the relation of writing to literature.

23. This is a reference to Foucault's text on Maurice Blanchot, "La Pensée du dehors," in *Critique*, No. 229 (1966). Here, too, he takes pains to keep self-reflexivity from becoming a strategy aimed at protecting the integrity of literature, of any interiority whatsoever, and argues instead that it is a means of linking up with the outside. Reflexive language, he argues, "must not be directed toward a confirmation of the interior—toward a kind of certainty concerning the center from which it can no longer be dislodged—but rather directed toward an extremity where it will always have to justify itself. Having arrived at the limits of itself, it does not witness the emergence of a positivity that contradicts it but of a void in which it will disappear: and it is toward this

void that it must proceed, accepting to come undone . . . in a silence that is not the intimacy of a secret but the pure outside where words unfold indefinitely" (528).

4. Deconstruction and the Question of Literature

1. In *On Deconstruction: Theory and Criticism after Structuralism* (Ithaca: Cornell University Press, 1982), Jonathan Culler suggests that such "misunderstandings" can in part be explained by critics whose understanding of Derrida's work comes more from reading commentaries on his work (such as those of Geoffrey Hartman), than from reading his work itself. The specific issue Culler refers to in this instance is the notion of "free play" as it is misunderstood and attacked by Wayne C. Booth (132, note 7).

2. The most notorious of the attacks on Derrida's work by a supposedly respectable philosopher is, of course, John Searle's ludicrous and mean-spirited essay in *The New York Review of Books* (October 27, 1983), which is nominally focused on Culler's *On Deconstruction*, but whose real purpose is to settle the score with Derrida for "Limited Inc," *Glyph*, no. 2 (1977), his reply to Searle's "Reiterating the Differences: A Reply to Derrida," *Glyph*, no. 2 (1977). When Searle resorts to name-calling and supports his "argument" against Derrida by quoting what Foucault supposedly said to him in a private conversation and what some unnamed "sympathiser" with deconstruction really thinks (a four letter word), it is clear that he feels threatened by Derrida's work and has no valid argument to use against it. It is also clear to anyone who has read Derrida's work at all carefully that Searle has absolutely no idea what Derrida actually means by the term writing.

3. Derrida also reveals that his first thesis topic, chosen in 1957, was "The Ideality of the Literary Object," and he describes that project in the following terms: "This title was somewhat more comprehensible in 1957 in a context that was more marked by the thought of Husserl than is the case today. It was then for me a matter of bending, more or less violently, the techniques of transcendental phenomenology to the needs of elaborating a new theory of literature, of that very peculiar type of ideal object that is the literary object, a bound ideality Husserl would have said, bound to so-called 'natural' language, a non-mathematical or non-mathematizable object, and yet one that differs from the objects of plastic or musical art, that is to say from all of the examples privileged by Husserl in his analyses of ideal objectivity" ("The Time of a Thesis," 37).

4. Gasché is simply paraphrasing Derrida in those instances when he addresses the question of deconstruction directly. The following is probably the most representative of these direct explanations: "Very schematically: an opposition of metaphysical concepts (for example, speech/writing, presence/absence, etc.) is never the face-to-face of two terms, but a hierarchy and an order of subordination. Deconstruction cannot limit itself or proceed immediately to a neutralization: it must, by means of a double gesture, a double science, a double writing, practice an *overturning* of the classical opposition *and* a general *displacement* of the system. It is only on this condition that deconstruction will provide itself the means with which to *intervene* in the field of oppositions that it criticizes, which is also a field of nondiscursive forces" ("Signature Event Context," *Margins of Philosophy,* translated by Alan Bass [Chicago: University of Chicago Press, 1982], 329).

5. Gregory Ulmer, in *Applied Grammatology* (Baltimore: Johns Hopkins University Press, 1985), asserts that "the methodologies in the two instances bear little resemblance to each other: the philosophical work is treated as an object of study, which is analytically articulated by locating and describing the gap or discontinuity separating what the work 'says' (its conclusions and propositions) from what it 'shows' or 'displays.' . . . Literary or plastic texts . . . are not analyzed but are adopted as models or tutors to be imitated, as generative forms for the production of another text" (x–xi). By essentializing the differences in strategies in this way, Ulmer is supporting the major argument of his book, namely that deconstruction and grammatology can be separated

199

the one from the other and that it is thus possible in reading Derrida to "set aside the philosophical investigations . . . while highlighting instead the meditation on writing as the clue to an applied grammatology" (8–9). In opposing "deconstruction" and "grammatology" or philosophy and writing (literature or art), Ulmer is, in fact, reestablishing the very opposition between theory and artistic or literary practice that, I am arguing here, Derrida's work is intent on undermining.

6. This is, of course, a reference to Paul de Man's critique of Derrida's reading of Rousseau, "The Rhetoric of Blindness: Jacques Derrida's Reading of Rousseau," in *Blindness and Insight: Essays in the Rhetoric of Contemporary Criticism* (Minneapolis: University of Minnesota Press, 1983). See also Derrida's reference to this essay in *Mémoires: For Paul de Man* (New York: Columbia University Press, 1986). Derrida says of de Man's "critique" of his reading of Rousseau: "Never has any appeared to me as generous in its rigor, as free of all reactiveness, as respectful of the future without ever giving way to complaisance, never has any criticism appeared to me so easy to accept as that of Paul de Man in 'The Rhetoric of Blindness.' None has ever given me so much to think about as his has, even if I did not feel I was in agreement with it; though I was not simply in disagreement with it either" (126). In terms of the specific issue of whether literary texts "deconstruct *themselves* by themselves," Derrida qualifies his agreement in the following terms: "I felt myself, up to a certain point, rather in agreement with this interpretation that I extend even beyond so-called literary texts—on the condition we agree on the 'itself' of 'deconstructs itself'" (123–24). But if the notion of "self-deconstruction" is extended "beyond so-called literary texts," then it cannot be considered a defining characteristic of literature. This has always been, I would argue, the chief difference or disagreement between de Man and Derrida, one that de Man makes abundantly clear in "The Rhetoric of Blindness."

7. This text has recently been published in France in Derrida's collection of texts on Blanchot entitled *Parages* (Paris: Galilée, 1986). It originally appeared in French in *Glyph*, no. 7 (1980) followed by an English translation by Avital Ronell. My references are to this translation.

8. Jonathan Culler rightly argues that "treating philosophy as a literary genre does not, for Derrida, entail the superiority of literary discourse or of literary knowledge, neither of which can resolve or escape intractable philosophical problems. Moreover, it would be precipitous to claim that philosophical texts are ignorant of something—their own rhetoricity—which literary texts understand" (*On Deconstruction,* 183).

9. I am indebted here to an exposé that Peter Connor gave on "Tympan" in a graduate seminar I ran on the place of a critical notion of aesthetics in the work of Merleau-Ponty and Derrida.

10. In his essay on Georges Bataille, "From Restricted to General Economy: A Hegelianism without Reserve (*Writing and Difference*), which in many ways sets the stage for his own approach to Hegel in *Glas*, Derrida analyzes Bataille's strategy of laughter as a means of confronting and breaking with the seriousness of the Hegelian dialectic: "To laugh at philosophy (at Hegelianism) . . . henceforth calls for an entire 'discipline,' an entire 'method of meditation' that acknowledges the philosopher's byways, understands his techniques, makes use of his ruses, manipulates his cards, lets him deploy his strategy, appropriates his texts. Then, thanks to this work which has prepared it—and philosophy is work *itself* according to Bataille—but quickly, furtively, and unforeseeably breaking with it, as betrayal or as detachment, drily, laughter bursts out" (252).

11. Alan Bass, in his translation of *Margins*, transliterates this archaic French verb used by Derrida and gives its meaning as "to criticize, to ridicule publicly" (x).

12. Derrida, in a discussion that is included in *The Ear of the Other*, edited by Christie V. McDonald (New York: Schocken Books, 1985), says this about *Glas*: "I think that a text like *Glas* is neither philosophical nor poetic. It circulates between these two genres, trying meanwhile to produce another text which would be of another genre or without genre. On the other hand, if one insists on defining genres at all costs, one could refer historically to Menippean satire, to 'anatomy' (as in *The Anatomy of Melancholy*), or to something like philosophic parody where all genres—poetry, philosophy, theater, et cetera—are summoned up at once . . . a graft of several genres" (140–41).

13. See Derrida's "My Chances/*Mes Chances*: A Rendezvous with Some Epicurean Stereophonies," translated by Irene Harvey and Avital Ronell—in *Taking Chances: Derrida, Psychoanalysis, and Literature*, edited by Joseph H. Smith and William Kerrigan (Baltimore: Johns Hopkins University Press, 1984).

14. Geoffrey Hartman, in *Saving the Text: Literature/Derrida/Philosophy* (Baltimore: Johns Hopkins University Press, 1981), argues along these lines that "there is a real danger of literature getting lost, running amok or running scared after Joyce's *Wake* or Derrida's *Glas*" (79). But in treating "*Glas* as a work of art" and, in order to do so, having "bracketed specific philosophical concepts developed by Derrida" (90), Hartman diminishes the dangers and risks of the experiment for both sides and ensures literature's ultimate victory over philosophy (Genet over Hegel) by making Derrida predominately into a writer of experimental fictions: an artist and not a philosopher. The question that Hartman never raises is whether it is really possible to bracket the "specific philosophical concepts developed by Derrida" in order to isolate the "literary" or "artistic" side of his enterprise. My argument is, rather, that the philosophical and the literary are so entwined in this and other texts that such an operation of bracketing or separating simplifies both the philosophical and literary implications of his work.

15. A recent essay by Anne McClintock and Rob Nixon, "No Names Apart: The Separation of Word and History in Derrida's 'Le Dernier Mot du Racisme,'" (*Critical Inquiry*, v. 13, no. 1 [Autumn 1986]) is only the latest in a long list of works which misunderstand Derrida's notion of textuality by conflating his notion of the general text with that of a particular text and then attack him for separating word and history (in this case the word is not just any word but *apartheid*). McClintock and Nixon are responding to Derrida's "Racism's Last Word"—translated by Peggy Kamuf and published in *Critical Inquiry*, v. 12, no. 1 (Autumn 1985), but originally written for a catalog accompanying an exhibit of anti-apartheid paintings. In their essay, they attempt to give Derrida a lesson in history so that he will be finally able to see, I suppose, what is really beyond the text: the historical-political world. In his respond, "But, beyond . . . (Open Letter to Anne McClintock and Rob Nixon)," translated by Peggy Kamuf for the same issue of *Critical Inquiry*, Derrida assures them that he is not "repelled by the word" *apartheid*, as they claim, but by the "thing that history has now linked to the word" (159) and that he needs no lesson in history from them. Derrida has this to say about the phrase "there is nothing beyond the text": "*Text*, as I use the word, is not the book. No more than writing or trace, it is not limited to the *paper* which you cover with your graphism. It is precisely for strategic reasons . . . that I found it necessary to recast the concept of text by generalizing it without any limit. . . . that is why there is nothing 'beyond the text.' That's why South Africa and *apartheid* are, like you and me, part of this general text, which is not to say that it can be read the way one reads a book. That is why the text is always a field of forces: heterogeneous, differential, open and so on. . . . That's why I do not go '*beyond* the text,' in this *new* sense of the word text, by fighting and calling for a fight against *apartheid* . . . (no more than anyone else can go beyond it, not even the most easy-to-recognize activists), but the strategic reevaluation of the concept of text allows me to bring together in a more consistent fashion . . . theoretico-philosophical necessities with the 'practical,' political, and other necessities of what is called deconstruction" (167–68).

16. Derrida could be considered, in "The Double Session," to be rewriting the schema of *The Birth of Tragedy*—but without the Nietzschean nostalgia for a pre-Platonic era (see Chapter 1) and placing an even greater emphasis on the original contamination of literature and philosophy on a mimetic stage which is, in fact, neither completely philosophical nor literary in nature: that is to say, neither Plato's stage nor Mallarmé's.

17. Derrida begins his text on Philippe Sollers, "Dissemination," by stressing the exemplary character of his "novel" *Numbers*: "The text is remarkable in that the reader (here in exemplary fashion) can never choose his own place in it, nor can the spectator" (290). It could be argued that in this text Derrida takes fewer precautions than in "The Double Session" and that Soller's text is treated to too great an extent as a model form of dissemination, as the ultimate dissem-

inating performance. Remarks such as these could be used to support notions like "applied grammatology" or "deconstruction as criticism," but only when taken out of context and generalized—something that Derrida's entire critical project constantly warns against.

18. The other major problem with Gregory Ulmer's *Applied Grammatology* is precisely the notion of application. Only if writing is first opposed to theory, literature and art to philosophy (deconstruction), can they be reduced entirely to an exemplary *practice* or pedagogy. Ulmer is interested in only one side of the contradiction indicated above and, thus, proceeds as if Derrida in his own writing practice had resolved the contradiction.

19. This, of course, is a reference to "Envois" in *La Carte postale* (Paris: Flammarion, 1980), where Derrida playfully analyzes the various possible relations of Plato and Socrates indicated by a postcard showing Plato behind Socrates and seemingly dictating to him over his shoulder.

20. Derrida gives the following description of the "logic of mimesis" in Plato: "1. *Mimesis* produces a thing's double. If the double is faithful and perfectly like, no quantative difference separates it from the model. Three consequences of this: (a) The double—the imitator—is nothing, is worth nothing in itself. (b) Since the imitator's value comes only from its model, the imitator is good when the model is good, and bad when the model is bad. In itself it is neutral and transparent. (c) If *mimesis* is nothing and is worth nothing in itself, then it is nothing in value and being—it is in itself negative. Therefore it is an evil: to imitate is bad in itself and not just when what is imitated is bad. 2. Whether like or unlike, the imitator is something, since *mimesis* and likeness do exist. Therefore this nonbeing does "exist" in some way (*The Sophist*). Hence: (a) in adding to the model, the imitator comes as a supplement and ceases to be a nothing or a nonvalue. (b) In adding to the 'existing' model, the imitator is not the same thing, and even if the resemblance were absolute, the resemblance is never absolute (*Cratylus*). And hence never absolutely true. (c) As a supplement that can take the model's place but never be its equal, the imitator is in essence inferior even at the moment it replaces the model" (187).

21. No one in recent times has pursued the problem of mimesis with more insistence and rigor than Philippe Lacoue-Labarthe. See especially "Typographie," in the collection entitled *Mimesis: Desarticulations* (Paris: Flammarion, 1975) and his recently published *L'imitation des modernes* (Paris: Galilée, 1986), and in particular the essays "Le paradoxe et la *mimèsis*," "Histoire et *mimèsis*," and his text on Jean-François Lyotard, "A Jean-François Lyotard—Où en étions-nous?"

22. In "Criticism and Crisis," the first essay in *Blindness and Insight*, Paul de Man, after pointing out that "what was considered a crisis in the past often turns out to be a mere ripple" (6), refers to Mallarmé's "Crise de vers" and gives the following definition of crisis: "We can speak of crisis when a 'separation' takes place, by self-reflection, between what, in literature, is in conformity with the original intent and what has irrevocably fallen away from this source. Our question in relation to contemporary criticism then becomes: Is criticism indeed engaged in scrutinizing itself to the point of reflecting on its own origin? Is it asking whether it is necessary for the act of criticism to take place? The matter is still further complicated by the fact that such scrutiny defines, in effect, the act of criticism itself. Even in its most naïve form, that of evaluation, the critical act is concerned with conformity to origin or specificity. . . . For that reason, the notion of crisis and that of criticism are very closely linked, so much so that one could state that all true criticism occurs in the mode of crisis. To speak of a crisis of criticism is then, to some degree, redundant" (8). De Man's main purpose in this essay is to show the limits of the process of demystification and argue that the "rhetoric of crisis," like all forms of rhetoric for him, "states its own truth in the mode of error. It is radically blind to the light it emits" (16). De Man claims that only literature, "free from the fallacy of unmediated expression" and characterized by "the self-reflecting mirror-effect by which a work of fiction asserts, by its very existence, its separation from empirical reality" (17), escapes demystification because "it is demystified from the start" (18). Here is another of the places where Derrida's and de Man's work can be seen both to overlap in terms of a similar concern with the problem of self-reflection in literature and, at the same time, radically differ in terms of the crucial issue of the privileged status of literature.

23. Allan Megill begins his interpretation of Derrida in the following way: "Derrida contends that his writings are meaningless—that they are, in the literal sense of the word, nonsensical. At any rate, this is what Derrida appears to be contending. But perhaps I have gotten it wrong" ("The Deconstruction of Crisis," *Prophets of Extremity*, 259). And gotten it wrong Megill most certainly has! And the way he has gotten it wrong certainly doesn't inspire confidence in his ability to read Derrida with any success at all. But, as I have already mentioned in another note, Megill's book is terribly uneven, and after this "nonsensical" start concerning Derrida, he does manage to get some things right about Derrida. In fact, Derrida even emerges as the philosopher with whom Megill claims to have the most affinity and on whom he relies to undercut the notion of "prophecy" he associates with Nietzsche, Heidegger, and Foucault. See, especially, his analysis of the differences between Foucault and Derrida in terms of their respective approaches to history and, as concerns crisis, his claim that Derrida distrusts this notion insomuch as it implies a linear reading of history: "It is not surprising that his evocations of crisis are peculiarly strained. . . . The logic of his stance and the sensitivity of his intelligence oblige Derrida to say simultaneously that there is a crisis and there is not a crisis. . . . The crisis theme is consistently counterpointed and undermined" (292).

24. At the end of his essay on Foucault's *Madness and Civilization*, Derrida evokes a notion of crisis in which "reason is madder that madness . . . and madness is more rational than reason" and which is not that of one finite historical era but "has always already begun and is interminable" ("Cogito and the History of Madness," *Writing and Difference*, 62). Derrida goes on to praise Foucault for having mobilized in his work all of the potentialities of this word: "Here, the crisis is on the one hand, in Husserl's sense, the danger menacing reason and meaning under the rubric of objectivism, of the forgetting of origins. . . . But the crisis is also decision, the caesura of which Foucault speaks, in the sense of *krinein*, the choice and division between the two ways separated by Parmenides in his poem, the way of logos and the non-way, . . . the way of meaning and the way of nonmeaning; of Being and of non-Being. A division on whose basis, after which, logos, in the necessary violence of its irruption, is separated from itself as madness, is exiled from itself, forgetting its origin and its own possibility. Is not what is called finitude possibility as crisis? A certain identity between the consciousness of crisis and the forgetting of it? . . . Crisis of reason, finally, access to reason and attack of reason. For what Michel Foucault teaches us to think is that there are crises of reason in strange complicity with what the world calls crises of madness" (62–63).

25. In his essay on Edmund Jabès, Derrida analyzes Jabès's association of the poet and the Jew in terms of the problem of the site: "When a Jew or a poet proclaims the Site, he is not declaring war. For this site, this land, calling to us from beyond memory, is always elsewhere. The site is not the empirical and national Here of a territory. It is immemorial and thus also a future. Better, it is tradition as adventure. Freedom is granted to the nonpagan Land only if it is separated from freedom by the Desert of the Promise. That is, by the Poem. When it lets itself be articulated by poetic discourse, the Land always keeps itself beyond any proximity, illic. . . . The Poet and the Jew are not born *here* but *elsewhere*. They wander, separated from their true birth. Autochtons only of speech and writing" (*Writing and Difference*, 66).

26. Derrida has at times even spoken out quite harshly against the privileging of this term over all the others. For example, in "The Time of a Thesis: Punctuations," he claims that he has never liked the word deconstruction: "I use this word for the sake of rapid convenience, though it is a word I have never liked and one whose fortune has disagreeably surprised me" (*Philosophy in France Today*, 44). In roundtable discussions published in *The Ear of the Other*, Derrida is even more explicit: "Here you are referring to a diagram of deconstruction which would be that of a technical operation used to dismantle systems. Personally, I don't subscribe to this model of deconstruction. . . . That is why the word 'deconstruction' has always bothered me. I had the impression that it was a word among many others, a secondary word in the text which would fade or which in any case would assume a non-dominant place in a system. For me it was a

203

word in a chain with many other words—such as trace or differance—as well as with a whole elaboration which is not limited only to a lexicon, if you will. It so happens—and this is worth analyzing—that this word which I had written only once or twice (I don't even remember where exactly) all of a sudden jumped out of the text and was seized by others who have since determined its fate in the manner you well know. Faced with this, I myself then had to justify myself, to explain, to try to get some leverage. But precisely because of the technical and—how shall I put it?—negative connotations that it could have in certain contexts, the word by itself bothered me. . . . For me, 'deconstruction' was not at all the first or last word, and certainly not a password or slogan for everything that was to follow" (85–86). In another discussion he adds that he does not want to repudiate the word, however: "I don't think I have ever repudiated anything. What I meant to say yesterday on the subject of deconstruction is that the fortune of the word surprised me. If I had been felt all to myself, if I had been left alone with that word, I would not have given it as much importance. But finally, rightly or wrongly, I still believe in what was bound up with this word—I am not against it" (142).

27. For example, in *The World, the Text, and the Critic* (Cambridge: Harvard University Press, 1983), Edward W. Said claims to be troubled by what he calls Derrida's "involuntarism" (188) and argues that Derrida's "work embodies an extremely pronounced self-limitation, an ascesis of a very inhibiting and crippling sort. In it Derrida has chosen the lucidity of the undecidable in a text, so to speak, over the identifiable power of a text" (214).

5. Disruptive Discourse and Critical Power

1. *Madness and Civilization: A History of Insanity in the Age of Reason*, translated by Richard Howard (New York: Vintage, 1973); *The Order of Things: An Archaeology of the Human Sciences*, translator not indicated (New York: Vintage, 1973); *Discipline and Punish: The Birth of the Prison*, translated by Alan Sheridan (New York: Vintage, 1979); *The History of Sexuality, v. I: An Introduction*, translated by Robert Hurley (New York: Vintage, 1980). Two other volumes of *The History of Sexuality* appeared shortly before Foucault's death—namely, *L'usage des plaisirs* (Paris: Gallimard, 1984) and *Le souci de soi* (Paris: Gallimard 1984) translated by Robert Hurley as *The Use of Pleasure* (New York: Pantheon, 1985) and *The Care of the Self* (New York: Pantheon, 1987)—and another volume will be published posthumously. Even though this has not been the general reaction to these last two works, and, even admitting the possibility that they make specific contributions to our understanding of the sexual practices and the discourse on sexuality of the Greeks and Romans, these works seem to me to lack the critical force of Foucault's previous work—which is the principal reason they will not be considered here.

2. The complete reference to the text is *I, Pierre Rivière, having slaughtered my mother, my sister and my brother. . . A Case of Parricide in the 19th Century*, edited by Michel Foucault, translated by Frank Jellinek (New York: Pantheon, 1975).

3. This could be compared to the laughter provoked by reading Borges, which he claims is the starting point of *The Order of Things*—see Chapter 3 for a discussion of its place in this work.

4. The nature and status of this exclusion is, of course, the focus of Jacques Derrida's critique of *Madness and Civilization* in his "Cogito and the History of Madness," in *Writing and Difference*, translated by Alan Bass (Chicago: University of Chicago Press, 1978).

5. *Histoire de la folie à l'âge classique* (Paris: Gallimard, 1972), 38. *Madness and Civilization* is regrettably a translation of only the abridged 1018 edition of the text, and many of the most interesting passages in which Foucault situates his own perspective have been left out of this version. All references to the French edition will be to the second edition indicated above, which also includes two appendices: "La folie, l'absence d'oeuvre" and "Mon corps, ce papier, ce feu," Foucault's polemical "response" to Derrida's critique.

6. "I mean that the silence of madness is not *said*, cannot be said in the logos of this book, but is indirectly, metaphorically made present, if I can say this, in its *pathos*—taking this word in its best sense. A new and radical praise of madness whose intentions cannot be admitted because the *praise* [*éloge*] of silence always takes place within *logos*, in a language that objectifies. 'To-speak-well-of' madness would be to annex it once more, especially when, as is the case here, 'speaking-well-of' is also the wisdom and felicity of 'speaking-well. . . . Therefore, if Foucault's book, despite all the acknowledged impossibilities and difficulties, was capable of being written, we have the right to ask what, in the last resort, does he lean on to support this language without recourse or support: who enunciates the possibility of nonrecourse?" (*Writing and Difference*, 37–38, t.m.).

7. Derrida raises the question of the historical status of a text such as this one that attempts, in a certain sense, to write the history of history in order to transcend it: "If this great division is the possibility itself of history, the historicity of history, what does it mean, here, 'to write the history of this division?' To write the history of historicity? To write the history of the origin of history? . . . If there is a historicity proper to reason in general, the history of reason cannot be the history of its origin, which requires *already* the existence of the historicity of reason in general, but must be that of one of its determined figures" (*Writing and Difference*, 42–43, t.m.).

8. Shoshana Felman, in "Madness and Philosophy *or* Literature's Reason," which is her analysis of the place of fiction in the Foucault-Derrida dispute, argues that "it is in fact to *literature* that Foucault turns in his search for the authentic voice of madness—to the *texts* of Sade, Artaud, Nerval or Hölderlin. . . . For Foucault, literature gives evidence *against* philosophy"—in *Yale French Studies*, no. 52 (1975), 220. In pointing out what she sees as an equivalency of madness and literature in Foucault's work, Felman's purpose seems to be not only to rescue Foucault from Derrida's critique, but also to praise and defend the powers of literature in her turn: "But the requirement of Foucault (that of the impossible philosphy of madness: of pathos) is the requirement of literarity *par* excellence—the search for metaphor and for a maximum of *resonance*" (226). In the volume in which this essay appears, she, in fact, goes much further than Foucault when she claims that madness "says itself, makes itself heard, and subsists as a speaking subject only in and by the literary text"—in *La folie et la chose littéraire* (Paris: Seuil, 1978), 14. For if madness is the "absence of the work" for Foucault, it most certainly is also the absence or fragmentation of the "speaking subject," as well as the transgression of the literary text as literary and as a specific text or work.

9. *Language, Counter-Memory, Practice*, edited by Donald F. Bouchard (Ithaca: Cornell University Press, 1977). Within a Marxist content (and probably more indebted to Bakhtin than to Foucault), Richard Terdiman explores some of the critical and historical possibilities of the term "counter-discourse" in his recent book, *Discours/Counter-Discourse: The Theory and Practice of Symbolic Resistance in Nineteenth-Century France* (Ithaca: Cornell University Press, 1985).

10. The phrase "corps à corps" recurs in Foucault's *History of Sexuality*, but in a different context. It serves to distinguish the link between truth and sex in Greece from the confessional link established between them in our own society: "In Greece, truth and sex were linked, in the form of pedagogy, by the transmission of a precious knowledge from one body to another [*corps à corps*]; sex served as a medium for initiations into learning. For us, it is in the confession that truth and sex are joined, through the obligatory and exhaustive expression of an individual secret. But this time it is truth that serves as a medium for sex and its manifestations" (61).

11. There is something "Bakhtinian" in Foucault's description of the theater of *supplice*. But if for the former it is the laughter and multiple languages of the carnival and the marketplace that testify to the fundamental heterogeneity and heteroglossia of the social fabric and are, thus, signs of potential and actual resistance to authority, for Foucault it is in the violence of public torture and executions that this resistance manifests itself. Foucault argues that revolts did, in fact, often occur: "Preventing an execution that was regarded as unjust, snatching a condemned man from the hands of the executioner, obtaining pardon by force, possibly pursuing and as-

saulting the executioners, in any case abusing the judges and causing an uproar against the sentence—all this formed part of the popular practices that invested, traversed and often overturned the ritual of the public execution" (59–60).

12. The book is divided into two parts: Part I, "The Dossier," includes Rivière's memoir and the documents associated with it; Part II, "Notes," includes the various readings given the memoir and the documents by Foucault and the other members of the seminar. Calling the second part "Notes" really does not get around the fact that these readings are in fact *interpretations*—they are simply interpretations whose chief purposes is to oppose previous interpretations and, in some sense, "free" the documents from them so that they can be seen in a different light.

13. Derrida—since it is Derrida who is in question in Foucault's reference to writing—in "Cogito and the History of Madness" had already questioned Foucault's tendency to indict psychiatry as being responsible for the entrapment of madness: "Does it suffice to stack the tools of psychiatry neatly, inside a tightly shut workshop, in order to return to innocence and to end all complicity with the rational or political order which keeps madness captive? The psychiatrist is but one delegate among others. Perhaps it does not suffice to deny oneself the conceptual material of psychiatry in order to exculpate one's own language. All our European languages, the language of everything that has participated, from near or far, in the adventure of Western reason—all this is the immense delegation of the project defined by Foucault under the rubric of the capture or objectification of madness. *Nothing* within this language, and *no one* among those who speak it, can escape the historical guilt—if there is one, and if it is historical in the classical sense—which Foucault apparently wishes to put on trial" (*Writing and Difference*, 35).

14. Patricia O'Brien's analysis of Foucault's position on crime entitled "Crime and Punishment as Historical Problem"—in the *Journal of Social History*, v. 11, no. 4—originally called my attention to the problem of the beauty he ascribes to this memoir and thus to the privileged status he gives to Rivière's discourse and acts. As O'Brien forcefully argues, Foucault's exemption of Rivière's document from the conflict within discourses raises serious theoretical and methodological questions: "Although he [Foucault] sees deviance as a product of power, he enshrines individual criminal action. Authenticity of action is introduced here, creating important methodological problems. . . . The beauty of the text implies its underlying authenticity and historical transcendence. In looking at the conflict within discourses, the discourse of the madman is exempted from the process. . . . The implication is that there is a validity to the document that exists someplace outside the power relationship. The avoidance of the 'trap' is based upon a mystical sense, a terror, of the inviolability of the document" (514).

15. The translation reads, "The discourses . . . which we wished to use as our starting point to talk about it," which is the opposite of what the French says: "ces discours . . . dont nous voulions parler à partir de lui." I have had to modify almost all of the quotations taken from this translation; it is full of such mistakes that drastically change the sense of Foucault's comments.

6. Borderline Aesthetics

1. Hegel in his *Aesthetics*—translated by T. M. Knox (Oxford: Oxford University Press, 1975)—also goes on to point to the limitations of both the empirical study of art and its abstract theorization: "Eaach appears to exclude the other and not to let us reach any true result. On the one hand we see the science of art only busying itself with actual works of art from the outside, arranging them into a history of art, setting up discussions about existing works or outlining theories which are to yield general considerations for both criticizing and producing works of art. On the other hand, we see science abandoning itself on its own account to reflections on the beautiful and producing only something universal, irrelevant to the work of art in its peculiarity, in short, an abstract philosophy of the beautiful" (v. I, 14). The solution, for Hegel, lies, of course, in the reconciliation of these extremes in a philosophical (that is, dialectical) concept

of the beautiful: "The philosophical Concept of the beautiful, to indicate its true nature at least in a preliminary way, must contain, reconciled with itself, both the extremes which have been just mentioned, because it unites metaphysical universality with the precision of real particularity" (22).

2. For Derrida: see also "Economimesis," in *Mimesis: des articulations* (Paris: Flammarion, 1975), translated by Richard Klein in *Diacritics*, v. 11, no. 2 (Summer 1981), "D'un ton apocalyptique adopté naguère en philosophie," in *Les Fins de l'homme* (Paris: Galilée, 1981), and *"MOCH-LOS ou le conflit de facultés,"* in *Philosophie*, no. 2 (1983). For Lyotard: *Just Gaming*, translated by Wlad Godzich (Minneapolis: University of Minnesota Press, 1985), "Introduction à une étude du politique selon Kant," in *Rejouer le politique* (Paris: Galilée, 1981), *Le Différend* (Paris: Minuit, 1983), "Judicieux dans le différend," in *La faculté de juger* (Paris: Minuit, 1985), and *L'Enthousiasme: La critique kantienne de l'histoire*, (Paris: Galilée, 1986). For Nancy: *Le discours de la syncope: 1. Logodaedalus* (Paris: Flammarion, 1976), *L'Impératif catégorique* (Paris: Flammarion, 1982), and "L'Offrande sublime," in *Poésie*, no. 30 (1984).

3. Those who have attempted to derive an aesthetics, a methodology of reading, or a school of deconstructive literary criticism from Derrida's own work on art and literature should perhaps have read more carefully his remarks on Kant. It seems to me that a critical reading of Derrida should have as one of its goals to make a practical criticism derived from Derrida's work very difficult, if not impossible to realize. Rodolphe Gasché in his recent book, *The Tain of the Mirror: Derrida and the Philosophy of Reflection* (Cambridge: Harvard University Press, 1986) argues in a similar vein that "Derrida's marked interest in literature, an interest that began with his questioning the particular ideality of literature, has in his thinking never led to anything remotely resembling literary criticism or to a valorization of what literary critics agree to call literature" (255). My only problem with Gasché work is that in arguing against the literary appropriation of Derrida and for what he claims is a more serious philosophical reading of his work—a task Gasché, surprisingly enough, attempts to accomplish with almost no references to other philosophers and theorists who have also treated Derrida's work in a serious "philosophical" way— he fits Derrida too nicely into a particular philosophical tradition and makes him too much of "a philosopher." Through his meticulous and rigorous philosophical reading of Derrida, which is largely thematic in form, Gasché could also be criticized, perhaps, for providing the means for a practical *philosophical* methodology or school to be derived from Derrida's work. In my mind, his book on Derrida, as important as it is, amounts to a "philosophical appropriation" of his work, which is potentially just as limiting as the literary appropriation Gasché rightly criticizes.

4. Derrida's reading of Kant and Lyotard's (see Chapter 7) both emphasize the critical place of the aesthetic in Kant and the links between the aesthetic and the extra- or paraesthetic. But it is in dealing with the question of Kant's humanism that Derrida's strategy for reading Kant probably differs the most from Lyotard's. Lyotard, of course, also recognizes the limiting effects of Kant's humanism—especially in terms of Kant's Idea of totality, which Lyotard would replace with an Idea of the multiplicity and diversity of ends (see, for example, *Just Gaming*, 88). But he tends to emphasize what, in Kant, can be freed from the *telos* imposed by his notion of Man; Derrida tends to emphasize the way such a notion limits even the most critical of Kantian concepts.

5. In "Economimesis," Derrida argues: "Under the cover of a controlled indeterminacy, pure morality and empirical culturalism are allied in the Kantian critique of pure judgments of taste. A politics, therefore, although it never occupies the center of the stage, acts upon this discourse. It ought to be possible to read it"—in *Diacritics*, v. 11, no. 2 (Summer 1981), 3.

6. Derrida's preface to *La vérité en peinture* is entitled "Passe-partout," a term of passage and movement which suggests the multiple locations critical discourse must occupy in order to deal with art. Derrida refers to his own critical discourse in this collection as a kind of "passe-partout" in the various senses of the term: a pass-key that opens different locks, a border or mat within the frame separating the painting from the frame as well as joining them together, and

literally something that provides passage everywhere. Derrida warns, however, that this term should be taken neither as a "universal key," nor a "transcendental passage," nor a "password to open all doors, decipher all texts, and oversee their links" (17). The *passe-partout*, "open in its 'middle,'" has as its primary function "to let the work appear, . . . and it remains a structure with a mobile foundation; but in order to let the work appear, it does not form a frame in the strictest sense but a frame within the frame. . . . The internal borders of a *passe-partout* are often mitered" (17–18).

7. Jonathan Culler, in *On Deconstruction*, argues that this reliance on the authority of the text avoids confronting the paradoxical nature of the distinction between criticism and literature, metalanguage and language, inside and outside: "Literary works themselves contain metalinguistic commentary: judgments of their own plots, characters, and procedures. Curiously, the authority of critics' metalinguistic position depends to a considerable extent on metalinguistic discourse within the work: they feel securely outside and in control when they can bring out of the work passages of apparently authoritative commentary that expound the views they are defending. . . . This is a paradoxical situation: they are outside when their discourse prolongs and develops a discourse authorized by the text, a pocket of externality folded in, whose external authority derives from its place inside. But if the best examples of metalinguistic discourse appear within the work, then their authority, which depends on a relation to externality, is highly questionable: they can always be read as part of the work rather than a description of it. In denying their externality we subvert the metalinguistic authority of the critic, whose externality had depended on the folds that created this internal metalanguage or pocket of externality. The distinction between language and metalanguage, like the distinction between inside and outside, evades precise formulation but is always at work, complicating itself in a variety of folds" (199).

8. The poet is compared to the child at play in "Der Dichter und das Phantasieren" ("Creative Writers and Day-dreaming") in the following terms: "The creative writer does the same as the child at play. He creates a world of phantasy which he takes very seriously—that is, which he invests with large amounts of emotion—while separating it sharply from reality. Language has preserved this relationship between children's play and poetic creation. It gives [in German] the name '*Spiel*' ['play'] to those forms of imaginative writing which require to be linked to tangible objects and which are capable of representation" (*The Standard Edition of the Complete Psychological Works*, [London: Hogarth, 1953–74], v. IX, 144). The creative writer, thus, reveals his phantasies in play, but in a disguised form. For Freud, in this essay, it is the content of the phantasies that can be analyzed. What remains a secret is the "art" of the writer: "How the writer accomplishes this is his innermost secret; the essential *ars poetica* lies in the technique of overcoming the feeling of repulsion in us which is undoubtedly connected with the barriers that rise between each single ego and the others. . . . He bribes us by the purely formal—that is, aesthetic—yield of pleasure which he offers us in the presentation of his phantasies. We give the name of an *incentive bonus*, or a *forepleasure*, to a yield of pleasure such as this" (153).

9. As is the case for Romain Rolland in *Civilization and its Discontents*, the artists, poets, and novelists Freud evokes in his work are both "friends," "great men" with whom he identifies positively—"One of these exceptional few calls himself my friend in his letters to me. . . . The views expressed by the friend whom I so much honour . . . caused me no small difficulty" (*S.E.*, v. 21, 64–65)—and rivals for the truth.

10. This is a reference to Derrida's "Spéculer—sur 'Freud,'" in *La carte postale* (Paris: Flammarion, 1980). Parts of this essay have been translated in two different journals. The first part as "Speculations—on Freud" (with the quotation marks around Freud omitted), in *Oxford Literary Review*, v. 3, no. 2 (1978), and the second part as "Coming into One's Own," in *Psychoanalysis and the Question of the Text*, ed. by Geoffrey Hartman (Baltimore: Johns Hopkins University Press, 1978). Derrida's project in "Speculations" is to respond to the following questions concerning *Beyond the Pleasure Principle*: "How must this text proceed, with what step [*pas*] above all, in order one day—today, against so many readings that are as partial as they are canonical,

that is to say, academic—for us to become sensitive to the essential impossibility of stopping at a thesis, at a conclusion posed in the scientific or philosophical mode, or in the theoretical mode in general?" In attempting to move "beyond the pleasure principle" and beyond any thesis supplied by theory, Derrida cautions against identifying the "athetic" principle with fiction or literature: "This textual process that cannot be dominated by any instance as such (especially not by the theoretical instance in its scientific or philosophical mode), I shall not be in too much of a hurry to call it 'fictional,' or even worse, 'literary'" ("Speculations—on Freud," 79, translation modified and completed).

11. As Derrida points out in "Coming into One's Own," Freud refused to be considered an artist or a poet (the thesis of Havelock Ellis) and continually defended the scientific status of psychoanalysis and the results that would outlive him and his name (142).

12. Weber describes the principal question he pursues in *The Legend of Freud* (Minneapolis: University of Minnesota Press, 1982) in the following terms: "Can psychoanalytical thinking itself escape the effects of what it endeavors to think? Can the disruptive distortions of unconscious processes be simply recognized, theoretically, as an object, or must they not leave their imprint on the process of theoretical objectification itself? Must not psychoanalytical thinking itself partake of—repeat—the dislocations it seeks to describe? . . . . For the enterprise of constructing a theory of the unconscious inevitably entails the struggle to wrest meaning from a process that entails the deliberate dislocation of meaning. It is the mark, the stigma of this struggle that I have sought to retrace" (xvi).

13. In "The Frame of Reference: Poe, Lacan, Derrida," *Yale French Studies*, nos. 55–56 (1977), Barbara Johnson tries to show that Derrida's reading of Lacan is an oversimplification that is similar to the pattern of "blindness" Paul de Man, in *Blindness and Insight*, argued was at the basis of Derrida's reading of Rousseau: "Derrida is thus framing Lacan for an interpretative malpractice of which he himself is, at least in part, the author" (478). Her argument—that the totalizing characteristics Derrida finds in Lacan's approach to Poe are neither essential to Lacan's reading of this specific text nor to his philosophical-psychoanalytical project in general, but are rather projected onto it by Derrida himself—constitutes, however, a kind of denial (*Verneinung*) of key elements of Lacan's reading. When she claims that "Lacan's apparently unequivocal ending says only its own dissemination, while 'dissemination' has erected itself into a kind of 'last word'" (504), the reversal is quite clever but does not, I feel, stand up to scrutiny. Johnson's analysis is much more "insightful" when she discusses the problem of the frame in the Lacan-Derrida dispute and its relation to literature—even if she still feels that Lacan is being framed by Derrida and has not committed the "crime" of which he is accused: "Interestingly enough, one of the major crimes for which Lacan is being framed by Derrida is precisely the psychoanalytical reading's elimination of the literary text's *frame*" (479).

14. Included in *La carte postale*, this text was translated as "The Purveyor of Truth," in *Yale French Studies*, no. 52 (1975).

15. See Derrida's "Géopsychanalyse: 'And all the rest of the world. . . ,'" in *Géopsychanalyse: Les souterains de l'institution* (Paris: Editions Confrontation, 1981) in which he criticizes the International Psychoanalytical Association for its refusal to name the geographic-political area, Latin America, where an important psychoanalytical organization coexists and has direct relations with states practicing torture on a wide scale. His text is, as he says, a "call to name Latin America," in order to "measure up to what has been uncovered there, to respond to what menaces psychoanalysis, limits it, defines it, disfigures it or unmasks it" (30). He argues that "the psychoanalytical medium is permeated by this violence. All intrainstitutional relations, the entire clinical experience, all relations with civil society and the State are marked by it, either directly or indirectly. This is as much as to say that there is no simple interiority of the analytical medium" (29).

16. Barbara Johnson, when she is not trying to make Lacan into a better version of Derrida than Derrida himself, very successfully captures the paradoxical logic of framing in Derrida's

work: "The total inclusion of the 'frame' is both mandatory and impossible. The 'frame' thus becomes not the borderline between the inside and the outside, but precisely what subverts the applicability of the inside/outside polarity to the act of interpretation" (481). In "Envois," Derrida refers to Johnson's critique of his reading of Lacan on pages 162–64 and concludes by characterizing her position in the following fashion: "Lacan meant in truth what I said, what I shall have said, in the name of dissemination. How about that! As for me, all the while appearing to speak of dissemination, I supposedly reconstituted this word into a last word and thus into a destination. In other words, if this can be said, Lacan already meant what I said, and I am only doing what he says to do. And low and behold, the trick is played, destination is palmed off on me and dissemination is reversed for Lacan's benefit" (164).

7. The Aesthetic and the Political

1. Hegel makes this claim in his *Aesthetics: Lectures on Fine Art*, translated by T. M. Knox (Oxford: Oxford University Press, 1975), and by this he means that art no longer "affords the satisfaction of spiritual needs which earlier ages and nations sought in it, and found in it alone. . . . It has lost for us genuine truth and life, and has rather been transferred into our *ideas* instead of maintaining its earlier necessity in reality and occupying its higher place. . . . The *philosophy* of art is therefore a greater need in our day than it was in days when art by itself as art yielded full satisfaction. Art invites us to intellectual consideration, and that not for the purpose of creating art again, but for knowing philosophically what art is" (10–11). In his critique of the philosophical *knowledge* of art, Lyotard is overtly anti-Hegelian and is attempting to make speculative philosophy in a certain sense a "thing of the past," especially as concerns art.

2. Translated by Régis Durand and included as an appendix to *The Postmodern Condition*, translated by Geoff Bennington and Brain Massumi (Minneapolis: University of Minnesota Press, 1984), 81.

3. It should be emphasized from the start that the postmodern, for Lyotard, is not an historical category, the period coming after the modern, but rather a critical element of the modern: "A work can become modern only if it is first postmodern. Postmodernism thus understood is not modernism at its end but in the nascent state, and this state is constant" ("Answering the Question: What is Postmodernism?," 79).

4. In another essay on the problem of narrative—"Narrative, Heterogeneity, and the Question of the Political: Bakhtin and Lyotard," in *The Aims of Representation: Subject/Text/History*, edited by Murray Krieger (New York: Columbia University Press, 1987)—I analyze the risks of cutting narratives off from their various contexts through an overly rigid pragmatic strategy. This is the problem, which Lyotard himself recognizes, with Lyotard's frequent use of Cashinahua narratives as an exemplary form of narrative pragmatics because they situate and undermine the autonomy of the narrative function and emphasize, rather, the "receiver" function of narrative. His point is to highlight the difference between these narratives and those dominant in modern Western culture in order to argue for a critical notion of justice: for if the "speculative game of the West is a game without listeners," then the "game of the just" is one in which "one speaks as a listener and not at all as an author. It is a game without an author" (*Just Gaming*, 72, t.m.).

5. Geoff Bennington in "August: Double Justice" (*Diacritics*, v. 14. no. 3 (Fall 1984) argues that there is an unintended oscillation between prescription and description in Lyotard's use of the rules of language games and that ultimately the opposition between them is undecidable. This, he claims, means that "no continuous refinement of the entities of the language-game game could account for all its moves" (68). Thus a certain undecidability would also lead to literature, whose "murkiness" as concerns knowledge and the strict application of rules could be considered one of its critical advantages.

6. In *Instructions païennes*, for example, Lyotard describes the "political" power of "little nar-

ratives" in the following terms: "If the network of uncertain and ephemeral narratives can eat away at the grand, instituted narrative apparatus, it is in multiplying the somewhat lateral skirmishes, as pro-abortionists, prisoners, draftees, prostitutes, students, and peasants all did in your country during the last decade. One invents little stories, even segments of stories; one listens to them, transmits them, and acts them out at the right moment" (34–35). He refers to May 68 as a "narrative explosion" consisting of "thousands of unknown narrators, *narrataires*, and actors beginning to recount, listen, and act out stories without having obtained permission or authorization to do so" (26). And referring to "Socialisme ou Barbarie," the radical political group of which he was a member from the mid-fifties to the mid-sixties, he credits it with having "saved the honor of narrating" by transmitting the stories coming from Russia, Eastern Europe, and China which were critical of communist bureaucracy—even if the narratives that the members of the group themselves gave of these accounts had "practically no listeners" (28).

7. This is Lyotard's response to a question raised after his talk, "Discussions, or phraser 'après Auschwitz,'" given at the Cerisy Colloquium in 1980, which was devoted to the work of Jacques Derrida. It is to be found in *Les fins de l'homme: à partir du travail de Jacques Derrida* (Paris: Galilée, 1981), 314.

8. Philippe Lacoue-Labarthe, in a talk given at the Cerisy Colloquium devoted to Lyotard's work, questions whether language games or any other categorization of language can be considered neutral: "I am not sure, in any case, that the confidence regarding the relative 'neutrality' of language games would stand up to [a critical investigation of the deeper ground of language such as Heidegger's]. It would be necessary, in fact, to examine a certain language, if not language itself, and what is presupposed by every conception of language. What would one find under pragmatics, under the theory of enunciation, or even under the tranquil certitude that there are statements, propositions, 'ordinary language,' etc.?" (translated by Christopher Fynsk as "Talks," in *Diacritics*, v. 14, no. 3 [Fall 1984], 29–30). The same kind of criticism could obviously be made of Lyotard's philosophy of phrases.

9. Critical experimentation does not, according to Lyotard, lead to eclecticism—which in the form of "kitsch" constitutes a "realism of money" and thus is the opposite of a questioning of foundations. Kitsch has a definite public always in mind, the public of consumers: "It is easy to find a public for eclectic works. By becoming kitsch, art panders to the confusion which reigns in the 'taste' of the patrons. Artists, gallery owners, critics, and public wallow together in the 'anything goes,' and the epoch is one of slackening. But this realism of the 'anything goes' is in fact that of money" ("Answering the Question: What is Postmodernism?"—in *The Postmodern Condition*, 76).

10. Lyotard's chief dispute with Habermas is over the latter's positing of consensus as the regulating principle of communicational exchange and the political role he assigns to art, that of providing a way to unify experience. Lyotard argues in "Answering the Question: What is Postmodernism?" that "what Habermas requires from the arts and the experiences they provide is, in short, to bridge the gap between cognitive, ethical, and political discourses, thus opening the way to a unity of experience" (*The Postmodern Condition*, 72). The postmodern, for Lyotard, constitutes a form of dissension within the general consensus governing form, taste, and judgment in an attempt to give an indication, not of what is presentable, or even what should be, but rather of what cannot be presented: "The postmodern would be that which, in the modern, puts forward the unpresentable in presentation itself; that which denies itself the solace of good forms, the consensus of a taste which would make it possible to share collectively the nostalgia for the unattainable; that which searches for new presentations, not in order to enjoy them but in order to impact a stronger sense of the unpresentable" (81).

11. This text, originally published in *Esprit* (1980), appears in Vidal-Naquet's *Les Juifs la mémoire et le présent* (Paris: Maspero, 1981) and is followed by an appendix in which he attacks Chomsky's preface for Faurisson's *Mémoire en défense contre ceux qui m'accusent de falsifier l'histoire* (Paris: La Vieille Taupe, 1980). Chomsky, in his preface, defends Faurisson's right to do

research and publish against those he claims, accepting Faurisson's version of events, are trying to silence him—as if that were really what was at stake in this controversy. It is, in fact, Faurisson's work that has a silencing effect—silencing all those documents and all those testimonies attesting to the existence of the final solution—and not the work of those, who like Vidal-Naquet, claim that Faurisson and his American counterparts of *The Journal of Historical Review* (such as Arthur Butz) are "historians of the false." One can only wonder what really led Chomsky to write such a preface and use such questionable judgment in his defense of Faurisson's "right to publish" his despicable text, which no one, in fact, had tried to take away from him.

12. See especially Lévinas's *Autrement qu'être ou au-delà de l'essence* (The Hague: Martinus Nijhoff, 1978)—translated by Alphonso Lingis as *Otherwise than Being or Beyond Essence* (The Hague: Martinus Nijhoff, 1981). Lyotard, in *Le différend*, comments on the notion of obligation in Lévinas as a displacement of the priority of the self by the other: "In making the "I" its "you" [*tu*], the other makes himself master and the "I" his hostage. But he is not master because he dominates but because he makes demands. The "I" enclosed within its own state of mind and world knows nothing of the other and can know nothing of him. The appearance [in the sense of occurence, *apparition*] of the other is not an event of knowledge. But it is an event of feeling. The "I", placed in the position of a "you," is someone to whom a prescription is addressed, the simple prescription that there is prescription (and not only description, knowledge). The "I" in this situation learns nothing. . . . He doesn't even know what the other wants of him or even if he wants something, but he is immediately under an obligation to him" (164).

13. In "Economimesis," Derrida also insists on the central role of analogy in the *Third Critique*, but from a very different perspective: "Every time we encounter in this text something that resembles a discursive metaphor (nature says, dictates, prescribes, etc.), these are not just any metaphors but analogies of analogy, whose message is that the literal meaning is analogical: nature is properly [*proprement*] *logos* towards which one must always return [*remonter*]. Analogy is always language" (13).

14. This text in a slightly modified and expanded form can also be found in Lyotard's recently published *L'enthousiasme: La critique kantienne de l'histoire*.

15. In their "Ouverture" to *Rejouer le politique*, Philippe Lacoue-Labarthe and Jean-Luc Nancy present the critical project for the "Center for Philosophical Research on the Political," which they are in the process of inaugurating, in terms of the notion of "the retreat of the political": "This double demand—the recognition of the closure of the political and the unsettling practice of philosophy in terms of itself and its own authority—leads us to think in terms of the *re-treat of the political*. The word is to be taken in what is at least its double sense: retreat from the political in the sense of what is 'well-known,' the evidence (the blinding evidence) of politics, from the 'everything is political' through which our imprisonment in the enclosure of politics can be described. But it is also to be taken in the sense of retracing the political, re-marking it—that is, making appear what is for us a new question, the question of its essence. This could in no way constitute . . . a withdrawal into 'apoliticism.' . . . This is to say that the activity of re-treat is itself a political activity—by which it is undoubtedly a question of exceeding something of the political, but absolutely not in the form of an 'exit out of the political'" (18).

16. As Cecile Lindsay argues in "Experiments in Postmodern Dialogue," *Diacritics*, v. 14, no. 3 (Fall 1984), Lyotard's notion of experimental art already has to do with the creation of a public that does not exist as yet and that cannot be defined before the fact: "That newness then resides in the work's potential for *future* effects, for future moves calling forth addressers and addressees who did not exist as such before" (58).

17. Lyotard argues, in fact, that since the notion of a citizen is a political ideal of the republic, no one has the right to proclaim himself or herself a citizen—and yet, in the republic, everyone is obliged to be one: "The republican subject is not empirical man but emancipated freedom; the citizen is a rational being. He/she is not describable as an actual reality; no one can give an example of a citizen, no one can call himself/herself a citizen. It is a kind of ideal of political

reason" (in Etienne Tassin, "La déflexion des grands récits: entretien avec Jean-Fran̆cois Lyotard," *Intervention*, no. 7 (November–December 1983, January 1984], 57).

18. In *L'enthousiasme*, Lyotard has this to say about the differences between the beautiful and the sublime: "Enthusiasm as the *'Begebenheit* of our time' is phrased therefore according to the rule of an apparently antonimical and basically parathetical aesthetics. The aesthetics of the sublime is the most parathetical, the most extreme of all aesthetics. First of all because not only is the sublime a pleasure without interest and a universal without a concept, as is taste, but in addition it contains a finality of antifinality and a pleasure of pain, in opposition to the feeling of the beautiful, whose finality is without end and whose pleasure is due to the free agreement of the faculties among themselves. With the sublime, Kant advances very far into the parathetical so that the solution to aesthetic antinomy appears even more difficult for the sublime than for the beautiful" (72–73).

19. In "Préjugés: Devant la loi," a talk given at the Cerisy Colloquium on Lyotard, Derrida admits that he, like many others, had always kept the theme of judgment at a distance, and that the singularity of Lyotard's work is to have directed at contemporary thinkers the following "categorical challenge": "You have not finished, you will never have finished with judgment. Your epoch, which is also a crisis . . . retains something like an enormous prejudgment in the form of a paradoxical denial as concerns judgment itself. . . . If you think you have gotten rid of the problem, it won't leave you in peace just because of that. You are by it pre-judged, and, as concerns it, pre-judiced (*pré-jugé*). It is because it rests on nothing and cannot be presented, certainly not with philosophical guarantees, criteria or reason, but judgment is paradoxically ineluctable" (*La faculté de juger* [Paris: Minuit, 1985], 96–97).

8. The Undetermined Ends of Theory and Art

1. In terms of the critical effects of the question of art, see also the recent work of Philippe Lacoue-Labarthe and Jean-Luc Nancy. For Lacoue-Labarthe, see especially the chapters of *L'Imitation des modernes* (Paris: Galilée, 1986) on Hölderlin, Nietzsche, and Heidegger and his text on Paul Celan, *La Poésie comme expérience* (Paris: Christian Bourgois, 1986). For Nancy, see *Le Partage des voix* (Paris: Galilée, 1982) and *La Communauté désoeuvrée* (Paris: Christian Bourgois, 1986), especially Parts 2 and 3, "Le Mythe interrompu" and "'Le Communisme littéraire.'"

2. Foucault's "response" to Derrida is entitled "Mon corps, ce papier, ce feu" and is included as an appendix to the second edition of *Histoire de la folie*. "What is an Author?" (in *Language, Counter-Memory, Practice*) is just one of the essays in which Foucault attacks a notion of writing that he obviously associates with Derrida (especially, pages 119–20). Derrida in "Signature Event Context" (*Margins of Philosophy*) and "Limited Inc abc . . ." (translated by Samuel Weber in *Glyph*, no. 2 [1979]) questions the notion of speech acts as it is derived from Austin and used by Searle and Foucault. In an interview with Lucette Finas ("Avoir l'oreille de la philosophie," in *Ecarts* [Paris: Fayard, 1973]) to which he refers in "Limited Inc," Derrida states that "*Signature Event Context* analyses the metaphysical premises of the Anglo-Saxon—and fundamentally moralistic—theory of the performative, of speech acts or discursive events. In France, it seems to me that these premises underlie the hermeneutics of Ricoeur and the archaeology of Foucault" ("Limited Inc," 173).

3. In the discussion after Lyotard's talk, Derrida and Lyotard had the following exchange. Derrida addressing Lyotard: "I was still sensitive to it today, and I have always sensed it in reading you, but even today when I never felt so close to your work, you have a style, a tone or a way of breaking with nostalgia and everything it connotes or carries along with it, which is resolute, sharp, determined, etc., and I said to myself that at bottom that is what is at stake, and only that, in this question [of what separates us]." Lyotard, after a series of exchanges, replies that he "was hoping to get Derrida to agree with him by proposing a less nostalgic version of difference,

213

which he believed he saw emerging in the development of his work. Derrida acknowledges this displacement in his work but repeats: 'In your work it is the side that breaks cleanly with nostalgia' that one especially sees" (*Les fins de l'homme*, 312–13). In "Préjugés, devant la loi" Derrida praises Lyotard's critical use of a notion of judgment without criteria but also explains why he himself had always "kept this theme at a distance" (in *La faculté de juger*, 95).

I N D E X

Adorno, Theodor W., 29, 49–52, 170, 186, 192 n.1 n.4

aestheticism, 3–4, 7, 22, 27, 34, 45, 50–51, 83, 102, 108, 124–25, 128–29, 134, 136, 144, 179, 180, 182, 186, 189 n.2

aesthetic judgment, 23, 135–41, 176–81

alterity, 31, 33, 36, 40, 55–56, 74–77, 94, 110, 159

Althusser, Louis, 47–49

analogy, 174–182, 212 n.13

anti-representation (anti-mimesis), 54, 99, 101–2, 104

art (aesthetics, the aesthetic), 3–12, 18, 21–30, 36–39, 42, 44–51, 108–10, 121–22, 124, 126, 128, 132–44, 155–56, 160–69, 176–88, 192 n.1, 198 n.21, 206 n.1, 207 n.3 n.4, 213 n.18

Apollonian/Dionysian, 7–8, 10, 185–86, 190 n.11

archaeology, 54, 56, 58, 61–62, 67, 70–71, 74, 108, 110, 112–15, 197 n.16

Aristotle, 6, 13, 120–21, 161, 165

Artaud, Antonin, 72, 76, 90–91, 110–114, 117, 121, 128

Auschwitz, 169–173

authority, 145–46, 148, 150, 208 n.7

avant-garde, 25, 95, 155, 167

Bakhtin, Mikhail, 190 n.13, 195 n.11

Barthes, Roland, 70, 78, 189 n.1

Bataille, Georges, 67, 78, 90–91, 107, 112, 117, 121, 128, 198 n.20, 200 n.10

beauty (the beautiful), 108–9, 124–28, 136–37, 139–42, 178–79, 206 n.14, 213 n.18

being, 57, 67, 73–74, 88, 103, 112, 115–16

Benjamin, Walter, 3, 186

Bennington, Geoff, 210 n.5

Blanchot, Maurice, 3, 67–68, 78, 90, 105, 107, 185–86, 189 n.1, 190 n.8, 196 n.10, 197 n.14, 198 n.23, 200 n.7

Booth, Wayne, 199 n.1

Borges, Jorge Luis, 55–58

category, 157–58, 161–62, 164–69

Cervantes, 112–13, 115

Chomsky, Noam, 211 n.11

closure, 37, 62, 93, 133, 137–39, 145, 187

cognition (the cognitive), 174, 176, 178

communication, 35–36

concept (the conceptual), 39, 134, 170, 174–78, 183

consensus, 169, 181, 211 n.10

Copenhagen School, 86–87

counter-discourse, 117, 205 n.9

crisis, 36, 38, 102–5, 202 n.22, 203 n.23 n.24

critical aesthetics (or poetics), 36–38, 51

critical theory (critical thought), 28, 49, 50–51, 53, 55, 61, 64, 67, 69, 71, 131–32, 135, 157, 163, 175, 178, 184

Culler, Jonathan, 199 n.1, 200 n.8, 208 n.7

Dällenbach, Lucien, 194 n.1

deconstruction, 14, 16–17, 26–27, 34, 36, 41, 53, 78, 81–82, 89–94, 104, 150, 191 n.17, 192 n.3, 193 n.6 n.11, 199 n.4, 200 n.5 n.6, 201 n.15, 203 n.26

deconstruction-as-criticism, 82, 84, 202 n.17, 207 n.3

deconstructionists (literary), 82, 104, 187

Deleuze, Gilles, 190 n.12, 198 n.20

de Man, Paul, 7, 11–19, 21, 190 n.11, 191 n.15 n.16 n.17 n.18, 200 n.6, 202 n.22, 209 n.13

Derrida, Jacques, 3, 22, 78, 81–105, 111, 131–54, 186–88, 189 n.1, 191 n.17 n.19, 192 n.21 n.3, 193 n.5, 198 n.22, 199 n.1 n.3 n.4, 200 n.5 n.6 n.10 n.12, 201 n.14 n.15 n.16, 202 n.19 n.20 n.22, 203 n.23 n.24 n.25 n.26, 204 n.27 n.4 n.5, 205 n.6 n.7 n.8, 206 n.13, 207 n.3 n.4 n.5, 208

n.10, 209 n.11 n.13 n.15 n.16, 212 n.13,
213 n.19 n.2 n.3; *La carte postale*, 103,
202 n.11, 208 n.10; *Dissemination*, 81, 95–
103; "Le facteur de la vérité" ("The
Purveyor of Truth"), 148–53; *Glas*, 93–95,
200 n.12, 201 n.14; *Margins of Philosophy*,
92–94; *Of Grammatology*, 85–89, 92, 96,
192 n.3; *Parages*, 105; *Positions*, 86, 90;
Speech and Phenomena, 92; *La vérité en
peinture*, 132–44; *Writing and Difference*,
89–91, 133, 187
Descartes, René, 111, 124
desire, 38–48
Dews, Peter, 192 n.5
dialectic, 32, 36–37, 39, 42, 47, 49–50, 55,
62, 67, 93–95, 117, 161, 170, 200 n.10, 206
n.1
Diderot, Denis, 112, 114, 118–19
différend, 31–32, 46, 166–77, 183, 193 n.13
discourse (the discursive), 24, 30–33, 36–
46, 51, 64, 68–71, 110–14, 126, 157, 162,
192 n.5
disinterestedness, 126, 137, 141, 178, 180
displacement, 103–5, 132, 141, 153, 187–88
disruptive discourse, 107–9, 124, 127
dissemination, 82, 201 n.17, 209 n.13, 210
n.16
dogmatism, 176, 182
double strategy, 94, 97
Dreyfus, Hubert and Rabinow, Paul, 196
n.14, 197 n.16

empiricism, 96, 131, 132
end of art, 5, 29, 42, 134, 183, 188
energetics, 38–39, 42
Enlightenment, 128–29, 172
enthusiasm, 179–81
episteme, 54, 56–63, 66–68, 87–88, 107,
114–15, 195 n.4
epistemological break, 58, 67
espacement, 193 n.5
ethical-political (the), 173, 181
exemplarity (the example), 98–99, 137, 150,
201 n.17
experience, 57, 79, 110, 116, 182, 194 n.3
experimental (experimentation), 156–57,
163, 167–68, 192 n.1, 211 n.9
extra-discursive (the), 108, 110–14, 128

faculties (Kantian), 173, 175–78, 182
Faurisson, Robert, 172, 211 n.11
feelings (sentiment), 171–74, 179–80, 183

Felman, Shoshana, 205 n.8
fiction (the fictive), 17–21, 152–53
figure (the figural), 24, 29–44, 51, 157, 192
n.3 n.5, 193 n.11
finality, 139–40
Fink, Eugen, 4–5, 190 n.4 n.6
form, 27, 39–41, 87, 134, 138–40, 178, 181
formalism, 54, 71, 82, 86, 96, 102, 136, 138–
39, 144–45, 150, 153, 163, 165
formlessness (the unformed), 42–43, 142,
181
Foucault, Michel, 3, 22, 53–79, 90–91, 101,
107–29, 185–88, 189 n.1, 194 n.2 n.3, 195
n.4 n.5 n.7 n.8, 196 n.9 n.12 n.13 n.14,
197 n.15 n.16 n.19, 198 n.20 n.21 n.22
n.23, 203 n.24, 204 n.5, 205 n.6 n.7 n.8
n.10 n.11, 206 n.12 n.13 n.14, 213 n.2; *The
Archaeology of Knowledge*, 69–71, 195
n.3, 196 n.13; *Ceci n'est pas une pipe*, 195
n.8; *Discipline and Punish*, 107, 109, 119–
24, 126; *The History of Sexuality*, 107,
109, 118–19; *I, Pierre Rivière. . . .* , 108–
9, 125–27, 206 n.12 n.14 n.15; *Madness
and Civilization (Histoire de la folie)*, 72,
75–76, 107, 109–19, 124, 187, 194 n.3, 203
n.24, 204 n.5, 205 n.6 n.7 n.8; *The Order
of Things*, 54–68, 71, 107, 109–10, 114,
118, 195 n.3 n.5, 196 n.9; *L'ordre du
discours (The Discourse on Language)*,
68–69; *Raymond Roussel*, 71–75
frame (of work), 131–33, 136–54, 208 n.6,
209 n.13 n.16
Frankfurt School, 47
French Revolution, 178–82
Freud, Sigmund, 32–33, 37–43, 49, 91, 116,
146–51, 208 n.8 n.9, 209 n.11

Gasché, Rodolphe, 82, 84, 191 n.16, 192 n.3,
193 n.6, 199 n.4, 207 n.3
Gearhart, Suzanne, 191 n.16
genealogy, 70–71, 108
Genet, Jean, 90, 93, 95
genre, 91, 157, 164–65, 167–71, 173, 176
German Romantics, 3, 190 n.13
grammatology (applied), 91, 93–94, 200 n.5,
202 n.17
graphic (the), 87–88

Habermas, Jürgen, 211 n.10
Hartman, Geoffrey, 199 n.1, 201 n.14
Hegel, G.W.F., 5, 23, 29, 32, 36–37, 39, 42,
47, 92–95, 131–32, 134–35, 137, 155, 161,
170, 183, 200 n.10, 206 n.1, 210 n.1

Heidegger, Martin, 3–7, 11–13, 18, 116, 132, 137, 165, 186, 190 n.5 n.6 n.7 n.8 n.9, 191 n.19, 192 n.3, 194 n.14, 197 n.14, 198 n.21, 211 n.8
heterogeneity, 157–65, 168, 176, 184, 205 n.11
historicism, 57, 62
history, 25, 57–58, 65, 108–14, 128, 134, 141, 143, 151, 169, 170–73, 175, 177–80, 182–83, 186, 188, 196 n.12, 205 n.7
Hölderlin, Friedrich, 72, 112, 197 n.19
humanism, 139–41, 207 n.4
Husserl, Edmund, 32, 90, 92, 137, 197 n.16, 199 n.3

Idea (Kantian), 174–75, 178, 180–84
idealism, 96, 180, 182
ideology, 157
imagination, 159–60
impasse, 104–5, 162, 182, 191 n.17
incommensurability, 164
indeterminacy, 157
injustice, 161–62, 168, 172, 183
inscription, 83, 89, 91, 96
inside/outside opposition, 135–39, 141, 143, 145, 151, 154, 208 n.7, 210 n.16
intertextuality (intercontextuality), 149–51

Jabès, Edmund, 90, 203 n.25
Jameson, Fredric, 194 n.17
Johnson, Barbara, 148, 153, 209 n.13 n.16
Joyce, James, 167
judgment, 137, 157, 168, 173–78, 184, 213 n.19, 214 n.3
justice, 160, 162–63, 169, 173–74, 178, 183–84, 210 n.4

Kant, Immanuel, 3, 23, 109, 132, 134–44, 157, 160, 165–66, 171, 173–84, 207 n.3, 207 n.2 n.3 n.4 n.5, 212 n.13
knowledge, 97–98, 155–57, 160–63, 171–73, 177, 184, 210 n.1 n.5

Lacan, Jacques, 70, 78, 148–53, 209 n.13 n.16
Lacoue-Labarthe, Philippe, 6, 11, 17–21, 190 n.9 n.14, 191 n.18, 192 n.20, 202 n.21, 211 n.8, 212 n.15, 213 n.1
language, 13–14, 19–21, 30, 32–35, 61, 64, 67–74, 77, 112, 115–16, 133, 165, 211 n.8
language games, 156–57, 160–64, 166, 183, 210 n.5, 211 n.8

Laplanche, Jean, 193 n.12, 197 n.19
Lanzmann, Claude, 171
Leiris, Michel, 78, 92–93
legitimation, 159, 161, 183
Lévinas, Emmanuel, 91, 133, 174, 212 n.12
Lévi-Strauss, Claude, 70, 90–91
libidinal, 24, 29, 32, 37, 39, 41–51, 183
Lindsay, Cecile, 212 n.16
linguistics, 30–34, 70–71, 164
linkage, 164–68, 170–76, 183
literariness (literarity), 54, 87, 144–45
literary criticism, 82, 84, 89, 104, 207 n.3
literature, 11–22, 53–54, 75, 82–84, 86–98, 100, 102–5, 110–11, 116–18, 123, 129, 144–151, 153, 160–63, 185–88, 199 n.3, 200 n.6 n.8, 201 n.14, 202 n.22, 205 n.8, 207 n.3, 210 n.5
Lyotard, Jean-François, 3, 22, 23–52, 135, 155–188, 189 n.1, 192 n.3 n.5, 193 n.6 n.7 n.11 n.14, 194 n.15 n.17, 195 n.8, 207 n.4, 210 n.1 n.3 n.4 n.5 n.6, 211 n.8 n.9 n.10, 212 n.12 n.16 n.17, 213 n.18 n.19 n.3; *Dérive à partir de Marx et Freud (Driftworks)*, 25, 27–28; *Le differend*, 157–58, 164–78, 181; *Discours, figure*, 24–25, 30–43, 51, 157, 187, 192 n.3, 195 n.8; *Des dispositifs pulsionnels*, 28–29, 43, 49–50; *Economie libidinale*, 24, 28, 43–51, 174, 187, 193 n.14, 194 n.15; *Instructions païennes*, 157–59, 161–62, 167, 173, 210 n.6; *Just Gaming (Au juste)*, 44–45, 157, 161–64, 167, 169, 184, 204 n.4 n.5; *The Postmodern Condition*, 157, 161–62, 164, 167; *Le postmoderne expliqué aux enfants*, 180

madness, 58, 67, 72, 74–79, 99, 107, 109–16, 119, 197 n.19, 203 n.24, 205 n.6 n.8, 206 n.13 n.14
Mallarmé, Stéphane, 34–37, 89–90, 98–103, 115–16, 201 n.16
man, 58–61, 65, 67, 115, 139–141, 196 n.12
margins (the marginal), 92–94, 108–9
Marx, Karl (marxism), 43–44, 46–49, 159, 193 n.14, 194 n.17
matrix, 39–41
McClintock, Anne and Nixon, Rob, 201 n.15
Megill, Allan, 189 n.2, 198 n.21, 203 n.23
Merleau-Ponty, Naurice, 3, 30, 32–33, 37, 186, 193 n.6 n.7, 195 n.6 n.8
metanarrative (metatheory), 157–59, 183–84, 188

Index

metaphysics, 6, 19, 24, 29, 100, 116, 133, 157, 165, 186, 190 n.6
mimesis, 97–104, 202 n.20 n.21
mise en abyme, 53–54, 72–73
model, 170, 177

Nancy, Jean-Luc, 135, 142, 189 n.1, 212 n.15, 213 n.1
narrative, 157–64, 183, 210 n.6; little narratives, 157–58, 160, 162, 164, 166, 210 n.6; grand narratives, 157–58
negation, 170, 172
negative theology, 49, 67
New Criticism, 82, 135–36
Nietzsche, Friedrich, 3–22, 24, 44, 72, 76, 87, 94, 110, 112–17, 185–86, 189 n.2, 190 n.3 n.6 n.7 n.8 n.9 n.10 n.11 n.12 n.13 n.14, 198 n.21, 201 n.16; *The Birth of Tragedy*, 4–5, 7–11, 190 n.11; *The Will to Power*, 5–8, 13, 186, 190 n.8

obligation, 166, 170, 174
O'Brien, Patricia, 206 n.14
Oedipal, 152–53
order, 56–59, 67–68, 71, 74
origin (of language), 69–74, 79

panopticon, 120, 122
paraesthetics, 3, 22, 42–43, 47, 51, 109, 128–29, 143–44, 155, 161, 182–88, 192 n.1, 207 n.4
paraexperience, 170, 195 n.3
parafaculty, 176
paraliterary, 104, 188
paralogic, 1, 175
parathetic (paratheory), 48, 51, 213 n.18
parergon, 137–38, 141, 143, 152–53
passage, 136, 140, 143–44, 176, 182, 207 n.6
performance theory (the performative), 93, 100, 134, 158–59, 213 n.2
philosophy, 1–24, 30–31, 34, 42, 88–98, 108–9, 111, 128, 131–33, 135, 141–42, 151, 155–56, 168, 170, 172–74, 176, 182, 186–88, 189 n.1, 200 n.8 n.10, 201 n.14, 206 n.1, 207 n.3, 210 n.1
phrases (philosophy of), 158, 164–69, 171–72, 175, 183
Plato (Platonism), 6, 8–10, 13, 97–100, 137, 201 n.16, 202 n.19 n.20
play (*jeu, Spiel*), 146, 190 n.6, 208 n.8
Poe, Edgar Allan ("The Purloined Letter"), 148–50, 152–53

poetics, 3, 36–37, 73, 120–22, 136, 147
poetics of absence, 67–68, 75–76, 79
poetry (the poetic), 8–10, 18, 33–38
politics (the political), 24–28, 43, 47, 108–9, 128, 134, 162–64, 166–69, 174–84, 186, 188, 212 n.15
Pontalis, J.B., 193 n.12
postmodernism, 155–56, 158–59, 161, 165, 167, 184, 210 n.3, 211 n.10
poststructuralism, 2, 78
power-knowledge, 118–24, 126–28
pragmatics, 157–64, 183, 210 n.4
prescription, 161–64, 210 n.5, 212 n.12
presentation, 142–43, 174, 180–84, 211 n.10
primary process, 41–42
progress, 178–79
proscription, 161–64
psychoanalysis, 42–43, 75, 125, 145–53, 206 n.13, 209 n.11 n.12 n.13 n.15
punishment, 119–24
purposiveness (without purpose), 139–40

Rajchman, John, 77–79
reason (the rational), 74–75, 110–14, 126, 170–71, 173–74, 203 n.24, 206 n.13
régime (of phrases), 164–65, 171, 173
representation, 53–55, 59, 61–66, 196 n.8
result, 170–71, 187
rhetoric, 11–17, 19–21, 46, 72, 144, 191 n.15
Ricardou, Jean, 194 n.1, 197 n.18
Rogozinski, Jacob 189 n.1
Rousseau, Jean-Jacques, 72, 86, 88
Roussel, Raymond, 68, 71–75, 197 n.18
Rousset, Jean, 90
rules, 60, 71, 74, 115, 156, 160–62, 166–67, 169–70, 173, 176, 183
Russian Formalists, 87

Sade, Marquis de, 67, 112–14, 117, 121, 128
Said, Edward, 196 n.12, 204 n.27
Sartre, Jean-Paul, 25
Saussure, Ferdinand de, 37, 70, 86
Schlegel, Friedrich, 190 n.13
sexuality, 118–19
Searle, John, 199 n.2, 213 n.2
self-reflexivity, 53–57, 60, 63, 66–79, 101–3, 109, 115, 129, 144–45, 150–51, 197 n.18, 198 n.23, 202 n.22
sensible (the), 32–33, 35–36, 39
sensus communis, 181
signs of history, 169, 171, 173–74, 178–80

silence, 107, 110–13, 126–27, 169, 171–72, 183, 199 n.23, 205 n.6, 212 n.11
Smock, Ann, 196 n.10
Socrates, 7–11, 60, 190 n.11 n.12 n.13, 202 n.19
Sollers, Philippe, 90, 201 n.17
sovereignty, 62, 65
speech, 81–82, 92, 193 n.7
specificity, 132–36, 141, 143–45, 154, 156
spectators, 178–82
speculation (the speculative), 146–47, 170–71, 174
structuralism, 2, 12, 33, 37, 53, 70, 89, 101, 193 n.5, 197 n.15
subject (the), 59, 117, 122, 140, 164, 195 n.4
sublime (the), 126, 135, 141–44, 177, 180–84, 213 n.18
supplice (theater of), 120–23, 205 n.11
surreflexion, 33–34, 193 n.6, 195 n.6
Snyder, Joel, 195 n.5

teleology, 165–66
Terdiman, Richard, 205 n.9
terror, 126–27
text (textuality), 81–90, 95–97, 101–2, 125, 149–53, 187, 191 n.14, 193 n.5, 201 n.15
theaters of power, 119, 121–22
Thébaud, Jean-Loup, 44
theory (the theoretical), 1–4, 21, 24–25, 30, 44, 47–51, 87, 89–91, 94, 96, 103–5, 128, 131–35, 139, 141, 143–45, 147, 150–56, 158–59, 161–63, 182–87, 209 n.10
totalitarianism, 159

totalization, 47–48, 85, 153, 158–59, 161, 163–64, 167, 175, 181
tragedy (the tragic), 7–10, 110–13, 116, 120–22, 190 n.12
transcendence, 66, 117, 127, 136, 174
transgression, 33–34, 67, 75–79, 107–10, 115–19, 125–29, 169, 198 n.20
trope, 16, 19, 72
truth, 148–52, 185–86

Ulmer, Gregory, 199 n.5, 202 n.18
unconscious (the), 39, 41, 147
undecidability, 104–5, 187, 191 n.15, 210 n.5
universality, 178–79, 181
unpresentable (the), 142–43, 173–74, 178, 180, 182–84, 211 n.10
unreadability, 104–5
unworkness (*désoeuvrement, absence d'oeuvre*), 68, 75–76, 187, 196 n.10, 197 n.19, 205 n.8

Valéry, Paul, 92
Velásquez, Diego (*Las Meninas*), 54, 59–66, 195 n.5
Vidal-Naquet, Pierre, 171–72, 211 n.11
visibility (the visual), 62–64, 193 n.11
void (the), 66–67, 72–76, 112, 115, 117, 199 n.23

Weber, Samuel, 147, 161–62, 209 n.12
Wittgenstein, Ludwig, 157, 164–66
writing (*écriture*), 78–79, 81–92, 94–95, 97–98, 100–2, 125, 187, 198 n.22